Are We There Yet, Ron

To Lynn

All the best

By
Graham Pollard

from

Graham

Ross

Published by LR Publishing

This edition published in 2008
By LR Publishing

ISBN 978-0-9555919-1-4

A CIP catalogue record of this title
Is available from the British Library

Paperback ISBN 978-0-9555919-1-4

By the same author

Left or Right Ron? – Impressions of Sussex on foot.
ISBN 978-0-9555919-0-7

Typeset Times New Roman 12 by author
Printed an Bound by PrintonDemand-worldwide.com
Published by LR Publishing, 4 Rockall Drive, Hailsham, East Sussex BN27 3BG

ACKNOWLEDGEMENTS

Being very naïve, I thought it would be a piece of cake to write a book. I was so wrong. Once the book was written I thought it would be so easy to get it published, after all, everyone who had read parts of 'Left or Right Ron?' kept telling me that I should get it published. If only I knew the trauma and anxiety that getting that book off the ground would cause. But, eventually, we did it. I say we, because without so many people assisting me in so many ways I would have given up months ago. So, what in the world possessed me to write another book?

My wife and children have given me endless encouragement. Having started our own publishing business they have stood by me through the rough times. To them I am eternally grateful for their patience, trust and understanding and can assure them that I will always love them dearly.

To Lyn, my self-appointed agent and proof reader, I promise to do this book differently. I will try very hard to ensure that I get my 'there' and 'their' in the correct places and can't thank you enough for ensuring that all punctuation is precise and proper and that any libel cases are nipped in the bud before we go to print.

To all the people we have met during the writing of this book I thank, whoever you are, for helping two Sussex men to understand their surroundings by giving advice and direction in times of being geographically challenged (lost!)

Finally there's Ron. I can't think of any other person I could do this with. He is my inspiration as well as being the thorn in my side. He keeps me going when I don't want too. He forces the amber nectar to be placed in my hand and always, always, gives me that little bit of encouragement to do things that, normally, I wouldn't dream of doing.

If anyone takes part in any of the enclosed walks please be aware that neither Ron nor I can be held responsible for any deviation, diversion or change to any of the walks. But Ron and I encourage one and all to get out and discover this beautiful Sussex countryside.

Thanks to everyone.

PREFACE

One of my recent discoveries, in the book world, is Candace Robb. She writes of murderous exploits in the City of York in the 1300's. One of her characters, Magda Digby, alias 'The Riverwoman' is one of my particular favourites. The way she is portrayed and the way her spoken words are written by the author are, in my opinion, true brilliance.

I was so fascinated with Candace Robb's portrayal of the walled City of York that I have visited it, many times whilst on holiday, just to see the various gates described in her books. But it is Magda that I really love. Everything to her is so basic, so simple and easy going. But she has her own problems and worries in her humble life. Magda cares for the people of York, and the surrounding areas. She is 'The Healer' and midwife. She uses old herbal remedies, passed down to her from previous generations, the ingredients being found in the York countryside. She speaks very descriptively using the old words 'thee', thou'st' and 'thy'. She does have a temper, but it is rarely seen in public. She always appears calm and confident.

She reminds me so much of Ron. The way he talks. His calmness. He has a simple philosophy on life in general. Our friendship, over the last few years has grown into something special. I have got to know Ron and his 'ways'. During our walks around Sussex, related in my first book, 'Left or Right Ron?' we talked to each other, joked about many things and discussed issues that only good friends can discuss with each other. Ron has become a true and valued friend to me. Again, whilst writing these pages both Ron and I have learnt so much about our home County of Sussex. Its countryside, its wildlife and its people are all to be seen. You just have to go out and find them.

I hope the next few pages reflects our friendship and understanding of each other as we continue our quest to discover parts of Sussex that have existed for centuries but have only just been found by two Sussex boys who are looking for that certain something?

Readers of our previous exploits will know that our walks are taken from publications. We carry out the walk as instructed and then write about the walk, what it was like and what we saw. Due to the outstanding success of the previous title 'Left or Right Ron?' these pages are familiar in content apart from the way each walk was chosen. Also, at the end of some chapters, if space permits, Ron has penned a few poetic words which tells of his feelings for the place we have visited. These chapters are all my own choosing and we have attempted to complete them in some sort of alphabetical order. (Or, at least, that was the idea.) Ron has had little to no input into where we walk. In fact most walks are a complete surprise to him until we get to the start. Some of these walks are around little known areas of Sussex; some are at places that even Ron didn't know existed. One up to the Townie!

Both Ron and I hope you enjoy the following pages.

Graham Pollard

CONTENTS

To all of our parents,
But especially Ken and Joan who passed much too suddenly
Sam, who is no longer with us but is always there,
Celia who has encouraged me and is my best critic
Annie and Ronald are forever in Ron's thoughts

Without any of them, we wouldn't be here!

Chapter 1 - Amberley

During the year 2006/07 Ron and I completed 52 walks around Sussex[1]. We followed different public footpaths around villages and out into the countryside. I wrote about what we found, what we discussed and some observations of things we saw but one of the places I would have liked to visit, but we didn't get round to, was Amberley. I cannot explain why because Amberley has been described by some as 'one of the most beautiful villages in Sussex'. So, I thought that Amberley should be the first place we will visit, at the start of our next venture.

The original estates of Amberley had been given to the Saxon Bishop Wilfred in AD680 and a church has been on this site since then. The present church of St Michael was built in the 12th century, believed to be on the orders of Bishop Luffa to serve as the church for his adjacent manor house.

But in Norman times churchmen were expected to be feudal magnates so the castle at Amberley, home of the Bishops of Chichester, is an illustration of this expectation.

Shortly after the Battle of Hastings, in 1066, King William distributed the titles and lands, won from the Saxon aristocracy. The main benefactors were his most loyal barons and clergymen, but in return they were required to provide him with military and administrative services. They had to supply men and arms to fight whenever and wherever the King required and also had to govern their lands, on the Kings behalf, applying the Law and collecting any taxes due.

It wasn't long before the church held 10% of the land of England and received 20% of the country's income. As time went on many churchmen, especially in the higher reaches, spent more time on their secular duties than on their spiritual ones.

So, King William instituted a reform where the bishops 'seat' must be in the largest centre of population in his diocese. The Saxon Bishop of Selsey, therefore, became the Bishop of Chichester. This required the building of a new cathedral at Chichester, along with houses and palaces for the Bishop and higher clergy. Bishop Luffa, in the year 1100, whilst building the cathedral at Chichester, also built himself a manor house at his feudal estate of Amberley. Over the next 250 years this manor house grew into the castle we see today.

Hilaire Belloc, one of my favourite authors, penned a poem, many years ago, titled 'West Sussex Drinking Song'[2] and the first verse mentions Amberley:

> *They sell good beer at Haslemere*
> *And under Guildford Hill.*
> *At Little Cowfold as I've been told*
> *A beggar may drink his fill:*
> *There is a good brew in Amberley too,*
> *And by the bridge also;*
> *But the swipes they take in at Washington Inn*
> *Is the very best Beer I know.*

Amberley was also the home of Edward Stott (1856-1918) whose paintings of English rural life around his home influenced some of the great painters of his time[3].

---

[1] 'Left or Right Ron?' by Graham Pollard, Published by LR Publishing – 2007 – ISBN 978-0-9555919-0-7
[2] 'The Sussex Bedside Anthology' by Margaret Goldsmith – The Arundel Press - 1950
[3] http://www.lbhf.gov.uk/external/beyondburnejones/ARTISTS/edwardstott.htm visited 11/02/07

Upon his death, the bachelor left most of his money to The Royal Academy for travelling scholarships.

The day before our arranged walk Ron tells me that he hasn't been feeling too good. "Got a lump", he tells me as he holds his stomach. "Have you been to see a doctor?" I ask. "I don't need one o'them," he replies. "Prob'ly indigestion, that's all." But it's unlike Ron to complain about his own health. He can complain about everything else but not usually how he feels. I'm in favour of calling the walk off but Ron insists that he will be ok. After some encouragement I have to agree that we will go on the condition that he tells me if he has a problem. "I'll be fine," he insists, "been lookin' forward 'ter this walk since you said we be goin'." So, a little reluctantly, we set off for Amberley one late, cold, February morning.

Amberley Church

Parking in Amberley is no problem at all. We find plenty of places in Church Street, right next to the Parish Church of St. Michael. But Ron's first words about this village, which is suggested as being one of the prettiest villages in Sussex is, "ain't it drab?" I'm not sure what I expected apart from thatched roofs, and lots of them, but I have to agree with Ron, it all looked pretty bland. Perhaps it was the time of year that made the place look boring. There were no flowers, no bright buildings. The stonework on the houses is all the same colour, brown. But I was always told that first impressions should be discarded. So we would continue by first having a look at the church, which thankfully, was open.

Church Interior

Inside the church was very typical of what we had witnessed in other churches during our travels around Sussex. But in this church the layout seemed to be an odd shape. If you sat in the right-hand pews you were unable to see anything of the altar; yet the outside of the church didn't appear to be the same shape? That doesn't sound right but perhaps you have to see it to understand what I am saying. But what can just be seen are the faded wall paintings that were all but destroyed during the restoration work of 1864.[4]

Behind the church are the walls of what used to be Amberley Castle, now it's a holiday place for the rich and influential. Viewing is possible but it has to be strictly appointment only. So be warned. We found a locked doorway, outside and

Black Horse, Amberley

behind the church, which leads into the 'castle', which was dedicated to Richard who was the Bishop of Chichester and Lord of Amberley Manor from 1244 to 1253.

---

[4] Dear Amberley by The Reverend E Noel Staines, published by Amberley Church Parochial Council- page 33

There are only a few churches, in Sussex, that are dedicated to St. Michael and I was interested to note that, originally, he was the guide and defender of goodness and that he held an important rank within the Archangels. Another very good 'thing' about St Michael is that the Feast of St Michael is held every year on the 29th September. My birthday. Coincidence or what?

Leaving the church we head up Church Street towards Hog Lane. At least that's where we think we're heading, because there isn't a single street name to be seen. "Perhaps another war has broken out and they've decided that removing the street names will confuse the invaders," I offer. From the map I have of Amberley we pass Hog Lane and should be heading towards The High Street. But, again, at the end of what I think is Church Street, there are no street names. Along Church Street (?) are various house names that give us some indication as to what the village was like some years ago. Names of houses include The Old Bakery, The Malt House, The Old Brew House and The Old Post House. Many of the places have thatched roofs but all the walls are the same drab colour.

Turning left into the High Street we pass what appears to be the only place, apart from the church and the pub, which seems to have outlasted the trauma of today's modern society. The village store sits back off the very short High Street with a sign asking you not to park your car outside (?) At the end of the High Street, on our right-hand side is The Black Horse Inn, with its adverts for home cooked food served after 12 o'clock. "But 'tis only 11.30," says Ron, "we'll 'ave 'ter call back later."

Amberley Wild Brooks

We turn right, into East Street (?) and head towards Hurst Cottages. To our left is the open wilderness known as Amberley Wild Brooks, a large 30 square mile area of tidal river marshes notable for fishing and boating. This place must be a haven for wildlife and birds and must look very impressive at high tide. Just beyond this area can be seen the railway line which was laid from Pulborough to Ford in 1863. It is reported in the book 'Dear Amberley'[5] that in December 1872 George Gearing went sailing after consuming two quarters of beer. On returning to land he met with two friends and they all went to 'Mr Ratley's shop' and drank a pint of elderberry wine each. George then headed home for Watersfield along this railway line. Later 'blood and material' were found on a train at Ford. A plate layer was sent back along the track and at 6.45 a.m. he found 'first a walking stick, 5 or 6

Stott Corner

[5] ibid

yards later a boot with a foot in it, 15 yards on the body of the deceased whom he knew, and 30 yards on, the other leg.' The verdict at his inquest was 'Accidentally run over by a train having fallen asleep across the line whilst in liquor.' In July 1890 a nine-year-old boy was killed whilst crossing over the line. As a result the Coroner wrote to the Railway Company and a bridge was constructed over the line.

It is just as we get to Hurst Cottages that we see our first street sign. "'Ave 'ter 'ave one 'ear," says Ron, "looks like council 'ouses, an' council always put signs up." But these houses must be worth a few bob. They're big, with large gardens and they're in Amberley.

We turn round and head back towards the village. I'm a little disappointed with Amberley. I was expecting a little more flavour. It's difficult to explain but I certainly don't think that this is the most beautiful village in Sussex. It does have some really nice thatched houses but it wasn't a homely type of place. Don't get me wrong, the few people we met were friendly enough but it didn't inspire me to want to live here. I'm beginning to think that Amberley wasn't the place to start our next venture when we find ourselves walking along Hog Lane and see a house called The Thatched House when it obviously wasn't. At least someone had a sense of humour.

At the end of Hog Lane, on the left, is a house called Stott Corner. As I'm explaining to Ron about the artist, an upstairs window opens and a man tells us "no it isn't my cottage, couldn't afford it. You'll be amazed at how many times I hear people talk about that artist." He then, for some reason, needs to explain to us that one of those 'nice council houses' in Hurst Cottages, at the end of East Street, was recently sold for £400,000. "Perhaps you can tell us why there aren't any street signs in Amberley," I ask. "Never noticed," is the reply, "I don't even know if this is Hog Lane or North Road. Perhaps it's because it is all private." Strange, I thought, he lives here and doesn't know the name of the road he lives in. And according to my map, there isn't a North Road. I leave Ron to chat and head down a

View from Amberley Mount

public footpath just to see where it went and to get away. Ron managed to drag himself away and meets me as I approach the Recreation Ground. "Did you ever play cricket or football here, Ron?" I ask. "Not that I can remember," he replies, "seems field ain't big enough fer a football pitch but they do 'ave one o' the prettiest pavilions I've seen, with it's net curtains an' all."

We turn left and walk along the main road for a few yards, until we come to Mill Lane, where we turn right. I will say now that this is not a walk for the faint-hearted. It is very, very steep in

Lost knickers?

places, it is very, very muddy, in other places but the views are astounding. We stopped at a house called Highdown to admire the countryside and the scenery took your breath away. You could see for miles, which is hardly surprising when you realise that we are heading towards Amberley Mount, one of the highest points in West Sussex.

Just past Highdown we turn off the lane and head even higher up, by following a well-marked bridle path. As we climb the next hill it is amazing at how many people we meet. This must be one of the most popular walks we have been on. There was

Abandoned machinery

never a moment when other walkers were not in view. Either above, or below us. All were happy to say a few words to us as we or they passed; Ron will speak to anyone. Yet only one group of people asked why Ron was dressed in a Sussex Smock.

Eventually we reach the summit. Here we are practically level with the gliders from the Southdown Gliding Club. These light planes are towed up by another aeroplane, which releases them to find the thermals, which keeps them in the air. The aeroplane returns to the airstrip, picks up another glider and gets him in the air. It seemed to be a continuous cycle because there was always some sort of plane in the air.

Whilst we were up there we saw no end of bird life, including one of Ron's favourites, the kite. The way that bird soars, with little to no effort is a true joy to watch even when the rooks were harassing it. "Them rooks always try ter scare the kites away," explains Ron, "but them kites are too shrewd to be worried about any rook. Look at the way 'e flies. Just a couple o' flaps with 'is wings an' 'e soars even 'igher." Ron's keen eyesight also managed to find a pair of ladies knickers, wound round some barbed wire. The 'Publication Laws' of England will not permit me to disclose what Ron thought might have happened to the young lady who lost this item of clothing in such a windswept environment.

Thankfully the saying 'what goes up, must come down' (and I am not referring to knickers) is true today as it's ever been. We turn right at the top of the hill, Amberley Mount, and head down towards a farm. The track we take is solid, so our descent is not difficult. On our right is a ploughed area that stretches for miles. It's difficult to imagine what would grow in this ground, but it is very fine soil and is mixed with flint and chalk. The farmer must have spent ages turning the soil to get it to look so good.

One of the things that really used to annoy me was to hear about poor hard up farmers. Whilst I will accept that some tenant farmers have problems I do think that a number of farmers just need to look around their own farms to realise that there is cash in trash. Don't leave it to rot, rust away into a pile of junk, get it and sell it. The

The long walk back

number of farms that we have passed through are all the same. Just tips for redundant machinery. Clear up the junk, improve your living environment and sell it. What's the problem? The farm we are about to come to is enormous. It must be worth, on paper, millions of pounds but when you get to the farm buildings it is wall-to-wall rubbish.

An eyesore. I took pictures but they are a very small portion of the machinery abandoned to rust on this farm.

At the end of the drive we find ourselves just a short distance from Highdown, the house near the start of our climb, in Mill Lane. Instead of walking back along Mill Lane we turn left and head towards the railway line at Amberley Station. On our left is a handy seat, placed in memory of Nesta Rhys-Davids who passed away in 1973. Sitting on this seat overlooking the village of Amberley was a welcome rest from the hills and dales of the last few miles.

View across river to Bury

We emerge, at the end of a lane called 'High Titten'. I have no idea why it is called 'Titten'. But 'High' it certainly was. We turn left here and head towards Amberley Living Museum. The museum is also known as 'Chalk Pit Museum' and is open, daily, throughout the year. It is a marvellous place to visit showing crafts of a bygone age, and the people who work there are always prepared to answer any questions from inquisitive youngsters. The entrance fee also includes parking and is well worth a visit, should you be in the area. Just past the museum is the railway station. We walk under the line and immediately turn right, heading towards the River Arun.

Remains of Amberley Castle

We follow the course of the river for about 1 mile until we reach a sign leading us towards Amberley Castle. It is at this point that a river crossing once existed, which joined Amberley to the village of Bury. The short journey, across The Adur stopped operating in the 1950's but it is clear where the ferry crossed. Now the ground is very wet

Amberley Thatch

and it is obvious that locals do not use the path. It is treacherous. The water, underfoot, is stagnant, and smells. It is also deep in places. At one point I went up to my knees in mud and the smell couldn't be described. Trust me. I now have wet feet, wet trousers and it smells vile. Ron is in hysterics.

The distance between Amberley and Bury is only a few hundred yards but within those yards I am soaked. Thankfully it is only a short distance, along an enclosed path, until we reach the outer walls of Amberley Castle. From here it is even less distance to the car.

Ladies and Gents

We, eventually, found our way back to The Black Horse and this time we ventured inside. I have to say that the welcome we received here made the trip more worthwhile. Although the Landlord was away we were warmly welcomed into this olde worlde pub. As Ron says 'a real pub'. On the wall are old photographs and antiquities of the area. I hate to think how many sheep bells, made by local Frank 'Grassy' Oliver, are hanging from the beams. I also found a photograph titled 'Amberley Parliament 1898' with a list of the names of the men in the picture. As we are sitting with our full glasses in hand, purely for research purposes only, Ron, on his return from the gents, suggests that I go to the toilets. "Take yer camera with yer," he splutters, "can't believe the pictures on the wall." I thought Ron might be on the turn, especially when he said, "I'll come with yer," and I'm sure the locals had their suspicions when we both left the bar and headed outside towards the toilets, with me holding the camera. But I drew the line at taking photographs of the pictures that were inside the cubicles. Some places it's best not to go! But I did find the signs amusing and it felt as if you were heading out into a forest just to go to the loo. When we got back inside the bar one of the regulars, who introduced himself as Andrew, asked Ron if he played sport. Ron doesn't need any encouragement to tell of his all round sporting achievements and proceeded to tell the gentleman. It would appear that Andrew is the sports coordinator for Amberley and he asked Ron if he would consider playing again, "Fer God's sake," chokes Ron, "I'm 60 bloody 2 years old. Yer can't be that desperate!"

We bid our farewells and head back to the car. Perhaps it was the time of year that makes Amberley appear a little drab, perhaps it wasn't. The people are friendly and those we spoke to in The Black Horse tell us that in the summer the village is alive with colourful flower gardens and hanging baskets. But, I'm afraid, I wasn't that impressed with the village.

We strolled around the village of Amberley
A quaint little place, with all that history
Our thanks to the patrons of The Black Horse pub
A good pint of Bombadier and a nice bit o'grub
AreSee©

Amberley Parliament 1898

Snaggey Syeral = Lime Burner	Ned Ruff = Farm Labourer
Mark Syeral = Hairdresser	Ted Ruff = Farm Labourer
Jimmy Adams = Carrier	'Doc' Hook = Blacksmith + Herbalist
Bert Wakeham = Lime Burner	George Philby = Chalk Pit
Dick Wakeham = Lime Burner	Tom Scutt = Chalk Pit
Steve Field = Bargeman	Taffy = Chalk Pit

And one other, who at the time of printing, has not been identified.

Chapter 2 - Billingshurst

Ron is not too well. The lump he discovered before our last walk at Amberley is still with him. We completed that walk in February and I have insisted that we do not walk again until it has been diagnosed. It is now June. He still has the lump, but no diagnosis. He has now been referred to a Hospital in Brighton for more tests to establish what this lump might be. "I lost me virginity in that 'ospital," complains Ron, "not natural ter put a camera up there. Still, it 'ad a bright side, Doctor was a pretty little female an' she explained what she was doin' whilst she was doin' it. But it sure ain't nat'ral."

To try and cheer Ron up I have relented. I have agreed to go for a walk, and after a little thought I have chosen Billingshurst. I have no special reason for choosing this place; it just seemed like a nice area to go to.

My first visit to Billingshurst was a few years ago when I was working for Royal Mail as a Planner and the new postal delivery routes had to be plotted for what was then called 'Single Daily Delivery' (SDD). The place was described, in many books, as a village but it seemed as if it is quite large. The village centre had that olde worlde charm with lots of small independent shop holders where the likes of Tesco's or Sainsburys and Asda have not encroached into The High Street. Perhaps the description of 'a village' should be changed to 'small town'? It will be interesting to see if it has changed

In 1662 the Reverend William Wilson was ejected from the Parish of Billingshurst because he would not re-establish the Book of Common Prayer after the dissensions of Oliver Cromwell's time. Several warrants were issued for Wilson's arrest, but he was never found. He was given refuge in the house of a Dr. Banks, another clergyman who (unlike Wilson) had accepted the Established Church and the Revised Prayer Book of 1662. Reverend Wilson died in 1670, aged about 40, but was not forgotten. On September 16th 1912 a service commemorating his ejection was held in Trinity Congregational Church, Billingshurst, when a tablet was unveiled to him recording 'his faithfulness to the claims of conscience.'[6]

Heading towards Great Gilman's Farm

The walk I have chosen is a little different from all our previous walks. Whilst we start at Billingshurst we do not actually visit any part of the 'village' but skirt the countryside to the west. The walk is said to be a 9½ mile circular and should take 4¾ hours to complete and the instructions were found on today's technical wonder – the Internet.[7] We have used this website without problems before so I am confident that all will be well.

We are joined, today, by Alan, who has read our exploits and wishes to take part in one of our little jaunts, fool that he is. I have seen Alan many times, walking along country roads around Hailsham with his thumb-stick but didn't actually meet him until the book 'Left or Right Ron?'[8] was released onto the unsuspecting public.

---

[6] People of Hidden Sussex by W Swinfen & D Arscott ISBN 0950951013 - 1985
[7] www.theargus.co.uk visited 24/06/2007

I collected both Ron, dressed in his Sussex Smock, and Alan, dressed as a Sussex squire, from The Kings Head (nothing changes) and head off. The discussion centres on the recent smoking ban in public places which didn't seem to be going down too well with some of the regulars at The Kings Head. The one thing that really, really annoys me is the ex-smokers who just have to have a go at people who smoke. Most of these people can't resist whining at smokers who, until they packed up were quite happy to blow smoke in my face when I was trying to kick the habit. One regular to The Kings Head, on the day that the ban was introduced, actually slagged people off for smoking the 'disgusting' weed, causing an argument between customers, and then went outside to light a cigar. He thought he was being funny but I can find no reason for this person's childish action. I personally do not smoke. That is my choice. If the place that I am in becomes smoky I leave. That is also my choice. When I did smoke I enjoyed a cigarette. Now I am unable to continue that enjoyment so why should I slag someone else off for something I am unable to do?

We also discuss the recent attempted suicide bombings at the airports, but anyone who knows Ron will understand that, due to publishing laws, I am unable to print Ron's views!

We arrive at Billingshurst at 2.15pm and park the car in a little side street behind Billingshurst Railway Station. Our first mission was to find Lower Station Road which, according to our instructions, should be very close to where the car was parked. As luck would have it a Police car was waiting at the level crossing gates so I asked the officer for directions. They say that you are getting old when the policemen look young. As I approached this officer he looked nervous, he was chewing his finger nail. He also looked about 12

Medieval hedge twig

years old. "Could you tell me where Lower Station Road is, please," I ask. "Your standing on it, sir," is the reply. The barrier went up and he was gone. Leaving me standing in the middle of the road. I walk back to Ron and Alan and we all head off towards the entrance to Great Gilman's Farm.

At the start of this walk the sun was shining. There were a few clouds but nothing untoward. But I noticed that Alan had on a heavy coat, a hat, and he was wearing wellingtons. Perhaps he was aware of something brewing. Ron had his smock on, carrying his usual carrier bag. I thought, what the hell, I'll just wear my fleece. No, I won't wear it, I'll tie it round my waist, the sun was very warm and I'll start sweating under the fleece. So that is how we set off.

We followed the road, as instructed, until we hit a gentle climb. On the right is a playing field. "Look at

Hairy Wound Wurt

[8] Left or Right Ron? Published by LR Publishers 2007 ISBN 9780955591907

the slope on that. Wouldn't need ter 'it the ball very 'ard ter get four runs out there," comments Ron. I'd noticed that Alan had said very little. But his breathing seemed a bit laboured. I hope he's going to be ok? We'd only gone a few hundred yards and I was starting to worry about him and we'd still got over 9 miles to go. "You ok, Alan?" I ask. "Yes, I'm fine," is the reply, "but I might 'ave ter find an 'edge ter slip be'ind in a second. Must 'ave been the 'alf pint o'bitter I 'ad afore we come out. Bladder ain't so good these days." With that he's disappeared behind the next hedge only to return with a smug, satisfied smile, "that's better," is all he says. Just past Great Gilman's Farm entrance, on the opposite side of the road, we find the stile that will lead us into open countryside.

Easily found stile

Once over the stile Alan and Ron become experts on foliage. I really mean experts. It's like walking with an encyclopaedia. Alan snatches at the hedgerow and says, "do you know how ter tell 'ow old an 'edge is?" He holds out two twigs. They both look the same to me. "This one," he says, holding out the twig in his right hand, "is a newer variety of this one," he produces the other twig in his other hand. "This one is the original, it's got rounded leaves which means it's been 'ere since medieval times. This one with pointed leaves 'aint so old, see," and he throws the 'new' twig to the ground. "You can always tell," he says. "Now come on let's see what else we can find."

It is about now that I notice a big black cloud heading in our general direction. "Don't like the look of that rain-cloud," I comment. "That's no rain cloud," says Ron, "tis a Wens'day an' it don't rain in Sussex on a Wens'day afternoon. You knows that." "I've got wet on a Wednesday before now, Ron," I reply "So's you might, from a sea fret or a cloud mist but it ain't rain." You can't argue with him but the cloud heading in our direction certainly looked black.

We follow the right field edge until we come to a three-way junction. We maintain direction as we go through a gate, cross the next field where we drop to another gate.

Ron and Alan are discussing the butterflies we are disturbing as we walk through the long grass. "Can't remember when I last saw so many butterflies," comments Ron. "It's surprising how many butterfly varieties there are," says Alan, "What's even more surprising is how many of them migrate." Naively I ask "Butterflies don't migrate, do they? I only thought they lived for a few days and then died." "You'll be surprised," says Alan, "how many do migrate. Some of our butterflies come over from France and they can live for a while." I am now bombarded with information about butterflies from both Ron and Alan. I vaguely remember something about elm trees and butterflies hovering above them and then there was a young moth of some sort only just been born lives on some grub or other and, finally it has been a good year for horseflies,

Alan exits the wood

apparently. But where that came from and who said it I have no idea. But it has started to rain! Not heavy, but it is raining.

We turn left along the field's edge and then find a sign leading us to a plank bridge and stile. This will lead us into Marringdean Wood. We follow the path crossing more bridges and stiles until we exit the other side, in a small meadow. Again, Alan picks a flower. "This is what is called Hairy Wound Wurt," he explains, "used to be rubbed into severe wounds and used as an antiseptic. Been used since ancient times," he continues, "Used with cobwebs, on battle wounds, it would congeal the blood." "How do you learn all these things, Alan?" I ask. "Always learnin' I am. Never too old ter learns. I reads things and finds things out. Me ol' mum used ter tell me all manner o'things when she were alive. Miss me ol' mum, I do." It is obvious that Alan's love for his mother is still strong. Which is strange because both Ron and I have lost our mother's recently and we are both still coming to terms with the loss. I will always remember my late father-in-law's words, 'you can have no end of fathers, but you will only have one mother'.

Ron wearing wet gear

It's the light rain that brings us back to today, as we exit the woods. "The rains getting harder," I comment. "That ain't rain but just a sea fret," insists Ron. "But we're nowhere near the sea, Ron," I reply putting my fleece on. "Then it must be a 'ill mist," says Ron. "You've got an answer for everything," says Alan as we head between two large oak trees and walk towards four large greenhouses, close to Jackman's Farm.

We pass the greenhouses and find the stile that leads us out onto the B2133. Here we turn right and look for a bridleway, on the left, leading us towards Steepwood Farm.

Our instructions take us to the top of the farm drive where the bridleway turns left, around the farm buildings, rising slightly before descending into Beedings Copse. And the rain is coming down hard now. It is throwing it down. "What do you call this, then Ron?" I ask. "I'll give in ter yer," he replies, "what's 'appened is the sea fret an'

the 'ill mist 'ave met and it's turned it inta' rain." What he does now amazes me. He puts down his carrier bag and proceeds to unwrap, not a cake or a bun or a drink, as in previous walks, but he actually has brought with him some wet weather clothing! I am gob smacked, of all the nerve. He's been telling me that 'it don't rain in Sussex on a Wednesday afternoon' and he's brought wet gear. I'll never believe him again. I am soaked. The rain has gone through my fleece and through my shirt. My trousers are wet through and sticking to my legs. All Ron does

Wild deer

is shrug his shoulders and giggles as we shelter under a large oak tree, waiting for the rain to pass. Alan says nothing.

I must admit that it was a short, but very sharp, downpour and after just a few minutes the sun was out and Ron had to remove the wet gear because he was beginning to sweat. We now enter Beeding's Copse through a deer gate and immediately take the left bridleway. It is whilst walking along this bridleway that we saw the wild deer. The field was awash with them. I have never seen so many deer,

Ragged Robin

just grazing, in one place. They were different colours, white, black, brown and grey. All were aware that we were about and some ran away behind trees but the sight was fantastic. Whether it was the thrill and excitement of seeing all these deer in one place or not, I don't know. But something, from this point on was not right.

For those who have followed our previous exploits will know that our sense of direction can be a little flawed. We also seem to lose our own bearings, but, more importantly signposts disappear. You will be happy to note that this walk was going to be the same. We should have followed the bridleway to Sand Pond Cottage. We never found the cottage. What we did find was a mass of horseflies who insisted on trying to eat all of us. Our next point to look for was Walnut Tree Cottage. That's right, we never found it, although Alan did find a walnut tree and promptly picked a walnut, bit the outer skin off, spat it out and hastily started rubbing the walnut over his face and hands. "It's supposed to repel the 'orse fly," he explains, "they used ter put walnut under the 'orses bridle ter keep flies off." After dousing himself, liberally with walnut you'd expect the flies to disappear but I noticed he was still slapping himself and swearing every now and again. Perhaps it didn't work.

Russian Rhubarb 'Gunnera'

We pass a large holly tree. "Used ter use that ter catch birds in the old days," says Alan, "boil the bark until it's thick and gooey and called it birdlime. Put a caged bird on the ground and surround the bird with twigs. Smother the twigs with the gooey birdlime and when the birds come down to

Foul pond

investigate they gets stuck ter the twigs. Just catch 'em an' cook 'em. Easy". Just past here Alan makes another find. "Look at this. I haven't seen this plant for years. It's called Ragged Robin, grows near ponds usually." "Why is it called Ragged Robin?" I ask. "It's not red and looks nothing like a bird." "Don't know why it's called that but I think it has somethin' ter do with the leaves. I'll look it up when we gets back." When we get back is right. Nothing looks like it should from our instructions. We should have found a four-way sign by now but we've seen nothing. And I'm getting worried. It's nearly 4.30 now and we're lost, and, according to our map we are not even halfway round. Another hasty look at our map and instructions tells me that we should be heading towards the B2133 again. Once we reach the road we turn right and then left into Oldhouse Lane. We walk on. We arrive at a pond. Perhaps this is part of Sand Pond Cottage. But no. I am amazed at the size of the leaves on a plant growing close to the pond. "That's what's called 'Gunnera', says Alan, "commonly known as Russian Rhubarb. The leaves get so large that if it rains you can shelter under 'em and not get wet." I notice that the horseflies are still biting. Ron's now started to scratch. The water in the pond looks a bit foul and it must be a haven for all sorts of wildlife. Some of it still insisted on taking chunks out of Ron and me. Perhaps the walnut on Alan was working?

At last we find the road. "We need to turn right here," I offer, "and then we should find Oldhouse Lane." But what we did find was the entrance to Steepwood Farm (see page 10). We had completed a complete circle and ended up where we had been over an hour ago. Ron can't stop laughing but Alan, being Alan, found something different to discuss. "I didn't notice that plant when we walked through earlier," he says.

"That's 'Dogs Mercury' that is," he continues. "Deadly poisonous it is. Used ter be used for poisoning the gentry, it was. Drop a few crumpled leaves in to a glass o'wine they did. Never used ter wake up. Real deadly." I'm now thinking of taking some. According to the map we now need to turn back along the B2133, and head towards Broadford Bridge to find our Lane. But it's getting late. Why don't we just continue along and up the B2133 and get to Billingshurst. After all, the signpost says that it is only 2 miles up the road. What possessed me to say "Let's see if we can find Oldhouse Lane, it can't be far down the road?" And off we went. And you will never guess what. We never found the Lane, we walked for over two hours and never saw another person until, in desperation I said, "Shall I knock on this door and ask directions?" "I think you'd better," chuckles Ron "or we'll be out 'ere fer days." He loves every minute of this. Alan gives me some comfort when he admits that our map 'ain't too good' and 'we can't blame Graham for there not bein' some people about'. I'm not sure how hard I hit this front door but a man from the opposite side of the road came out and asked if he could help. Ron is now in hysterics and can't say anything. But once we explained to the gentleman that we were lost and needed to get back to Billingshurst he obliged with directions.

We had to cross various fields and tracks

Dogs Mercury

How the others live

until we reached what would look like a private driveway. This driveway would lead us back onto the main road and, eventually, to Billingshurst. On the way Alan couldn't resist more lessons in our wildlife. He noticed what I thought was a brown butterfly sunning itself in the late afternoon sun. "There's a Five Spot Barnet Moth," declares Alan. "I've got a Bald Spot Barnet," replies Ron with that stupid grin of his. But I could see that Alan wasn't that impressed with the joke as we eventually arrive at the 'private driveway'. Looking up this driveway to the house at the end I am very jealous of anyone who has to live in this sort of tranquillity. It really is one of the prettiest places I have seen and must be worth a lot more money than any of us will ever see.

Five Spot Barnet Moth??????

We come to the end of this drive to be confronted with a house whose burglar alarm is raging war. The noise is very loud and it is obvious that the neighbours are getting a little annoyed with their peace and quiet being destroyed by this alarm. A few of them have obviously made the decision to break into the house and halt the alarm. One has scaled the walls and entered into the property by an open window and it is only a few minutes and the alarm is stilled. We heard the cheers from the neighbours as we approached Billingshurst and where we had parked the car. It is now 7pm and we have been walking for 5 hours.

I have learnt so much from Alan and probably forgot as much again. All the time we were walking, and that was for over 5 hours, Alan and Ron didn't stop talking about what they could see. I have tried to capture their observations in these pages but I am certain that some has slipped away and missed being written down. I can only apologise to them both if anything of paramount importance has been missed.

And finally, the picture above was taken at some point on our walk. I asked Alan what the picture was and he reliably informs me that it is a picture of the Five Spot Barnet Moth. I have enlarged the picture and looked at it through a magnifier but I still can't see the bloody moth! Can you?

We walked the woods and fields of Billingshurst
This is the walk we got lost the worse
We went out for a relaxing stroll
Walked for five hours, never saw a sole
Arsee©

Chapter 3 - Saltdean

This is another walk which is slightly different from the others. We have been invited by a fellow walker to follow a route taken when he walks his dogs. Our guest today is Ron, no not our Ron, but another Ron. Hopefully this Ron will not be the same as the other Ron. Am I making it clear, so far? Perhaps I should number them Ron1 and Ron2 just to make it easy? We'll see how it goes as we put pen to paper. With Ron(2) will be Hannah, a greyhound and Bing, an English Pointer who are prepared to walk with us on what looks as if it will be a pleasant day.

Saltdean is one of those places that you pass through and keep going. Before Ron(2) asked us to join him the only thing I could tell you about Saltdean was that it had a Lido, a lovely open swimming pool, and it was on the way to Brighton along the coast road. As you will be aware once we have a walk in mind I try to find out something about the place we are to visit. Saltdean was no different.

Literally, Saltdean simply means 'the salt dean or valley' and was first shown on a

Hannah, Ron (2) and Bing

map of 1740 as Saltdean Gap, because it formed a small break in the cliffs.[9] There are other reported reasons for the place being called Saltdean; one is that during a terrible storm, in the late 1700s' the sea water polluted the grass so badly that the sheep were unable to graze. The sheep that did manage to survive became a very hardy breed, now known simply as Southdowns. The Southdowns Sheep Society will tell you that this is pure fantasy as they attribute this particular breed to John Ellman from Glynde.[10]

Apart from these snippets I was unable to find that much about Saltdean. I'm hoping that the walk will uncover some more secrets as we go. I will just say here, that this walk is not for the faint-hearted. It is very steep in many places, both inclines and declines can be very tiresome. But once at the top the views are some of the very best I have seen. I will make no excuses for the number of photographs taken on this walk because I have tried to capture the natural beauty of Sussex in this chapter. The scenery is outstanding.

Another difference to our other walks is that this one was to be done in the morning. Not a weekday but, would you believe, on a Sunday. Not only was it a morning walk but an early morning to boot. I picked Ron (1) up at 7:15am and headed off towards Saltdean. The arrangement was to meet Ron (2), and his dogs, behind Saltdean Lido at 8:00am. This is where we arrive at just before 8:00. My timing is spot on.

From the outset Ron (2) had advised us that the walk he was to take us on could, depending on the weather, last 1 hour or up to 3 hours. We should have no problems

---

[9] Sussex Place Names by Judith Glover, Published by Countryside Books, Newbury, Berkshire 1997
[10] www.southdownsheepsociety.co.uk/history visited 23/07/2007

getting lost because no map was required as Ron (2) knew where he was going because he first completed the walks in this area some 40 plus years ago with his father, I was going to enjoy this.

Long bridleway towards Pickers Hill

Pickers Hill Farm

Ron (2) arrives complete with animals in the back of his car and advises us to follow him to the top of Saltdean Vale, where we park both the cars opposite a bridleway and both Ron (1) and I are introduced to Hannah and Bing.

We head along the bridleway with both Hannah and Bing (I love that name for a dog) on leads. There are a large number of potholes along this tarmac bridleway and due to the very heavy rain over the past few days they are all full of water. "Bing will walk in every puddle," explains Ron (2) "but Hannah hates the water so she'll walk round the puddles." Ron (2) had problems with leads crossing over as Bing went one-way and Hannah went the opposite.

Shortly after entering the bridleway we pass the Saltdean United Football ground and I just knew Ron (1) would have a comment. "Use ter play on that pitch," says Ron (1), "worst pitch in the league it was." "Why was that?" I ask. "Well just look at it," Ron (1) says, "full o' lumps an' bumps, practically unplayable it was, never liked comin' 'ere." "Which league do they play in?" I ask, "County League when I was playin' but I'm not sure what league they're in now". "Did you usually lose here?" I ask but apparently Ron (1) didn't hear the question or he decides to ignore me.

We now pass, on our left, what used to be the farm cottages for Pickers Hill Farm but Ron (2) thinks they are probably in private hands now as the only person working the farm is a man called Eric and he's part-time.

After walking into the farmyard and turning right and then left around the buildings we now follow a wide path, up the hill towards a gate. As I said earlier this walk is not for the faint-hearted. The theory that what goes up must come down is tested to the full. Once we arrive at the gate Ron (2) advises that the path goes all around the outside of this enormous field and as we need to get to the furthest corner we would cut across the middle. Again this is uphill and once we get to the top I'm beginning to wish I hadn't brought my coat with me. We can clearly hear a skylark whistling away as soon as we enter the field. It's as if we had turned on a switch. Apart from this bird it is total peace and quiet. "I've been known to just stop here, lie down in the sun and just listen," says Ron (2) and we can really understand why. On reaching the next gate we pass through and keeping the fence on our left continue to another gate. Ron (2) now tells us that Hannah, that's the greyhound, had a big problem with her left leg. There was thought that the leg would have to be amputated but the skill of a local vet managed to save the leg and, apart from some disfigurement she seems very able to walk. "She won't run far, just plods along," he says. All the while Hannah follows his every footstep while Bing is full of energy and bounces along at top speed only coming back to us when Ron uses his whistle. We pass through yet another gate and follow the path keeping the wire fence, this time, on our right-hand side. The panoramic view from up here is breathtaking and, according to Ron (2) only a taster of what is to come.

In the distance can be seen a derelict couple of barns, "Always reminds me of that Hitchock film 'The Birds'," says Ron (2) and a little way in the distance you can see hundreds of birds sitting on the rafters of the buildings. As if Bing knew what we were looking at he raced across the field and put the birds to flight. Hannah just plods along behind Ron.

Shortly after we pass the barns, on our left, Ron (2) says that we are approaching Harvey's Cross. Now I thought he meant a crossroads but couldn't see a road in sight. What Ron meant

Ron ponders

was simply a cross. But not an ordinary cross. This one was placed here in memory of John Harvey Esq., who died, suddenly at this very spot on the 20th June 1819.

The cross in memory of John Harvey

According to the memorial tablet John was from Ickwell Bury in Bedfordshire[11] which is today, *the* place to go for yoga exercises because it is said to be beneficial for the relief of pain caused by Multiple Sclerosis & Muscular Dystrophy. Unfortunately the memorial is a little worse for wear. It was only erected about 15 years ago and it is already overgrown with weeds and needs some TLC. I would also like to think that the damage to the stone cross is not due to mindless vandalism but Ron (2) believes that some vandals could be responsible. Next to the memorial is a stone seat which was donated by the Rottingdean Windmill Walk. To be honest if Ron (2) hadn't pointed it out I wouldn't have seen it because of the overgrowth.

Just past this memorial the path divides to the right and to the left. We now take the left fork. I will remind you of this particular path later because we come back this way on our return to the car.

Stone memorial of church

The skylarks are still singing their song on the wing as we now head down a steep hill, through a gate and we maintain direction, still downhill, into what is known as Balsdean Valley. To our right is a field

[11] www.mssociety.org.uk/document

full of sheep who are not too worried about the two Ronnie's and me but are very wary of Bing, who still hasn't stopped trying to run although, because of the sheep, he is now on his lead. We now reach a gate where, according to the signs the North Brighton Countryside route goes left but we turn right and head along the Southdowns Way Circular. It is now that we meet out first person. A somewhat elderly gentleman is jogging down the hill towards us wearing a day glow yellow jersey and black shorts. "'Ere comes a fit young man," says Ron (1), "must be in trainin' fer a marathon." All the runner says as he sweeps past is "Love the smock," and he's gone.

All that remains of Balsdean

Old broken machinery

We enter the Nature Reserve

We now discuss the behaviour of joggers, runners and walkers at some length. I, personally, can find no enjoyment in going on a long walk on your own. I need someone to talk to and discuss things with. Ron (2) obviously enjoys walking, especially with his dogs. He finds that he talks to them and they keep him company. Ron (1), on the other hand, can't understand why anyone would want to jog in the countryside. "You look at any jogger," he says, "they never look 'appy. Puffin' an' pantin' like they do can't be good for 'em. An' look at the funny colour they go after a few yards. An' what for? Ter get 'ealthy, tis all. Don't look too 'ealthy ter me. All that sweatin' an' lookin' at yer watch ter see if yer any quicker than the last time. Stupid if yer ask me. Yer can't see this beautiful countryside if yer racin' about like a loony. Might as well take a long walk, like us, an' admire the scenery." Next time you see a jogger, take a close look, and I think you may find that Ron is right. But each to their own.

We follow the wide track as it meanders through the valley. Ron (2) tells us that we are approaching what used to be the village of Balsdean. "It was in the early 1940's," says Ron "that the Canadians came over and used Balsdean for target practice. I can remember walking along here, with me dad, and there used to be a large metal water tank that was riddled with bullet holes. It's gone now but so have most of the buildings." The path now bears right and we now come off the track to our left and walk on the grass, "What are you looking for?" I ask Ron (2). "There was a stone here, somewhere, which marks the place where the altar of the church used to be. It's been so long since I've seen it I can't remember exactly where it is." But it didn't take him long to find. The photograph isn't that clear but the stone is inscribed with the words 'This plaque marks the site of the altar of the Norman church of Balsdean'. The church is mentioned in a document dated 1117 and 1147. Another document states that in 1579 the Vicar of Rottingdean was required '..to hold a service four times a year in the chapel of the 'village' of Balsdean'. In a visitation report, dated 1724 and written by Bishop Bowers, under the heading of Rottingdean, refers to a '..a farm called Baseden in which there is an old chappel(sic) and chappel yard and a small parcell of land leading up to the hill belonging as is said to the Vicar and called the Butt, but never enjoyed by the present vicar'[12]. There is nothing else here, apart from a derelict barn. The stillness is breathtaking in itself. There is no sound apart from sheep bleating in the distance and the rustle of trees. Yet there is a beauty here. There is something that I can't explain on paper, a feeling, all is at peace.

Numbered pegs

Ron brings me back to reality by finding some abandoned machinery, "a good mechanic could get that goin' again. Might have ter give ol' Des[13] a call."

We now follow a path, again uphill, to our left. Ron (2) knows this area as the 'S' bends. "Me and me mates used to come up here and play," says Ron (2) as he reminisces in the past. We pass through a gate and are now in a field full of sheep. People who know me and have read about our previous exploits[14] will be aware of my relationship with certain animals. But I think I have the solution to all my troubles. Get a dog. Even with Bing firmly kept on a lead these sheep were not interested in me but kept their beady eyes on Bing who was still trying to run about like a mad thing. Hannah still plods behind Ron (2). In the distance, to our left, Ron (1) has noticed more joggers and leads off again about how bad it is for you as we head around the field, keeping the fence on our right.

In the field corner we arrive at another gate which takes us into Castle Hill Nature Reserve. We ignore the path to our right but continue direction, again uphill. We pass some bright blue pegs in the ground, about 50 yards apart. All are numbered and, as we are in a nature reserve we have no idea what they were placed on the banks for. We did wonder whether to ask the owner of the Land Rover parked at the bottom of the field but he looked to be a little busy with a young lady so we thought better of it.

The track now goes up. And I mean up. Steeply up. I have to stop a number of times to get my breath. Ron (2) says that the views, when we get to the top, will be worth it. I can't understand why Ron (1) hasn't got the water out of his carrier bag. I'm gagging for a drink but I didn't like to ask. It isn't until we reach the summit of this mountain that Ron (2) gets out a bottle of water for the dogs and Ron(1) says that he's left our water at home. We've been walking three hours and now he tells me that he's left the water at home. Still the dogs needed to quench their thirst, lucky sods. Just where we stop to let the dogs drink is the exit from the Nature Reserve and Ron is beside himself. "I don't bloody believe it," he chokes, "look what those mindless bastards have done ter the sign." The exit sign is covered in graffiti. "They must 'ave

---

[12] Excavations at Balsdean Chapel, paper written by N. E. S. Norris F.S.A and E.F Hockings

[13] Des used to be a regular at The Kings Head, now only seen on odd occasions

[14] Left or Right, Ron ? published by LR Publishers, 2007

come all the way up 'ere just ter spray that sign with paint. Tis not right". I have to admit we are in the middle of nowhere. In every direction I look are green fields, nothing but fields and you had to agree with Ron (2)? Why people have to damage property like this is beyond me. It takes Ron a few minutes to calm down and we eventually move off to our right. "The views up here will certainly make up for your disappointment," says Ron (2) and what we are about to see is some of the most breathtaking scenery I have ever seen. I will just let you look at the pictures.

In the distance my eyes are drawn to the pathway we are taking. I can see, along this path some of the biggest cattle that I have ever seen. Ron (1) sees them at the same time as me, "Some o' your friends up a'ead," he chuckles. Ron (2) looks in the same direction, "Don't you like cattle?" he asks. "If it's big an' can run towards 'im, Graham ain't too keen." "I'll be ok. Bing and Hannah, as well as you two will be between me and them when we get there," I say, more pleading than anything. But they did look big, very big, and as we approached them they didn't move, they just swung their heads in our direction and

Beautiful View

eyed us. But I tried to show no fear and bravely, if not with a bit of a shake, we passed the cattle and kept our direction keeping a fence to our right.

Just as we reach a large dew pond, which Bing had to try out, there is a gate

Graffiti covered sign

Just before we go downhill

where, once through the path turns sharp right and we head towards what looks like a wooden enclosed area, which turns out to be another pond that Bing has to try. Hannah is still plodding behind Ron (2).

We are now, at last, heading downhill and eventually get to the part of the walk, at the start, just past Harvey's Cross. It's been sometime ago so you will be forgiven if you can't remember.

The return to the car is the first part of our walk in reverse. As we have been walking for over four hours conversation is very limited. But Bing is still on the run and Hannah is still plodding behind Ron (2) and that is the way it remains until, at last we arrive back at Saltdean Vale.

This has been a very tiring walk. It is very steep and, although it was a very warm day there was, thankfully, a breeze which helped keep us keep cool. Ron (2) obviously knows his way about these parts and it was great not to have to keep looking at a map with the hope that we wouldn't get lost. If you are thinking of completing the walk be prepared to have to slog it out, but as Ron (2) says the views are really worth the effort. We also learnt about Balsdean, the destruction of the village by the Canadians and we have seen a memorial to John Harvey, who dropped dead on the same spot as his memorial all those years ago.

I am shattered and can't wait to get home for a long soak in the bath. "If you want to come on any other walks with me," suggests Ron (2), "just give me a call, I know lots of other walks that might interest you." We both thank him for the offer but I think that this walk is going to take us some time to get over. But thanks for the very kind offer, Ron.

Are we high up????

We walked the Downs of Saltdean
Found the lost village of Balsdean
Look at the pictures, I think you'll agree
We saw some fabulous scenery
Arsee©

Chapter 4 - Cuckoo Trail

Those familiar with our walks will know that we have nearly completed the Cuckoo Walk apart from the bit from Polegate into Hampden Park and from Horam to Heathfield. Today we are completing the Hampden Park end of the trail.

It has been suggested that some of our walks cannot be carried out by everyone and that we should undertake a walk that can be completed by someone who is less

Rodney's Invalid Buggy

able than Ron and me. So today we are joined by Rodney who is unable to get about without the assistance of his invalid buggy. The walk has been organised and studied, in detail, by Rodney so there is no way that we will be getting lost. So for today I do not need a map. Rodney is a volunteer 'Ranger' for East Sussex County Council and is very familiar with the area.

I have to admit to one or two reservations. For one thing part of the walk is carried out in an area known as Shinewater. Some of the locals tend to steer a wide berth around the estates in this area, because it was known as a bit of a trouble spot. I have to say that I used to live in an area known as 'Town Farm', or 'Sin City' as it used to be called, in Hailsham which had the same reputation as Shinewater and I have to admit that although some areas were not desirable I never experienced any trouble. I am also a little worried that the walk will lack any historical interest, although I have uncovered some interesting facts about the park. Ron thinks I will be pleasantly surprised. We will see.

One thing that I will mention now is that Ron, at last, (we are now nearly into September) been given the 'all clear' with his lump. It is nothing more serious than a hernia which will, of course, need surgery. Apparently a bed is not, currently, available anywhere in the country, a surgeon cannot be found for months, who has the time to perform the delicate operation for him, nor can any nursing staff be located who have the expertise that is needed, should the operation be carried out at short notice. Unless, of course, he can scrape up £5,000 in cash, and then everything can be located and he will be operated on before the end of the week. What a wonderful medical system this country has??

Route 21 sign - at the start

For now though I am hoping that this gentle walk will not cause him any discomfort. Rodney says that it is mainly on the level, obviously it has no stiles to climb and the pathways are made up, i.e. no mud.

Due to my work commitments I have arranged to meet them both at the start of the walk, at Levetts Road, in Polegate. The start time is 1.30 and we are all present and on time.

The Polegate, Cuckoo Trail sign

Mobile phone mast

Ron explains about the book

From Levetts Road we head away from Polegate until we reach Aberdale Road, just a few yards away. Within these few yards Ron has managed to pick up, from the paths, a total of 7 pence. "Go on like this an' I'll 'ave bus fare ter get 'ome," he chuckles. We turn right, into Aberdale Road and follow the road to the left where we find the public footpath which is designated Route 21. "This wide path," advises Rodney, "will eventually lead us to the Cuckoo Trail and then on to Shinewater," and then he's gone. I'm not sure how fast his buggy can go but he left me and Ron standing. It is now, as Rodney disappears in the distance, that I confide my fears and doubts to Ron about this walk. "Don't you worry," says Ron, "I think you'll be pleasantly surprised. 'Tis a lovely day, it's a Wen'sdey afternoon an' not a cloud ter be seen. You'll enjoy it. Trust me."

The wooden sign we are greeted with after a short distance along this path is a little confusing to me. It tells me that we are on the Cuckoo Trail, at Polegate. Yet the first sign told me that we are on Route 21. I don't know how that works. We can't ask Rodney, he's nowhere in sight. But as we turn the bend the view across to the downs is stunning, spoilt only by the many electricity pylons that seem to be everywhere these days. When we walked along Aberdale Road, at the start, there is a pylon on the corner. Surely there must be another way, other than these monstrous eyesores. Anyone who carries out walks in the countryside will be aware of what I mean. And then, to top it all, a little further along the path is yet another of today's technological eyesores: the mobile phone mast!

One of my work colleagues asked me the other day if I could suggest a place where she could gather stinging nettles, to make twine (?) and some sloes, to make gin. I have found the ideal place for her to collect both. To the right of us now are the tallest stinging nettles I have ever seen and to our left is a sloe tree (?) full to the top with fruit. Just a little further on two cyclists, who look like grandfather and grandson, are busy picking blackberries and putting them into plastic containers. The elderly gentleman spots me with a camera and asks, "If I set my camera up could you take a photograph of me and my grandson, cycling towards you?" "No problem," says I. "'E's used ter takin' photo's," says Ron. "Speak to 'im nice an' e'll put yer in 'is next book." Ron never misses a chance to make a sale and explains to the gentleman, as he rummages in his

Views towards the South Downs

Stile in need of repair

cycle bag to find his camera, where he will find our first book[15]. "I've set the camera up," he informs me, "its set on f8 and focused at 20 feet," as he hands me an old 35mm Cannon camera. "All you do is look through the view finder and click when I say." He backs away from me with his grandson, climbs aboard his bike and slowly, cycles towards me. "Now," he says as he approaches. I press the button and hear a distinct click. I hand the camera back to him and hope that he gets the picture he's hoping for. "Looks like we might o' sold another book," says Ron, as our new found friends cycle off in the distance, "we should 'ave brought some books with us." "Haven't you got some in the carrier?" I ask. "Only the one," he replies, "an' I need that ter show 'em what the book looks like, don't I? Can't sell the only one I got with me. That'd be silly." And you can't argue with that, can you?

Apart from the fabulous views of the South Downs over to our right I notice that, to our left are derelict buildings, probably used by farmers but now just left to fall down. Brings me to one of my pet hates, poor hard up farmers, but here and now is not the place to discuss my theories. Perhaps it will come up again in a later chapter?

A short distance on from here and we catch up with Rodney who has had to pull over his buggy for an intake of nicotine. "Are you allowed to smoke in that confined space?" asks Ron. "Its o.k." replies Rodney, "providing I undo both of the side flaps. That way I get a through draft and I don't get to inhale the same smoke twice." He's got an answer for everything. And, for once, someone has an answer for Ron.

"This is where the Cuckoo Trail meets Route 21," advises Rodney. I didn't say anything about the sign confusion I found at the start. "The railway line to our right," he continues, "is the line from Polegate. As we get a little closer to Shinewater we will have to go over the line from Hampden Park to Hastings."

We walk on and it is very evident that a major road is on our left. The constant traffic noise, at times, is very loud. Also, along this part of the walk, we notice other walks branching off to the left and the right. As I said earlier, Rodney is a volunteer for the Council and one of his responsibilities is to inform the council if he see's anything not quite right and we are now on 'his patch'. So when he saw a stile that was in need for repair he took a photograph and noted where the stile was. "I'll

One of the many water features

[15] 'Left or Right Ron?' by Graham Pollard and published by LR Publishing

e-mail them about that when I get home."

I was impressed, and if all our public paths could be looked after in this way then it would make walking our beautiful countryside much more enjoyable. Another thing both Ron and I had noticed was the amount of water there is. Whether they were all man-made rivers or natural they all had one thing in common. A lack of warning signs of any description. On all the walks that Ron and I have completed, wherever there was water, it would be politically correct for the authorities to warn the public of the dangers of drowning. But that is common sense, I hear you say. And you would be right but as tax payers and users of our water industry doesn't it comfort you to know that you're well-earned money has been spent on thousands of signs that warn you that if you fall into the water there is a possibility that you will drown. Yet here, in the midst of one of the largest estates in the area are water features with not one warning sign. I wonder why?

Overgrown path

The path we are on now climbs slightly and the road is very close to the path. Traffic hurtles down this road at a fair speed; luckily a slight bank and a crash barrier are between us and the traffic. As the path levels off it bears slightly right away from the road then turns slightly left joining another path on our right. "We'll be coming back this way after we've walked round the Park," Rodney informs us. All along the path I've noticed large holes in

View across the lake

the ground covered with grills or mesh. "They're used for draining the rainfall into the lakes," says Rodney. "When it rains the water comes off the roads and goes down the gullies into the Park lakes. Otherwise this area would be flooded during the winter months." All of a sudden Rodney has his camera out and is focusing on what appears to be an impassable path. "Have to tell them about that as well when I get back," says Rodney.

We now come to a small bridge and I notice that there is another sign for Route 21 (?) and in front of us is the very large industrial estate at Hampden Park and we head towards it. Just as I was getting a little disappointed at being so close to a built-up area we turn left and walk pass the Route 21 sign and head under the main road. Here, again is a small river, without warning signs, running to our left. Just before this is a sign, which looked very new, welcoming us to 'Shinewater Park'. Until this day I have passed this park hundreds of times, on the road now above us, and never realised it was a Park. I have seen the water as I drive towards Asda on our weekly shopping trip. I have admired the scenery from above but never, until today, ventured into the area. I didn't realise what I was missing. The area is a credit to the planners, a credit to the area and the people of Shinewater must be congratulated for the way it is kept. During the excavation work for this Park they found artefacts that date back to 600 BC. An ancient trackway was located during the excavation work and because the find is considered of National importance, and for its own protection, the location of the actual trackway is not pinpointed.[16] The Park was constructed in the mid 1990's and consists of two lakes, Shinewater and Hydneye, which were excavated, originally for floodwater storage. Shinewater Park was officially opened in 2002 and is jointly managed by East Sussex County Council and Eastbourne Borough Council and won a commendation from the Civic Trust in 2004.

The walk all around the Park is approximately one mile. It is completely level and the going is as easy as you want it to be. But it is an unforgettable one mile. The park has everything that could be needed. It has play facilities for young children, all enclosed. It has play areas for the older children, including skate ramps, a basketball area and a football pitch. Dogs are asked to be kept under control and the people using the park respect it. It was clean. The only area we saw litter was an area that was close to the road so it may have been thrown from passing traffic but all in all I was impressed. The paths through the park will lead you to little quiet areas; people were fishing,

Rodney, never far from the ladies

mums and dads playing with their children who looked as if they were having fun. Not stuck indoors with a television or a computer screen.

Ron has found a new friend

Toward the end of our walk around the Park we met Penny. One of the softest Rottwiellers that I've seen. At first she is scary. She bounds towards you, barking After all she is BIG but once she's made friends with you she really is a softy. Ron, as always, had to make friends with her and her owner, Ann, was only too pleased to let Ron play. We stopped and chatted for a while, about books mainly, Ron still selling (Ann is an author) and it was strange but at this point everything in the world was good. Children at play, parents looking after their youngsters, children laughing, and dogs not held by a leash but under control. The way things should be. The way things used to be, not so many years ago.

As we leave the Park a young mum is teaching her two young children how to fish. The whole scene was one of togetherness and it touched me in a way that surprised even me.

Before we knew it we were back at the point that Rodney said we would be returning to, so the remainder of the walk was the reverse of the first three pages of this chapter. So I will not bore you with anymore.

Other than to thank Rodney for what turned out to be a very pleasant walk there is little more that can be said apart from Ron, of course, who rightly pointed out when we got back to the car, "said you'd be pleasantly surprised, did'n I?" And I certainly was.

---

[16] 'Welcome to Shinewater Park' - leaflet from Eastbourne Borough Council

Chapter 5 - Didling

When I was looking for another walk, I was hoping to find something just that little different. A favourite book in my possession is called 'Hidden Sussex'[17] and it lists many places that are off the beaten track and sometimes I happen to come across the not too familiar place name. Didling falls into that category. Who has heard of it? Everyone has asked "where is the next walk to be, then Graham?" I have replied "Didling" and everyone has said '"where the hell is Didling?" Until now I had no idea. But it is an actual place in Sussex, West Sussex to be exact and is part of the Parish of Treyford. "Where the hell is Treyford?" I hear you ask, welllllll it's near Iping. I know, I know, now you're all asking; where the hell is Iping? Well, it's actually reasonably close to Woolbeding. I could go on for ever, but…...

Let me put you out of your misery. Didling is a small village near Midhurst, with a population, in 1801, of 83 people[18]. I have the 1891 census for the whole of Sussex on disc and the population of Didling during this census year had gone down to 63[19]. So we'd better get to Didling before the last person leaves and turns the lights out.

Finding an actual walk for Didling was surprisingly easy. I went on my favourite Internet search engine, typed in the village name, and up popped a circular walk[20] which started at Elsted, passed through Didling and Treyford and ended back at Elsted. A circular walk of four miles. Being tight with money I did begrudge having to pay £1.50 to obtain this walk from the Internet but I have to admit, when I downloaded it and printed it off, it did seem as if you had your money's worth. Not only do you get a description of the entire walk, you also receive a map of the area, as well as photographs that have been taken by fellow walkers. We can't go wrong. Can we????

I connected Satellite Navigation to the car and at 8.30 on a cold Saturday morning Ron, Lyn and I set off towards Elsted. Ron still has no news regarding his operation and is dressed in his usual Sussex smock, carrying his usual carrier bag. Lyn puts a few copies of 'Left or Right Ron?' in the boot, just in case she sees an opportunity to make a sale. The drive to Elsted takes us along both dual carriageway and minor roads. The trip is over an hour and is spent with idle chit-chat about life in general. Those who know of our exploits will be aware that we have done some silly things in the past. These include ice skating, horse riding and one very silly walk where I was dressed as a fairy. I've usually had a few pints of the amber nectar before I would volunteer us for something silly. So on the way to Elsted we happened to pass a private airfield that was advertising free glider flying lessons. I looked at Lyn without saying a word to her, but she quickly said, "Keep your gob shut, there's no way your getting me up in one of those bloody planes!" I don't know why she should say that. I have not talked us into anything silly since the start of this book. But it is early days, so who knows?

Satellite Navigation (SatNav) is only as good as the person who operates it. The fact that we didn't end up in Elsted and had to ask a postman for directions gives you some idea of how good I am with SatNav. But, eventually, we arrive at the car park of The Three Horseshoes public house, where we park the car. "We can only park here if we intend to use the pub on our return," I say. Ron looks at me with that silly grin and

---

[17] Hidden Sussex by W Swinfen and D Arscott a BBC Radio Sussex Guide ISBN 0950951005 Pge 53

[18] West Sussex Land Tax – Sussex Record Society ISBN 0854450491, Pge 99

[19] Sussex 1891 Census – Sub District Harting 3 , RG12-0849 © S&N British Data Archives 2002

[20] http://www.walkingworld.com/findawalk/findawalk.asp visited 3/09/2007 Walk ID 2478 cost £1.50

says, "Is there ter be any chance that we don't sample the 'ospitality of this fine place? 'Ave ter call in on the way back," he says, "wouldn't be polite ter just drive off."

The Distant Harting Downs

Our clear and numbered instructions tell us to walk through the pub garden until we reach the far left corner where we will be greeted to wonderful views of the Harting Downs which is one of the largest areas of ancient chalk downland owned by the Trust. This local nature reserve and SSSI (Site of Special Scientific Importance) has traditionally been grazed by sheep and continued grazing is vital to maintain the range of species. Small hummocky mounds, the nests of yellow meadow ants, are a sign that the grassland has not been ploughed for a long time, if ever, and those areas of downland that were ploughed in the early 1970s are now reverting to pasture. The area is part of the South Downs ESA (Environmentally Sensitive Area). [21].

Unfortunately for us the fog was a little dense and although the Downs could be seen they weren't that photogenic. It is now that Lyn starts to get a bit 'girlie'. She's cold and wonders if she should go back to the car to get her jacket. After a bit of 'should I shouldn't I' conversation with herself she decides that she would go without,

Lyn struggles with the stile

"perhaps it'll warm up soon, after all the forecast says the temperature will be in the 60's." So we continue by bearing left, through the gap in the hedge, and head, with the hedge on our left towards some fingerposts and a stile. Perhaps it's our imagination but if the height of the first stile is anything to go by we could have some problems. Especially with Lyn. She seems to have a problem with 'getting her leg over' and struggles getting over this first stile.

We turn right here and walk across the field. Our instructions advise us to keep a look out for deer that are free to roam this part of the walk, but we are unable to see any. I hear giggling behind me and turn to find Ron, rummaging in his carrier bag. "What are you looking for, Ron?" I ask. "Lyn wants ter know what I carries in me bag, so I was just showin' 'er a little somethin'," I hate to think

The undergrowth takes over?

what he's about to show Lyn but he surprise me and produces a miniature bottle of whiskey. "Always prepared fer all 'ventualities. Keeps somethin' different in me bag on every walk so's I keeps people guessin'. Never know's what I got, see. Surprise me-self sometimes." Again, you can't argue with Ron's logic. But what I have noticed, is not deer, but how the walk started like every other we have been on. The grass is mowed and the hedges trimmed, until you are a few hundred yards from the start and the grass gets longer, the stinging nettles get taller and the undergrowth starts to take

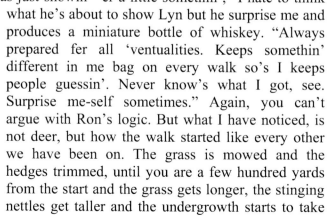

---

[21] http://www.nationaltrust.org.uk visited 09/09/2007

over. The place where we cross a small stream is a little precarious. The wooden planks are a little uneven and slippery but once over this obstacle we need to walk on the right hand field edge, next to a little stream. To be perfectly honest I didn't see a stream.

Another tall, overgrown stile

We need to pass the cattle

Didling Church entrance

Our instructions, that I printed off at home, are numbered one to nineteen. We are at instruction number three and find the signpost to New House very easily. We walk past the cottages and through the farmyard, expecting an irate farmer to come out and tell us to get off his land but we passed through without problems. Walking towards us is what Ron describes as 'a meaty wench' and her companion. As they walk past we give them a cheery greeting. As Ron is dressed in a Sussex smock the man says, "I have to ask, why the smock?" Ron explains what we are about, produces a business card from his pocket and offers to sell the couple a copy of Left or Right Ron? "We'll post it to yer if yer not local," offers Ron. The couple are from Hampshire, completing Sussex walks whilst on holiday and yes, they will look on the website on their return to home.

As we continue on our walk I notice that we have a herd of cattle in the next field and I am hoping and praying that we do not have to enter. But not only do we have to pass through this field but the stile we need to get to is the other side of the young cattle. I don't like cattle. In fact I am not impressed with any animal that can harm me in any way. "Just keep walkin'," says Ron, and then he says those comforting words, "they won't 'urt yer." But as we skirt past them they start to get up and head towards us. "They're coming," I choke and Lyn races past me like she's doing the 100 yard dash and has cleared the stile before I had even got there. "You had no trouble getting over that stile Lyn," I pant, climbing over the stile with Ron laughing behind us. "I just need the right encouragement," says Lyn.

I am confused by the next few directions because we appear to miss out instruction four and five but find ourselves, after wandering across the next field, at the point of instruction number six. "How did that happen?" I ask. Both Ron and Lyn look less than impressed.

The next stile we reach is just as high, if not higher, than the others. The person who wrote the instructions for this walk explains that she took her Labrador dogs with her and that they struggled with the stiles. Lyn said that they had four legs and

Ron needs to sit

The tub font

couldn't manage so how was she supposed to get over them. Ron did offer some assistance but Lyn, suddenly, managed to get over the stile before he got too close.

We are now on a road heading towards Didling. If I have one criticism about our instructions it is that the walker is not instructed to have a look at Didling church. If you do not look at the church you miss a real treat. Our instructions tell us to look for a sign and driveway to Woolbeeding Farm which is on our right. Unfortunately a no entry sign is on the gate explaining that entry is prohibited due to disease control. "That's no problem," says I, "if we walk along the road, we will come to the church and we can pick the walk back up when we come out. The road runs parallel to the path." So we head for the church.

From information gathered from the Internet[22] the Church of St Andrew is said to be 13th century and made of rubble and plaster. It is located at the end of a short drive and has to be seen to be believed. There is no electricity here and the only light available is by candles which are strategically placed at the end of the wonderfully ancient pews. As we walk towards the church a gentleman and his wife are getting out of a car parked next to the entrance. We must have looked a strange sight because the couple seemed to hesitate when they saw us approaching. "Wonderful morning," Ron says in his cheery manner. "Surely is, that," comes back an American accent. "It looks a wonderful little church," continues Ron. "Yes it is," says the man as he follows us up the short path, "and it's open," he continues. We all leave our thumb-sticks and drink containers in the porch-way as we enter through what looks like an original wooden door.

. Hanging from a wall, inside, is what is described as The Didling Prayer which reads:

Loving Father, we praise and thank You for this tranquil place of worship which has witnessed to the Christian Faith for centuries.

As the Shepherds of old who tended their sheep in the Downs remembered the Great Shepherd of the sheep, so may we too faithfully and lovingly fulfil Your commands, remembering that we are also Stewards of Your great county.

So Lord, as we recollect with gratitude all those who have loved and served You here, we pray, like St Andrew, we too may be worthy disciples and forever seek to proclaim in our lives the Good News of our Lord and Saviour Jesus Christ.

The inside is gorgeous and still reflects its old age. Candles are positioned on the end of each of the 400 year old pews and hang from the ceiling. "There ain't many

[22] http://www.crsbi.ac.uk/ed/sx/didli/index.htm visited 08/09/2007

Preparing to draw

churches that I 'ave ter sit down in," comments Ron, "but this just 'as ter be one ov'em." And Ron plants himself in one of the front pews and just looks around. "Bet this place can tell some stories," he says

The font, found opposite the entrance has to be one of the plainest fonts I have ever seen. Just a very irregular, unlined tub set in a circular plinth. A notice in the church says that the font is 'Saxon' and is hewn from a block of Brackelsham stone; who am I to argue? The church is tiny and services are now only held here on the first Thursday of each month which is surely a sign of the times. How long will it be before this old church and its congregation are no more?

As we leave, our American friend is setting up his easel, preparing to draw the church in ink. "Tis a beautiful place and a pleasure to be able to see inside," says Ron. "I first came to this church when I lived in Didling over 58 years ago and it hasn't changed a bit," says the gentleman. I notice his wife is now sitting in the car, reading a book, as we head back up the road to rejoin our walk.

It must have been a few hundred yards along the road, towards Treyford, when Lyn calmly asks, "Where's your thumb-stick, Graham?" And it suddenly dawns on me that I've left it at the church. "I'll go back an' fetch it," says Ron, "No you won't, I left it so I'll go and get it. I'll catch you up. There's a junction up ahead, I'll meet you there." So back I go. I'm tempted to cut across the field to get back to the church but decide that I'd better keep to the main road. When I get to the church the gentleman is still drawing and I offer my humble apologies for disturbing his concentration. "That's ok," he says as I explain that I left my thumb-stick leaning up against the porch wall. I collect my stick and as I walk back past the artist I glance at his drawing. It's good; in fact it was very good. Almost completed in black ink with my stick, drawn leaning up against the porch. "I thought it added a little to the ambience of the picture," he said, "gives it that little bit extra." I asked if I could have his name and address so that I could get a copy of the picture but he declined to give it to me so I sneaked a picture of him drawing a picture of the church as I left.

A familiar bridleway

I caught Ron and Lyn up along the road as we headed for the junction where, hopefully we would pick up the walk. Our last instruction was at number eight and we should pick it up at number thirteen. Whilst we missed five markers I feel that we saw the best of the scenery by visiting the church. At this junction is a small bridge over a stream. We couldn't resist the temptation of playing Pooh sticks. This game is now becoming a bit of a habit whenever we see moving water. The only problem with this particular game was that we didn't take notice of what our Pooh sticks looked like so, theoretically, we all won.

Not only did we find the continuation of the walk but we also found Lyn a walking stick which had obviously been left by a fellow walker. Hopefully I can use the fact that she took the stick, at some time, when she is having a go at me for taking apples from a tree or sweet corn from a plant.

I must say that Treyford was a bit of a disappointment. Simply because, apart from the scenery, there was nothing. Anyone coming from the area and reading this will probably tell me that there is plenty there but we missed it. If that is the case then I apologise but, again, the instructions didn't point out anything for us to see so we kept on walking.

The bridleway we are now on is typical of all bridleways with a canopy of trees and a solid path to walk on. In the distance, as we come out of the shadows of the bridleway, there are spectacular views of the Harting Downs again. A few weeks ago my daughter returned from America with pictures of what is called The Ozark Mountains which are in South West Missouri and are regarded as huge. They give tourists train rides around this 'mountain range'. My daughter explained to them that for once, something in England was larger than something in America. "Them ain't mountains," she

Taller than the Ozarks

bragged, "back in England we've got hills that are bigger than that." And when I showed my daughter the picture from the end of our walk we compared it to the Ozark and the Downs are definitely bigger.

We continue along our path until we reach a road leading us back to The Three Horseshoes. But before we head off for some light refreshment we decide to go and have a look at Elsted Church. This church sits back off the road and is reached by a short road leading away from a small green. Although the surroundings of the church are pleasant it was not a church that appealed to us. The seats were single chairs (no pews) which spoilt the overall appearance for me. The font was, however, particularly pretty by its location near a window but, overall, not my ideal place of worship. What is even more disappointing is that we were so unimpressed with the church we didn't find out who it was dedicated to.

Font showing chairs

Another thing that was a little disappointing is that neither of the churches we visited had leaflets which could explain items found within them. Since starting these walks I have amassed quite a collection of these leaflets and found them very interesting, especially if they point out items that you would not necessarily have seen. It makes you think that you've missed something.

We wandered over to the Three Horseshoes at about 1.30 and it was packed, inside. We had to queue from just inside the doorway to get to the bar. The staff were both pleasant and very polite as they received order after order and once we were out in the very well-kept garden food was efficiently and handsomely presented. The aroma from the many flowers in the garden was very evident. I wasn't that sure about the toilet facilities outside but Lyn tried the modern version, in the bar, and they were fine.

This was a pleasant walk and one that I would happily complete again. Ron liked the real ale from The Three Horseshoes and the church at Didling was a real find.

I'm not sure where the next walk will be. The only certainty is that the place will start with the letter 'E'. I'm thinking of a place called Ebernoe, which is near Balls Cross, and Kirdford. You know where it is really. You've probably passed a sign for it many times but, just in case it's slipped your mind the next chapter will remind you.

Outside Toilets (no longer used)

We picked a place that was fair to middling
A tiny place by the name of Didling
The Church was old and very quant
Just waiting for the artist to sit and paint.
Aresee©

Chapter 6 - Ebernoe

O fairest of damsels, how can you say No?
With you I do intend to Horn Fair for to go,
We'll join the best of company when we do get there,
With horns on their heads, boys, the finest at the fair[23].

St James's Day, July 25th, is the date for the traditional Horn Fair Day at Ebernoe. The above is the last verse in a folk song in celebration of the event. Some believe that the fair originated from some pagan ritual in which a cuckold husband was paraded through the village wearing sheep horns on his head. When I first heard the term 'cuckold' I had no idea what it meant. When I looked up the word in my dictionary[24] it said: *n. a man whose wife has committed adultery.* It must have been a difficult time to find out your wife was unfaithful but to have to be paraded through your home village was a bit over the top. The Fair continues to this day but it is now celebrated (?) with the spit roasting of a horned sheep, for the spectators of a cricket match (far more British, ay what!). The batsman with the most runs from the winning team, at the end of the day, is awarded a trophy of a sheep horn. This year (2007) the winner of the horn trophy was Martin West with 78 runs.[25]

During the reign of Henry VIII the Ebernoe Manor was, originally, in the hands of William of Arundel. But around 1542 Henry VIII took the Manor as part of a large 'forcible exchange'. The Crown retained it until 1592 when it was passed to a Mr John Brown who subsequently sold it, three years later to a Mr John Smith.[26]

Ebernoe is also mentioned in another book in my possession[27] when, in the great storm of September 1968, the West Sussex Fire Brigade answered 396 emergency calls in under 24 hours. One of those calls resulted in the rescue of people from the upper stories of their homes in Ebernoe.

Ron overlooks Ebernoe cricket pitch

I will admit to not knowing where Ebernoe is located, until now. Just before our walk, I was strolling around Hailsham and decided to pop into the local newsagents to look at some magazines. (No not the smutty top shelf type!) I picked up the September copy of Sussex Life. Normally I wouldn't bother with this magazine, although it is a very popular title with a large amount of information about our county in its contents. Most of the houses advertised inside the magazine (there are 48 pages of 'houses for sale') are around, or well over, £500,000 (half a million pound +) I think this gives the wrong impression of Sussex overall. Anyway, in this September's edition is a house for sale in, would you believe, Ebernoe. It's a Grade II listed property and is described as being 'off the beaten track'. It is reasonably (?)

---

[23] Last verse of Horn Fair folk song – www.folkinfo.org/songs/displaysong.php?songid=456

[24] The Collins Compact Dictionary – Reprinted 1990 – ISBN 0 00 433149-4

[25] http://en.wikipedia.org/wiki/Ebernoe_Horn_Fair visited 21/09/07

[26] 'People of Hidden Sussex' by W Swinfen & A Arscott. BBC Radio Publication 1985 Pge 64

[27] 'The Sussex Weather Book' by B Ogley, I Currie & M Davidson-Froglets Publications Ltd, Westerham, Kent 1991 pge 108

priced, according to the agent, at £1,150,000 (One million, one hundred and fifty thousand pounds). This just goes to prove that Ron and I move in some pretty well-heeled places.

Our walk, today, is taken from the Internet and is a seven mile circular walk around the parish of Ebernoe[28] calling briefly at a place called Balls Cross. Ron still hasn't had his operation but he assures me that he'll be ok. "It's not just while we're walking that worries me," I explain to him, "it's how you feel when you get home, on your own." "There ain't no need fer yer to worry," he says, "'cause when we gets 'ome I'm off up the town ter find out 'ow Sussex 'as got on in the cricket." Again, you can't argue with him.

I collect Ron at 8.30 on a bright Saturday morning. He's dressed, as he said he would be throughout these walks, in his Sussex smock. Complete with plastic carrier bag. "'ad a good night up the 'ead," says Ron, "only lost the darts match six – three." "And that's good, is it?" I ask, "cor' I say it was, thought it'd be nine – nil but we won three o' the games. Surprised ourselves, we did. I won my game," he continues, "just needed double 9, dropped in as sweet as anythin', beat 'Biscuit', I did." I now have a picture of Ron playing darts against a chocolate

The lone house on the green

digestive, but, apparently in this case 'Biscuit' is the nickname of an opposing dart player. I'm scared to ask him how he managed to get that nickname.

Why is this here?

Our trip to Ebernoe takes us over an hour. I haven't got SatNav with me today but I'm relying on a map which, unfortunately, doesn't give Ebernoe. But I do know that it is near Petworth and Balls Cross both of which are on the map so we should find it ok (?) shouldn't we?

As we arrive at Ebernoe we are greeted by the cricket pitch. In fact that is the only thing that does greet us, apart from the house seen in the distance. There is no street sign to say that we are in the correct location; in fact there is nothing, but a house and cricket green. "This must be it," I say as I park the car behind the cricket pavilion. "Let's 'ope the walk is a bit more excitin' than the village," says Ron. According to the instructions for the walk there should be a schoolhouse, a church and a manor house. But as we stand looking at the large expanse of green we can see no other buildings. "Ain't even a pub," comments Ron, "not the sort o'place fer me then!"

Our instructions tell us to head for the far eastern side of the green. "Which way is east?" I ask. I have no idea on direction. I have toyed with the idea of buying a compass but I'm not sure I'd be able to understand how to use it. I understand the

[28] http://www.theargus.co.uk/whatson/walks/westsussex/ebernoecircular/ visited 15/09/07

logic of north, east, south and west but when you're lost in the middle of a wood how do you know which direction you need to go to get back to your car?

Ebernoe House to our right

Stinging nettle clearing

Tame (?) pheasant

Feeding Station

Ron tells me the direction and we head off, along the road towards, hopefully, the start of the walk. As we pass along the road, on our right we see a partly demolished wall. "I wonder what that wall was for." I ask, as we walk over to inspect it. The wall is about 8 feet long with a small archway with a padlocked gate. The ends of the wall have been demolished; the weeds have overgrown parts so, although it looks impressive, it is in need of a little TLC. Perhaps it is of some historic interest to the parish of Ebernoe. If it isn't then why is it still standing?

No walk of ours would be the same without being a bit geographically challenged. Normally it happens when we are a way into a walk, but this time we get confused at the start. We can't find 'the signed footpath' we need to take 'through the woods, with Ebernoe House on the right'. We have arrived at the driveway of what we assume to be Ebernoe House (no house name board). When I check our instructions they clearly say to go to the eastern corner of the cricket pitch, so why are we walking along the road? We go back to the cricket pitch, and there, in the corner is our sign, leading us into the woodland with Ebernoe House on the right!

Our instructions tell us that this walk is well signposted throughout the seven miles. Both Ron and I have commented, many times, that walks in the West Sussex area are much better signposted than those in the East of our county. Let's hope that this is true for this walk. I have a suspicion that we will not meet many people today because the walk is described as mainly woodland.

As we walk amongst the trees, past Ebernoe House, it suddenly hits you how quiet it is and how fresh air smells. That may sound silly to those who have never experienced it but as soon as we started to walk along this path both Ron and I commented on the fresh air. "It's clean an' fresh," says Ron, "really lovely, an' 'ave you noticed 'ow the temperature as dropped?" It is very difficult to write about smells and temperatures but as we walked everything within these woods was peace and tranquillity. We both stopped, just to listen and take in the beauty. Our next instruction was to continue until we reached a three-way junction where we drop left and pass through a clearing. Finding the junction was no problem and the way was clearly signed. The clearing, however, was somewhat overgrown with some of the nastiest stinging nettles that we have come across. "I was thinking of wearing shorts for this walk," I tell Ron. I'm glad I didn't, because these nettles had managed to penetrate my trousers and had stung my knees. "Got me shins too," says Ron as we approach a wooden bridge at the far side of the 'clearing' both rubbing our legs and hoping for some kind of relief.

From here we continue over a stile and cross the middle of a field. At the other side is a sign which directs us along the field edge, over a stile and we come to a farm drive. This is known as Mercers Furze. Another word I had to look up was 'Furze'

Colhook Farm pond

My dictionary tells me that it means gorse, so why didn't they call it that? "'Ave yer noticed 'ow many pheasants are roamin' around 'ere?" asks Ron. We drove past some pheasants on the way here that were so tame we had to drive round them but I really hadn't noticed any since the start of the walk. "We must be close to a shoot," says Ron, "I've seen loads o' pheasants runnin' fer cover. Poor buggers don't stand a chance out 'ere. Feeds 'em all up, they do, then scare the 'ell out of 'em and just shoots 'em out the sky, that aint sport." The subject has touched a sore spot with Ron. "Look at 'em," he continues, "there's that many, you could shoot one and it'd fall from the sky and crush 'alf a dozen when it 'it the ground." Just as he

Our next venture?

spoke, we turned left along the drive, and was greeted by 10 to 15 of these much shot at species. Ron is not happy as we pass a feeding station, "it ain't natural," he says. "But it's been going on for years, Ron," I comment. "Don't make it right though, does it?" Again you can't argue with him.

We now turn left and walk along a bridleway. Again the direction is clearly signposted so we have no difficulty in following the instructions. This bridleway is just over three-quarters of a mile long and brings us out at a clearing with a large pond with a weeping willow. What our instructions don't tell us is that we are at Colhook Farm which has to be one of the prettiest places we have come across for some time. As we approach the edge of the water we obviously disturb whatever was in the pond because the water becomes very cloudy and plants start to move under the water. Ron says that he has seen goldfish but I couldn't see anything at all. "There," he says again, "just come up to the surface, goldfish see?" "No, Ron, I can't see anything but cloudy water," I reply. The more he yelled 'there' the less I could see,

Do you see what Ron saw?

so after taking a few photographs we cross the road and re-enter the wooded path and continue on our way with Ron still muttering, "I can't believe yer didn't see the fish," under his breath.

Again the sign for the bridleway are easily followed as we continue along towards Blackwool Farm. But before we reach the farm we both notice what could be our next venture; ballooning. People who are familiar with our exploits will know that, should the amber nectar flow freely at our favourite Inn, I tend to volunteer us for some silly things to do. But now I am not with glass and it's Ron who suggests a flight in a hot air balloon. "Be a giggle," says Ron, "you an' Lyn would enjoy it an' you could write about it later," he continues. "In fact," he says, "it could be a start fer another book, alphabetical sport, 'a' could be anglin', 'b', balloonin', 'c'," he stops to think, "that could be canoein'," "I'll not go canoeing," I interrupt, "I can't swim," "We'll think o'somethin' else fer 'c'," Ron is in full swing now but I had to stop him when he got to 'H' and suggested hang-gliding. All of a sudden I'm not too keen on his idea and steer him left, along the drive towards, what could be part of my favourite piece of the walk, water. Although I can't swim, water has always fascinated me. It's both powerful and beautiful at the same time and I have always enjoyed taking photographs of reflections in water. I am pleased to say that the Hammer ponds along this part of the walk did not disappoint me.

But I must just say that a few yards before these ponds Ron stopped me in my tracks by grabbing hold of my arm, scaring the life out of me, and said, "look at the

Hammer pond

size o'that giant, 'avin' a pee," I looked up to see the next picture and I'll leave you to decide on what you can see.

We pass the ponds and head into the farm buildings. Ron sees a lady in a Land Rover. She's pulled over and speaking to a man who is felling trees, "I don't suppose you got the cricket scores, 'ave you, me dear?" Ron asks. I'm not sure what the reply was but Ron mutters, "I only asked," as we head for the Fishing Hut where we pick up the next path on our walk.

This path takes us, for about half-a-mile through more woodland as we head towards Balls Cross. Just the mention of The Stag Inn at Balls Cross has put a step into our pace. Our instructions advise us to stay on this track and ignore all turnings until we reach a track joining us from the left.

Woodpecker hotel

This track will, eventually take us to High Buildings Farm. Before we reach the farm Ron notices what he describes as 'a high rise woodpeckers apartments' as he points to a tree that has eight holes in it. The driveway leading to the road is another half-a-mile long. Before we reach the road, a car, with some youngsters in, drives past. The young lady in the back seat, seeing Ron in his smock, waves frantically out of the back window. "She's obviously impressed with your debonair and rugged good looks, Ron," I say. "That's a young lady with good taste," he replies as the car turns left at the end of the drive. Before we reach the road the car has reversed back to the drive, "can't keep away from me, can she?" says Ron, as the car speeds off in the other direction. "Or it could be they took the wrong direction," I say. "Believe whatever yer want to," says Ron, "but I know she's taken with me smock."

Ron Heads for The Stag

We now turn right and head towards the junction at Balls Cross. I recognise the road as the one we headed down when we were looking for the start of the walk. At the top of the hill is the junction where we turn right and in just a few yards, we are at The Stag.

Fallen tree

Before we order a drink Ron asks the men outside if any had the latest cricket score. Apparently Sussex had won their last game of the season but needed Surrey to stop Lancashire getting 480 odd runs. If Surrey stop Lancashire then Sussex would win the Championship for a second year running. Ron was getting frustrated at not knowing what was happening. "Don't know about the score," say one of the regulars, "but I'll put me radio on in the car so's you can find out. What station is it on?" "Southern Counties," says Ron as they head towards the man's car. Within seconds Ron's back, "don't believe it," he says, "Lancashire are only goin' for it. They're 260 fer 2. You see, Surrey'll throw it away, just so's Sussex can't win." The fact that he now had a pint of beer in his hand didn't seem to make much difference to his temperament. But, slowly, with the radio turned up loud, Ron started to relax, telling the regulars what walk we were completing and why. Apparently there was a wedding in the area and the little pub started to fill with very well-dressed wedding guests. Before we left I managed a look inside the pub and was pleased to see that the bar was probably the same now as it was years ago. All oak beams, full of old photographs and pictures. Not only of scenes from the area but also characters and sporting teams from the past. One such photograph was of Thomas Payne who passed away on Christmas Eve 1926 and was the Postmaster. The picture shows Thomas unlocking a pillar box. Should you be in the area why not give The Stag a

Wood carvings

- 46 -

Ron attending to one of the signs

visit. We were welcomed as if we had used the pub for years and not just two strange people who just happened to drop by. It has a comfortable feel about it and the natives are very friendly. Food is available but, due to a power cut, not on the day we visited.

We leave the pub and turn right, heading along the road looking for a house, on our left, called 'Hollands'. If I have just one little criticism about our instructions it is that we are not told of the houses between the pub and Hollands. We seemed to be walking for some time before coming to our next path. We passed a number of houses before we reached Hollands and I was beginning to think that someone had changed the name since writing the instructions and we had walked too far. Just a little criticism but I feel that it should be mentioned. We now turn right and enter woodland known as Langhurst Common.

Worrying sign

Thankfully in another field

The path twists and turns but, again, is well signposted, even if the signposts require some of Ron's attention. On more than one occasion he had to stop and ensure that the finger arm was pointing in a straight line by applying a wedge here and there. It was along this path that we made our first real mistake. Some way into the wood the path bears to the left and right and, of course, we take the wrong way. But it is evident that you've made a mistake because if you bear left you, like us, end up in a field and there is no mention of this in our instructions. So we retrace our steps and head in the correct direction. One of the things that Ron has told me is that near our home is a wood called Abbots Wood and the woods we have passed through today remind him of Abbots Wood as it used to be. Within our wood, near Hailsham, there used to be a tree that had, carved in the bark, the names of some of the Canadians who were stationed near Hailsham. Unfortunately, the tree has been removed and is no longer a part of the history but as we approach the edge of Langhurst Common we come across a tree, very similar to the Abbots Wood tree. Complete with carvings. Ron had to stop and admire.

We continue until we arrive at a three-way signpost. We take the left path and we are advised that we are now on the same track we walked earlier on our outward journey. I'll take their word for it because it all looks the same to me. We are told not to come off this track until we meet another three-way sign, on a right-hand bend, with Sussex Wildlife Trust plaque attached to the post. We should reach this sign in about 100 yards. "Would you say that this sign is about a hundred yards away from

Boundary line across the main road

our last turning?" I ask Ron, as we look at a three-way signpost, on a bend, but without a Sussex Wildlife Trust plaque on it. "I'd say tis a good 'undred yards," replies Ron, so we turn left. Perhaps someone has removed the plaque I think to myself but no. We've gone wrong again so back we go to the original sign and continue a further few yards, round the bend, until we meet a sign with the plaque attached. Why weren't we told to ignore the first turning and continue to the next I do not know but it would have been easier? Our next instruction has me a little worried. We are about to enter an area known as Ebernoe Common which has been purchased by The Sussex Wildlife Trust and is used for grazing animals. This means that animals are grazing, free to roam the area as they want, and I don't like animals so I am looking in every direction as we pass through the common. Thankfully the only animals we encountered were in another field so I had no real reason to worry. That is until we reach the other end of the Common where a large sign assures us that out of the 16 species of bats that inhabit Britain, 14 of those species are found in this Common.

It is now that we hear a single church bell. A bit eerie since reading about the bats but as we pass a sign pointing to Furnace Field we can see the church up the slope to our left. The congregation are singing 'we plough the fields and scatter' which I thought strange for a wedding service but it was obvious, from the ribbons on the cars in the car park, that a wedding ceremony was taking place. "Got to admire the couple getting' married," says Ron, "why's that?" I ask. "Must 'ave been difficult ter find a partner out 'ere in the middle o' nowhere but it must 'ave been 'arder ter find the church," giggles Ron. The church is, literally in the middle of nowhere. All there is next to it is what is described on our instructions as a Schoolhouse. But why would they need a school with only a church, a manor house and a cricket pitch in close proximity?

We decide to walk past the church quietly without disturbing the ceremony and, after bearing left onto the road we find ourselves walking past Ebernoe Manor and towards the famous cricket pitch. We now notice that the main road runs through the outfield of the pitch. "Can you imagin' a ball 'urtlin' through the air towards yer, as yer stand on the other side o' the road, 'catchit!' shouts the skipper, 'sod off' yer shouts back, 'a bloody cars commin'" Ron can't control himself and is now practically crying with laughter. Some people reading this aren't going to believe the part about the road and the pitch so I have taken a photograph of the white boundary line which crosses the road and rejoins the green on the other side.

Throughout this walk, apart from a couple of places we did not see a sole. Yet it was both pleasant and tiring. When I got home I ached in a few places.

Getting home was a story in itself. As I said I didn't have SatNav with me and, yes, I got lost. First I headed up the wrong way on the A283. Then I went round Petworth three times before heading in the wrong direction again but we eventually made it home.

It wasn't until late in the evening that we found out that Sussex had won the Championship with Lancashire missing their target by 20 runs. So, good ole Sussex, triumphed again.

Our next walk will be a bit closer to home and start with the letter 'F'. Hopefully Ron will have seen the specialist and a date will have been set for his operation. Tomorrow is Ron's birthday so a few drinks will be shared in The Kings Head that night. Next weekend is my birthday so we might not sober up until the following weekend.

Ebernoe Church

The walk's picked, it's off we go
To the obscure village of Ebernoe
The cricket pitch 'as a road running through'
In the church the Bride and Groom say "I do."
Aresee©

Chapter 7 - Friars Gate

A decision was made to visit Framfield some time ago. Whilst looking for walks for this book I have tried to find towns or villages that have certain criteria. I would prefer them to be little known places, have some interesting history, or facts, and have a circular walk that can be completed by both Ron and me. Unfortunately the letter 'F' has caused a little head scratching. Although there are a number of places starting with the letter in Sussex, trying to find anything interesting about them has proved difficult. Some of my choices have included *Fairlight*, with its country park and a memorial to a man known as Grey Owl, *Fairwarp* and its radio masts, *Falmer* with the village water pump, *Faygate* has one of the first AA (Automobile Association) signs attached to the front of an Inn, *Felpham*, home of William Blake, painter, poet and mystic. There is *Fishbourne*, and it's Roman Palace, *Fittleworth*, the home of Elgar when he composed his Cello Concerto and *Ford*, with its Open Prison. I also considered *Frant*, because the place is associated with the name Budgen and this surname appears in my family tree. Also considered for some time was the village of *Fulking*, for the sole reason that I like the sound of the word. But if I found anything historic about these villages, I couldn't find a walk and vice versa. To be honest I couldn't find that much about *Framfield*, but I did find little snippets about the place and I have a circular walk[29] of 5¾ miles which includes Blackboys.

In 1792 it is recorded that eleven out of fifteen persons from Framfield, whose united ages amounted to 1,034 years (average age of 69) offered to play a game of cricket '..against an equal number of players of the same age from any other part of the County.'[30] Unfortunately I am unable to find out if the game ever took place.

The only reference I have to famous (?) people of Framfield is that of Richard Realf who was born, in the village, on the 14th of June 1832. He published his first book of poems in 1852, titled '*Guesses at the Beautiful*' before emigrating to Kansas, America, where he was involved in the anti-slavery movement. He started a newspaper and came into contact with John Browne, who was hung for treason in 1859. Richard, due to domestic troubles, committed suicide on the 28th of October 1878 in California.[31]

The Half Moon, Friars Gate

The current church, at Framfield, was started in 1288 but in 1509 a fire destroyed all the wooden parts. Some repairs were carried out but it wasn't until 1891 (382 years later) that the then High Sheriff of Sussex, Robert Thorton, had the tower rebuilt to its current glory. Within the current church is a brass of Sir Edward Gage, the Sheriff of Sussex who, in 1556 had the dubious honour of supervising the burning at the stake of the Lewes Martyrs[32].

---

[29] www.theargus.co.uk visited 21/09/07
[30] Sussex by SPB Mais Published by Richard Press and reprinted in 1950 – Chapter VI - Page 152
[31] http://www.theweald.org/N10.asp?NId=1405 visited 30/09/2007
[32] http://www.villagenet.co.uk/ashdownforest/villages/framfield.php visited 30/09/2007

And then it all changed. My birthday arrived and again, two sisters on my school bus, Halle and Ellen, who very considerately bought me a new book on pub walks[33], which included Friars Gate. "I've never 'eard of it!" comments Ron as did many others. So it was an ideal place for our walk.

Some may be aware that I am interested in Family History and that one valuable source of information is the census. I thought that the first census to be made public was completed in 1841 and a new census was released every ten years i.e. 1851, 1861, 1871, 1881……….. But I have managed to find a census, on the internet,[34] for Friars

Gate which is dated 1838 (?). It lists only the heads of the households and, in 1838 Friars Gate consisted of ten properties. House names or numbers are not included but occupations and birth years of the head of household are given. The one which caught my eye was a gentleman named William Avis who was born in 1797 in Withyham. His occupation is listed as 'maker of cricket balls' and was employed by Mr Duke. It really makes you wonder how; nearly 200 years ago William made a living, in a hamlet of only ten houses, selling the cricket balls he'd made.

Wide Forestry Track (?)

Incidentally there is no mention of The Half Moon public house in this census, but this is where we find ourselves on a cold, frosty October Saturday morning.

Before we start on the walk I will give a brief update on Ron's medical condition. Put simply, there is no update. He still has the lump, he still suffers from it and he still awaits the pleasures of our wonderful National Health system (after nearly a year from the original diagnosis) and because of this the walk we are about to complete is only 4¼ miles[35] of 'easy underfoot and enjoyable'. We will see.

Our instructions tell us to leave the pub ("but we 'aven't even been in it yet!" complains Ron) and turn right into the road,

walking up the hill, until we will reach a wide forestry track on our right. We didn't find a track but we did find a private road with signs warning us that it was a private road with another sign forbidding us to ride bikes and that, although signed as a private road, was, in fact, a public footpath. There was not one sign that said it was a forestry track, so why does it say this in our instructions? We turn right onto the private road and head through the outskirts of one hundred acre wood (Winnie the Pooh). The

The Pooh walk leaves to our left

path/road/track continues for ½-a-mile and the temperature has dropped considerably. In some of the many clearings the views are remarkable, even with the mist in the distance.

---

[33] Pub Walks in East Sussex by Mike Power – New Edition – Updated April 2003

[34] http://theweald.org/Census38.asp?MemoId=C0Cr02 visited 17/10/07

[35] Pub Walks in East Sussex by Mike Power, Walk No 16 Page 40

Our instructions now tell us to take a right fork where the road / track / path will lead us towards a house. Immediately after taking the fork we need to look for a narrow path, on our left, which will lead us through the fields and around the house and, hopefully, we should rejoin the track/path/road through a gate at the end of the path. Again, our instructions fail to tell us that the house we have just passed round is Fishers Gate. Is there a reason for this omission?

Déjà Vous now comes into play. "We've walked along this track before," says Ron, and I must admit that it does look familiar, but I'm not sure. "'Tis where we saw that BT man asleep in 'is van," continues Ron, "you know, when we was with Lyn doin' the Pooh walk[36], in the first book." We now pass Buckhurst Farm and cottages and things are starting to look familiar to me now. The number of pheasants we see, the shoot area the pheasants are forced to fly over that has Ron complaining that 'that ain't sport!' It suddenly comes flooding back

Blue bellied Ram has been busy?

Parish Church, Withyham

The magnificent Sackville Chapel

but something I didn't remember from that walk is what I hear now; the peal of church bells. "Can you hear that?" I ask Ron, "I can 'ere a police car," he replies. "No," I beg, "listen, in the distance, I can hear church bells. We didn't visit a church here with Lyn," I continue, "how did we miss that?" We arrive at the point that the Pooh walk leaves via a stile on our left. "I remember now," I say, "we went over the stile, across that field and down to Pooh Bridge. Our instructions for this walk tell us to continue along the track for a few more yards and we will come to Withyham Church."

The Lake at Withyham

---

[36] Left or Right Ron? By G Pollard – Walk 25 Page 108

Just before we arrive at the church a flock of sheep are gathered in a field on our left. All Ron had to say is "the blue buggers been busy agin," and without looking I knew exactly what he meant. I can't remember who told me that one ram can service quite a few sheep in one day and this one had certainly been busy. "Looks like some o'them sheep enjoyed it, too," says Ron, "looks like a couple of 'em is covered in the dye." And the sound of church bells is getting louder. It is literally just a few more yards when we turn slightly to our right and the church comes into view. And what a wonderful sight it is, standing on a high mound, surrounded by trees, the Parish Church of St Michael and All Angels, complete with bells ringing, makes the hairs on the back of my neck tingle. The setting is idyllic, with a large pond visible down the road, and a few very old cottages leading towards the church. "Yer only need a pub close by an' you'd think you were in 'eaven," says Ron, "per'aps a cricket pitch by the lake down the road an' I could live 'ere fer ever."

Tidy leaf fall?

As we climb the steps to the church the bell ringing is very loud and non-stop. "They must o' been ringing them bells fer nearly 'alf an 'our," says Ron, "and they ain't stopped yet." Thankfully the church is open and we enter, very quietly, just in case a service is in progress but we had no worries. If you are familiar with our exploits you will be aware of what I mean when I say that some churches you have to sit in. This was one of those churches. We are warmly greeted by June whose pride and enthusiasm for her church is so very obvious as she explains little things about <u>her</u> church. All the time she is talking to us you realise that the church belongs to the parish and is loved by the parish. Her knowledge of the church shines through as she explains about the early church being struck by lightening on the 16th June 1663 and mostly destroyed. The church was rebuilt and opened for worship again in 1672. The font, placed by the entrance to the church as it is the 'gateway to the Church' is dated 1666 and was probably the first item to be replaced after the fire.[37] There is also the Sackville Chapel which does not fall under the jurisdiction of the Bishop but is privately owned by the Sackville family, represented today by William the 11th Earl De La Warr who is the patron of this church. We are informed, by June, that the bell-ringers are a group not usually at this church but are 'having a go' with the peal of eight bells. The original five bells melted in the fire of 1663 and had to be recast. A sixth bell was added in 1715 and in 1908 all six bells were recast and two other bells added to give the magnificent 8-bell peal we are now enjoying. June also explained that the paintings, screwed to the south wall, were not originals but copies. The original paintings, when they were removed to be cleaned were found to be by a famous artist and dated late 1300's early 1400's. The originals are now safely on display at Leeds Castle where they are on permanent loan.

We manage to drag ourselves away from the church and head down the road towards the lake. Here we turn right and head towards The Dorset Arms along what we assume is the main road. Traffic should be restricted to 40 miles per hour but the way cars were hurtling past us I don't think the speed limit was observed by many. If

---

[37] The Church of St Michael & All Angels, Withyham purchased at the church 60p

you do intend to complete this walk be aware of this traffic and the fact that, typical of many villages, pathways are few and far between. We had to cross this busy road a number of times to be on a made pathway.

At the Dorset Arms we turn right and head up a long, private roadway into Buckhurst Park. We can still hear the bells from the church. "They've been ringin'

now fer nearly an 'our," says Ron, "an' non-stop at that, their bloody arms must be droppin' off soon. Bet they've got arm muscles like Jonny Wilkinson's thighs," Ron giggles. "an' look at that," he says, pointing to some piles of leaves. "It's that posh 'ere that even the leaves fall in tidy piles!" Walking through the park we see one of Ron's favourite places, a cricket pitch. "I don't believe it," Ron chokes, "it only looks like some bloody idiot's tried to do wheelies on the outfield. Just goes ter prove," he continues, "even posh buggers can be stupid."

Reflections are fantastic

Our instructions tell us to head towards a lake where we need to bear right. When we arrive at the lake there are two right turns that we could take. One leads us to the estate office, the other takes us round the corner a little further and towards a fence. Again, the instructions aren't too clear. We assume that we shouldn't head towards the Estate Office and decide to take the other right turn. We both feel that the instructions should tell us what not to do as well as which way we should go. But perhaps we are being a little picky?

It is a now that disaster struck. Ron's cherished boots fall apart. Not both feet but his left boot is loosing its sole. 'Need some string, that's all," he says as he walks raising his left foot higher than his right. The noise he makes is a little like flip, scrape, flop as he drags the sole of his left boot along the gravel. I can't stop laughing and Ron has now started to swear. It's strange to hear Ron swear like this. He is normally calm and serene but now, everytime the sole of his left boot drags along the ground, a very, very naughty swear word is released. "Look on the bright side," I offer, "we're nearly at the end of the walk." But nothing seemed to

Beyond economical repair?

help. The fact that we couldn't find any string didn't help either. He just had to flip, scrape, and flop the rest of the way back to the car.

As we slowly approach the end of Buckhurst Park our instructions are to look out for path 43 which we will find on our right. You guessed it. We didn't find Path 43 but we did find some ramblers who bade us a cheery 'good morning' which seemed to raise Ron's flagging spirits a fraction.

The instructions now tell us to cross a field and head for a stile in the left corner. I can't see a stile. In fact we can't see a left corner either. Are we on the right path? Are we in the right field? We are to pass some dwellings. We can't see any dwellings until we get halfway across the field. Now we can see dwellings in front of us and to our left. "Which way shall we go?" I ask Ron. "There's a stile in front of us," he replies, "let's 'ead fer that." So that's what we do. And he's right. How does he do it? We arrive at a wooded path leading us down towards a road. Exactly, like it says, in the book.

All we have to do now is cross the road, head up Whitehouse Lane and back to the car. One thing which may be of some interest; the Half Moon pub has a sign outside advertising that they are 'Open All Day.' Be warned, they aren't. Ron was gutted. We arrived back at the car at 11.30 and they didn't open until 12. But the walk itself was very pleasant. We didn't get lost and we met June at Withyham Church. And, again, we have found some unspoilt Sussex countryside that we hadn't seen before and there are still miles of it left to find.

A pleasant walk with beautiful scenery
Lakes and fields and woodland scenery
Withyham Church set in a paradise locality
Thank you, June, for your hospitality
AreSee©

Chapter 8 - Litlington

Ron and I visited Litlington whilst walking for our previous title, Left or Right Ron?[38] It was during a walk from Alfriston, and the famous pie shop, that Ron said he would like to visit the Plough and Arrow, which turned out to be the Plough and Harrow. On that occasion, just as we reached the sign outside the pub which advises that 'all walkers are welcome' the door was slammed and bolted in our faces? So, why are we going back to Litlington?

One of our booksellers is a lovely lady called Christine. She works in Hailsham Club, known by the regulars as The Top Club, and has been instrumental in selling a number of our books for us. When I first met Christine her enthusiasm for our book was obvious, so much so that when we asked her if she would like to join us on one of walks she jumped at the chance, fool that she is. We asked Christine to choose the walk and would you believe it the walk she has chosen for us to complete is Litlington[39] and it was decided to complete the walk in the traditional style of a Wednesday afternoon. You may be aware of Ron's saying that 'it don't rain in Sussex on a Wednesday afternoon!' and he's been right more times than wrong.

The name Litlington is derived from a couple of Saxon words. *Tŭn* or farmstead owned by the settler *Lŷtela* whose nickname 'the small one' suggests he was of a diminutive stature even for those times. From *Lŷteling tŭn*, the place name has developed to Littelelington and Litlintone by the end of the 12th century appearing in its modern form in 1548.[40] I have read somewhere that Litlington is famous for its tea gardens. It will be interesting to see if they still exist.

Say 'hello' to Christine

In the 1786 a Mrs Maria Fitzherbert lived at Clapham House, Litlington. She secretly married the Prince Regent who later became George IV. They secretly married as Mr and Mrs Payne but not surprisingly I cannot find the marriage listed in any of my Sussex books. One of their children was said to have been born at Clapham House before George abandoned her for the Princess of Brunswick.[41] Again I am unable to find anything which substantiates this claim.

We are also to be accompanied this afternoon by my wife, Emelia. We are about to celebrate 35 years of marriage and she has stood by me throughout all those years, and without her encouragement and understanding of our walking efforts we would never have reached the printer. She had declined many requests to accompany Ron and me over the past year or so, and when I asked why she should agree to complete this walk she told me that, '…You seem to be able to read a map a little better these days so there's less chance of getting lost'. Oh, she of little faith!

I am now going to be brutally and truthfully honest. The walk picked by Christine is an extremely hard walk to complete. It is very steep in places and although, once at

---

[38] Left or Right Ron? Published by LR Publishers – Page 17
[39] Pub Walks in East Sussex by Mike Power – Walk 23 – Page 56
[40] Sussex Place-names by Judith Glover Published by Countryside Books - Page 137
[41] http://www.villagenet.co.uk/sevensisters/villages/litlington.php visited 21/10/07

the top, Lullington Heath is outstandingly beautiful, both Ron and I feel that, for the ladies, it would be a bit too much. So we are doing a slightly different walk. We will be starting in Litlington but the walk will be a little longer than planned, but it will be on the level. It will include a couple of churches with a stop at the pie shop, made famous in Left or Right Ron?[42] Hopefully the girls won't be aware of our plan until it's too late and they are reading this chapter in the comfort of home. Please forgive us girls but we were thinking of you, honest.

I finish work a little early so that I can get home in time to pick up Emelia, and then on to the Top Club by 12.30, to collect Ron and Christine. Ron is wearing his Sussex smock, as usual, and Christine has to have the brightest pair of wellies I've ever seen. "Ooh I have been looking forward to this walk," she gushes as she approaches the car. It was if she'd never been out before, all excitable and bubbly. But I have to admit that her footwear was nothing compared to Ron's.

Bright pink wellies

He had been struggling to get his boots repaired. It's not that Ron is tight with money, far from it, but he had a devil of a job to find a pair of boots that fitted him and he wasn't prepared to let them out of his sight for much needed repairs. So he attempted to repair them himself. The results are in the picture. Can you believe he would risk wearing them across a country walk of over 5 miles? We will see how long they last.

Ron's repair job?

As we head out towards Litlington Christine rummages for her tobacco pouch. "It's in here somewhere," she says. "I thought I'd roll a couple before we start the walk, just in case I fall over and get muddy hands." I'm sat in the front driving, Emelia is sitting next to me and I feel her eyes turn to me as if to say 'she can't be serious, surely?' "Do you smoke, Emelia?" Christine asks, "Yes," replies Emelia, "but I've already rolled a few." "God, it must be nice to be organised like that. I don't think about things until the last minute and sometimes it's too late." The remainder of the journey is made with Christine and Ron relating little stories about who's married, separated, dead, buried or cremated and who's living with who and how many children they had. It's as if they haven't seen each other for years and are catching up with old times. In a strange way it was nice to sit back and listen. All that history between two people, just tumbling out, as if it was only yesterday.

We wait for Ron

As I said earlier Ron and I have completed this walk before, but originally, we started in Alfriston, walked to Litlington and back to Alfriston in a large

[42] Left or Right Ron? Published by LR Publishers – Chapter 4

circle. For this walk we will be heading towards Alfriston, by following the River Cuckmere and then back to Litlington. It should only take a couple of hours and the weather is really nice. No sun but not too cold. After all, it is the end of October and the temperature is falling daily.

We park the car just past the Plough and Harrow and start heading towards the River. No walk would be the same without one mistake and would you believe the path I took everyone up was the wrong one. A lady pointed out that we were on private land and the public footpath was further up the road. But anyone can make a simple mistake. Ron just giggled.

Teasels (?)

"I need a fag," says Christine and produces a very bent, roll up from her bag. "I'll join you," says Emelia and they both 'light up'. "Cor," says Ron, "I do miss not 'avin' a smoke. I often think ov' 'avin a drag when we're on one of our walks." "Then why don't yer?" asks Christine. "Can't do that," he replies, "promised me granddaughters I'd not smoke again. I can't let them down." "I've rolled this one too tight," says Christine, "I need a bloody poultice on the back o'me neck to drag on this." I am in hysterics and have to stop to get my breath and Emelia's nearly crying. If they both carry on like this throughout the walk I'm not going to survive. Christine is the salt of the earth but I don't think she's stopped talking since she got in the car and she has one of the most infectious laughs I've heard for ages. I'm sure that she must be the life and soul of any party.

At the end of the path we turn left and then right over a small wooden bridge. We have to wait for Ron as he makes his wish by dropping a few pennies into the water. This had become a habit for Ron for sometime now. Over all our walks he must have thrown pounds into rivers and streams throughout Sussex.

We now enter an area known a Burnt House Brooks which covers 13 acres of land and is currently owned by The National Trust. As we walk along the river bank, towards Alfriston, Christine comments on the amount of sloes growing on the bushes. "Must be enough to make a few bottles of sloe gin," she says, "and look at all them teasels, you could make a fortune at florists, selling them. They look lovely at Christmas, painted silver with sparkly bits glued to 'em," She doesn't stop talking.

All the while we keep the river on our right-hand side. In the distance can be seen Alfriston church known to many as 'The cathedral of the Downs' with it's beautiful green in the front, known as 'The Tye' and its well-kept graveyard which is written extensively about in Left or Right Ron?[43] So I won't attempt to bore you with the same old descriptions.

Emelia's reason for a kissing gate

---

[43] Left or Right Ron? – Published by Lr Publishers – Page16

As we continue walking along the river bank Christine and Ron chatter away behind us. We pass through some kissing gates, used to ensure animals cannot get to other fields but people are free to pass through. When we tell the girls that we think the name is given to the gates because the gate kisses the two posts as it opens and closes Emelia has other ideas. Christine is handed the camera and a photograph is taken.

Previously on this walk we have met a few fellow walkers and today was to be no different. Everyone passed us with a cheery 'good afternoon' and it made a pleasant change to meet them rather than walk, in the middle of nowhere, without meeting a single person. We also met three swans as they gently swan along the river. Ron

Three male (?) swans

thought they must be young males as it would be unusual to see this many swans swimming together.

As we approach the back of St Andrews Church, Alfriston it is obvious that the church organ is in full voice. For those unaware of my phobia (?) it is church organs, although in one church I did manage to sit and listen to an organ being played without it affecting me. But that is unusual. What usually happens is that I cry my eyes out. I do not know why nor can I explain what comes over me. It's something that just happens. I get very emotional and have to leave. "Are you going inside?" asks Emelia. "Yes," I reply, bravely, "I was ok at that other church. I've got over my phobia now." But how wrong can you be. At this church the organ is halfway along the aisle on the left. Sitting at the organ is a gentleman, possibly we thought later to be the vicar, and he was playing that organ as if he was demented. It was a fantastic piece of which I have never heard. But it hit me. I had to get out of the church as tears welled up and I couldn't control my feelings. Why does this happen? I have no idea. After sitting outside for a few minutes the feelings and the tears subside and I'm ok again. Luckily, Emelia, Ron and Christine are aware of these feelings and when they return, from the church, nothing has to be said.

Alfriston is a lovely place to visit if you've never been there. Christine had been through the High Street and seen the 15th century market cross but was not aware of what lay behind the shops. Next to the church, in The Tye, is The Clergy House. A thatched building that is reputed to be the first property purchased by the National Trust for the exorbitant price of £10 in 1896. The floor inside the house is unusual in

Bacon buttie time

that it is made of chalk and sour milk. "Let's sit here for a while," says Christine and produces, from her carrier bag, a bacon sandwich for each of us as she heads for one of the wooden bench seats around The Tye. "Can you imagine what it was like here when women didn't have to work?" asks Christine. I decide to keep away from the subject. Ron has gone quiet. "It must have been great," she continues, "sitting up at them old windows, sewing by candle-light. Nothing else to do, sew, gossip, gossip, sew. What might be nice is to have a little teashop up this road. Sell sandwiches and cups of tea all day. That would be nice. Only have to work in the summer, take the winter off and go abroad, somewhere. I bet it would be a gold mine working a tearoom here, especially on a Sunday with everyone coming to church." I'm not sure how or when she ate her bacon sandwich because she didn't stop talking, but when I looked at her it had gone. Then up she and Emelia got for another ciggie. "Have a piece of bread pudding. Only me bags heavy and I've been told there's a chocolate shop here and I need to empty me bag so that I can fill it with chocolate."

Littered path +

She doesn't stop.

Opposite 'The Tye' is a very dark and narrow walkway through to the High Street. You have to take care walking through here as the path can be slippery and the steps are surprisingly steep. As we emerge onto the High Street we turn right and head towards the Market Cross, in the middle of the village. Before we get to this, on our left, is a shop called 'Much ado Books', should you require a copy of my first book you can purchase copies in the shop. (Sales pitch over)

A stop at the Post Office/Stores is always necessary at Alfriston so that both Ron and I can stock up on pies. We used to buy some for an old drinking friend from The Kings Head, Sean, so that he had them in his lunch box for work, but unfortunately he is no longer with us. Christine is desperate to get over to the Chocolate Shop which is opposite. She tells me that she eats chocolate nearly every day and has some in every room at home. When I suggested that it wasn't good for her to eat that much chocolate she just laughed and said the worse part of her love for chocolate was having to share it. With that she was in the shop trying out the free samples.

Leaving the shop we turn left and head down the lane past The Old Coach House and towards the River Cuckmere, again. When we reach the river this time we cross a small wooden bridge, over the River, and head down the path towards the road. Just before the road Christine advises us that she needed a toilet. Standing on the bridge, watching and hearing the water flow, apparently wasn't helping her need. "Just keep walking," she says, "I'll hold on."

The Church through the trees

We turn right and head along a narrow path towards a stile. When Ron and I were last here this path was full of snowdrops. Thousands of them. A blanket of white flowers. It was gorgeous. What greeted us now, as we turned the bend in the pathway, was disgraceful. Not only litter thrown on the ground but what looked like human waste in the middle of the path. It was disgusting. We should have cleared it up but none of us could bring ourselves to touch it. It was that bad. With only yards past this mess was, I think, one of the best pictures of the whole walk. Through the leaves of the trees can be seen St Andrews Church and I can still hear the damned organ. But I am not affected once outside the building.

We now cross a couple of fields, following the signs for the public footpath and emerge on the road, heading back towards Litlington. Since I have been married to Emelia several people have commented on the way we always seem to touch each other. Let me clarify that. I mean we hold hands, yes even after 34 years of marriage. We are not afraid to show our love and respect for each other. The touch, the peck on the cheek, not all the time, but every now and again. We do it without thinking. Then, every now and again, someone makes a comment, "My God, they're at it again," says Christine, "Why don't you go and hire a room for the night?" It's when people say things like that that you realise, perhaps, how often those moments are. But I will make no apologies. We've been like it for over 30 years and we're still together. So we must be doing something right.

As we walk down the road, towards Litlington, we pass Church Farm and immediately after it is Litlington Church. Again, when we first came to this church, I was unable to enter due to the organist. This time there is no organ playing so we ventured inside. It has that usual church smell and feel yet is missing something. To me the church doesn't appear to be loved. The church grounds are a disappointment, there are unkempt graves, grass not mown and

Inside Litlington Church

although the inside is pleasant and quaint I'm afraid I was not impressed. There is a plaque hanging from the wall dedicated and listing men fallen during the war years yet, in the churchyard, lays a soldier whose name is not on the plaque. I just wonder why?

Entrance to Litlington Tea Gardens

It is now just a short distance to the car, and as we arrive I look up the drive, to our left and see the sign for Litlington Tea Gardens. So they do still exist. That's wonderful.

The drive home takes us past Lullington Church which is reported to be the smallest church in Sussex. We are told that the pews, seating 15 people, were removed so that chairs could be installed which would increase the congregation to 23. Personally I like to see a church with pews but that's just me. As Christine and Emelia had never been to see the church we decided to stop on the way home and have a quick look. Both Christine and I noticed the very nice looking apple trees on the pathway, as we headed for the church and on the way back we decided that God had supplied so it was only right that we should receive, and they tasted beautiful.

Chapter 9 - Guestling

The walk beginning with the letter 'G' was another difficult one to choose. Not as difficult a 'Q' or 'Z' are going to be perhaps but the letter 'G' still gave me cause for concern. In the book I normally consult[44] there were only seven places in Sussex beginning with the letter 'G' (*Glynde, Goodwood, Graffham, Gravetye, Greatham, Groombridge and Guestling*) although, I'm sure, there must be lots, lots more because *Golden Cross* immediately comes to mind. But from these seven I have chosen Guestling because the walk associated with it looks a bit of a challenge and there is some history that can be found about the village and its church, although, in our walk we do not appear to see either (?)A few days before our walk, I was on one of my favourite websites and discovered that there was some connection between Guestling and Alice in Wonderland but, for some reason I no longer have access to the site. I can't remember what that connection was and to date I have not found another site with this information. So I do have a couple of little problems. Problem number one is the website I very often use, '*www.villagenet.co.uk*', to find out about the village we are visiting, will not give me access. I have tried many times, not only on my computer at home but also on the ones at work and they all tell me that I am not permitted to access the site from this server. My second problem is that Ron has a date for his operation and I'm a little worried that the walk may be a bit too much. He is insisting that he'll be ok but I have my doubts, he seemed to be struggling at the end of our previous walks. Again, with some persuasion from Ron, I have agreed to this walk and, perhaps, another just before Christmas. We'll have to see how he gets over his surgery before a final decision on the Christmas walk is made.

First, we must complete Guestling, which is a 6¼ mile walk, found at another of our favourite websites[45]. The instructions, which are written by Ben Perkins, tell us to start from the Fairlight Road Car Park and Picnic Site, which can be found a mile east of Hastings, beside the road to Fairlight Cove. I'm told that down Fourteen Acre Lane, Guestling is the home of Hastings Brickworks[46], where hand-made bricks, used

The view at the top of Fairlight

to restore such important places as Buckingham Palace and Hampton Court, are produced. It is said that the fastest brick-maker can turn out 1,600 bricks a day. Unfortunately, viewing around the factory is only after prior arrangement.

About a mile outside the village lies a house called 'Maxfield', where Gregory Martin was born in about 1540. Gregory became an author and Catholic scholar before becoming a tutor to the children of Thomas Howard, the then Duke of Norfolk. In the 1570's he, with two helpers, translated the Bible from the Vulgate[47] into English, a version known as the Rheims Bible. Gregory died on October 28th, 1582 and is buried at Rheims.

---

[44] Hidden Sussex by W Swinfen & D Arscott a BBC Radio Sussex Guide pages 70-71
[45] www.theargus.co.uk/walks visited 28/10/2007
[46] Ibid
[47] The *Vulgate* is the Latin version of the Bible made by Jerome towards the end of the 4th century

One person who can be found within the churchyard at Guestling is a labourer called Buffard who, during the Swing Riots of 1830, was wrongly convicted of the arson attack on the barn, lodge and stables belonging to Thomas Breed of Guestling. Buffard was tried and found guilty, despite his persistent declarations of innocence, and was hanged outside Horsham gaol. He was buried one week after his execution but no headstone has been found. This miscarriage of justice was only discovered when the real culprit confessed on his deathbed that he had taken and worn Buffard's boots on the night he fired the property.[48]

Guestling appears to be split into three separate places, or hamlets. There is

Is it a Swing or Kissing Gate?

Views from Mallydams Wood

Guestling, Guestling Thorn and Guestling Green. Why this should be I, personally, have absolutely no idea and, what is more, I can't find out why. It just is. To make things even stranger, although the walk is around Guestling we don't get to see it. How strange is that?

On a very cold and icy Saturday morning in November I collect Ron from his house and we head off towards Hastings. Ron plays darts for The Kings Head on Friday nights so I asked how the game went. "We only won again," says Ron proudly, "only the second game we've won all season," he continues, "'ad a lovely pint o'real ale. New ter the area, 'twas called 'Pickled Partridge' an' she was nice. Didn't get back ter the 'ead, till late. But we 'ad a bit ov'a celebration, on account o'the win." I was desperate to keep the conversation away from the pitiful display from our England footballers after being beaten by Croatia but it wasn't long before he found his voice. Because of this loss we fail to qualify for Europe 2008 and the Football Association have sacked all the staff. "Should sack all the bloody players," says Ron, "not an ounce o'pride in none ov 'em. Can't even sing the National Anthem 'cause they can't remember the bloody words. Get rid of all o' them foreign players in our league too. Give some ov our own youngsters a go.................," I try to ignore him, but it's very difficult.

Once through Hastings we arrive at Ore village and turn right, heading towards Fairlight. The road is quite narrow in places and we are constantly driving uphill. Working on our theory that what goes up, must come down, I have the feeling that this walk could be tiresome. We'll have to see. The car park/picnic area is on our left. The place is deserted apart from a young man learning to drive. He is going round and round the car park very slowly and getting some manoeuvring practice. We unload the car of our thumb sticks, Ron dons his

[48] 'Captain Swing in Sussex and Kent' by Mike Matthews – Hastings Press – page 83

smock and we head out of the car park looking for a swing gate, on our right. The gate we arrive at is a kissing gate, so why, all of a sudden, is it called a swing gate? When I asked Ron he suggested a few explanations including the swinging of hips, complete with a little demonstration, on how to enter and exit the gate but I think he was making it all up.

Once through the gate the view is really something to see. But it is only now that you realise how far up you are. It is freezing cold and both Ron and I put our thermal hats on as we head for a gap in the wooden railings and head along a fenced path which drops gently downhill. As we drop down the hill we can feel the temperature start to raise and the ground underfoot isn't so hard and crisp. This part of the walk is the '1066 Country

Fairlight Hall (?)

Walk' and is very clearly marked so we have no difficulty in following the track towards a road. If you go onto the internet and obtain this walk be aware of the map, which is supplied, because there are little bits missing. The road we now come to isn't shown on the map.

We come out onto a road with a drive to our right leading to Bekwain Lodge and Fairlight Hall. The stile we need to climb over is to the left of the drive and Mallydams Wood is on our right as we head along the right edge of a field of newly planted winter barley. Our instructions then tell us '....opposite the second stile into the wood turn squarely left across the field'. This would imply that there was more than one stile '....into the wood', so why did we turn left at the first stile we came too? It didn't feel right, as soon as we headed across the middle of this field, walking on the farmers newly planted barley plants. When we were halfway across Ron turned round and pointed out the second stile and a clear path through the field. That was the path we should have been on. So I will say sorry now.

Stone held marker post

Another wishing well

The temperature is starting to drop again. The faint sun, high in the sky is now blocked by cloud and it's getting chilly. This cold weather always makes my nose run and I'm forever having to find a hankie to blow my nose. It's after one of my many nose blowing sessions that Ron unexplainably says, ".... 'an them women say we can't do more than two things at the same time and ain't ambidextrous. We surely must be," he continues, "'cause we can blow our nose, break wind an' pass water all at the same time." Why he should say that I have no idea, but it did cause a chuckle.

In the distance, to our right, is what we think is Fairlight Hall. I notice the flag and say to Ron "I wonder why the hall has an

American flag on its flag pole." "Probably owned by some rich American," says Ron,

"'tis right what me ol' mum used ter say about 'em during the war. Oversexed, overpaid an' over 'ere." That's obviously not a subject to pursue, so we continue dropping downhill, with the hedge on our left until we reach the bottom of the hill and go through a gap in the hedge. Just the other side of the hedge is a marker post embedded in stones. This is one of the first signs we've seen since the start of the walk and it was a little reassuring to know that we were still heading along the right walk.

We now cross the next field, and pass to the left of a wooden power pole, and enter woodland. We follow the path through the woodland, crossing over two wooden footbridges. Ron always has to stop on a footbridge. If the bridge is over running water he always drops a coin into the water and makes a wish. He has done this ever since we

Dog friendly stile

started our walks. "Costin' me a bloody fortune, these walks are," he says as another coin of the realm disappears into the running stream. "Mind you," he continues, "t'is

A typical (?) Sussex view

really pretty 'ere so I think it's worth another 5p." He drops another coin into the water.

We exit the wood via a steep uphill path and head across rough pasture towards a gate. It is now that I should warn you about the word 'rough'. The description is not altogether correct. Because if there should be another word meaning 'worse than rough' that word would not describe how rough it was. I am wearing thick jeans and

Woodland path

The posing Robin

Chinese lantern

the thistles and thorns have gone through the material and I can feel stinging cuts. So be warned if, during the summer, you fancy completing this walk do not wear shorts. Your legs will be cut to shreds. We now walk across a drive and climb a stile to follow a well trodden path uphill, across a field to a second stile. The hill is so steep we couldn't see the next stile until we reached the top. After climbing this stile we continue uphill until the next stile. Again it couldn't be seen until the ground levelled out. By the time we reached the stile I am shattered. "Makes a change ter see dog friendly stiles," says Ron, "Sod the stile, Ron, I can't breath." But Ron insists on showing me that a walker, with a dog, just lifts the side of the stile by the handle and the dog can walk through without having to climb over with his master. "Just a shame they don't supply an oxygen cylinder," I gasp. "Might be a long way up 'ere," says Ron, "but just look at the view." I turned round and what I saw cannot be described. I will just say that this is just one of the reasons for putting my body through this torture is our beautiful Sussex countryside. I agree that other Counties have scenery but this is Sussex. It is my Sussex.

It must be fantastic to have a view, like this, out of your living room window. The people who live in the house, behind us, as we look down the hill, at the horses and the lake at the bottom are very lucky people indeed. After a few minutes to gain some oxygen in my lungs we continue, across the field, and drop down (thank God!) to join Pett Road. Suddenly Ron grabs my arm, "Look," he says, "It's a Green Woodpecker." I just manage to see the bird as it flies high into an old oak tree. This is only the second Green Woodpecker I have ever seen in flight. The first was last year whilst walking around Hooe and Northeye. They are really colourful birds.

Once onto Pett Road we turn right and shortly go left into Chapel Lane. We are instructed to look out for a signed path on our right which will lead us to a path to the right of woodland known as Glebe Wood. Due to hanging branches you really need to keep your eyes open. On more than one occasion I very nearly got hit in the face by holly branches. You can see from the picture that branches hang right across the path. The path isn't that long and just before we arrive at the road leading to Friars Hill I spot another of my favourite birds, a Robin. I believe there is some superstition about a Robin crying in your garden that has some connection with a death within the family but I, personally, find the bird so endearing. This one actually posed for the camera. He just sat there and let me click away. I'm really pleased with the picture.

Once onto the road we immediately turn left, and then left again and head through the hedge into a field with Glebe Wood again on our left. We appear to be heading back in the same direction that we had come but we are now on the other side of the wood. In the distance is a tractor cutting the hedge and on the hill to our right, in the distance, is the church. "I s'pect that'll be Guestling Church?" asks Ron. That it's a church is no mistake but our instructions now take us away from the church and towards Higham Farm. We are instructed to look for a stile in the far left corner of the next field, but we can't find it. It looks as if there was something in the corner but it has been fenced off. We turn right at the bottom of the field and head towards the farmhouse with the hedge on our left. A dog starts to bark and an elderly lady offers her assistance. "Are you ok?" she asks. We explain that we are looking for the

footpath and she informs us that the path has been diverted to this side of the property. With Ron dressed in his Sussex smock the lady's curiosity gets the better of her and she asks what we are doing. Ron, tells her of our quest to complete walks and of our writings. She wishes us well and directs us, to the end of her drive and turning right should get us back on track. At the end of her drive is a mass of red headed plants. "That's Chinese lantern, that is," says Ron, "called that 'cause ov it's shape. It's only got one seed inside the lantern. When the lantern dries out it looks like a

Cow dung path

spiders web 'oldin' the seed. Real pretty, it is." He's beginning to sound a lot like Alan (Billingshurst). But not to be outdone, when I got home, I looked up 'Chinese Lantern' and its Latin name is *Physalis franchetii*. Alan will be so impressed!

We turn right and head up the other end of Chapel Lane until we reach, what we think is, Guestling Green and the main A259. We now need to cross the road and head down the access drive opposite the small Green. Since the start of the walk we have met only one person, the lovely lady at Higham Farm. That was about to change. As we walk along the drive two dogs start barking and heading in our direction. Both Ron and I ignore the dogs and head towards the gate at the end of the drive. With dogs still barking at our heels and a woman calling them off, a man suddenly appears from around a barn and says, "You can't come down 'ere. This is all private property!" "But the footpath," says Ron, "Through the gate," says dog lady. "Not this way, it ain't!" storms angry man. "Through the gate, I said," says dog lady. "Through this gate 'ere?" asks Ron. "That's what I said," says dog lady as she grabs her animals and walks off. We couldn't get that gate open quick enough. Once through the gate we both comment on the nice people we meet on our walks and there's some not so nice. The path through this part of the walk is covered in cow sh$t so perhaps we should have worn wellies. But we manage to navigate around the mess and get onto solid ground where we find a plank bridge into the field to our right. We immediately turn left and continue along the left edge of the field crossing two more fields. It is now that I hear the gunshots. Far in the distance, but I can definitely hear gunshots. Ron makes no comment. Yet.

We cross some more fields before we enter more woodland. This area, according to my map, is known as Batchelor's Bump, but I do not know why. The gunshots are getting louder. Still Ron doesn't say anything. The woodland path winds through the wood to a stream crossing. Again Ron deposits some money and makes another wish. The gunshots have stopped. Everything is peaceful again and Ron seems to be ok as we leave the wood and continue, between two fences to join a lane. Again, this lane is not on our map, but the railway line we now walk under is marked.

After about 40 yards we bear left and walk along a track towards a cottage. We find the narrow path on our left which squeezes between gardens and descend, yet again, towards the stream before climbing through woodland towards a stile. It is once we are over this stile and walking across the next field, towards a gap in the hedge, that all hell breaks loose.

Stream crossing

Just to our right the sky is suddenly full of ducks. There must have been somewhere around fifty to sixty of them. Just as suddenly the guns started. And one by one the ducks fell to the ground. I just stood there, amazed. Ron went ballistic! Those that know Ron usually find him a calm individual but at that moment he exploded. I have never seen him so angry. As the ducks flew higher to get out of the range of the guns, so Ron's anger increased. "Call that bloody sport," he starts, "feed 'em up one minute, scare the sh$t out ov' 'em the next an' then blast 'em out the sky." His blood pressure has rocketed as the colour of his face gets redder and redder. "Calm down Ron, for God's sake," I plead, but nothing is going to stop him. "Look what's 'appenin'," he continues, "the duck 'as nowhere ter go but back to the pond. It's is 'ome. 'E can't land anywhere else but on the water." Ron is nearly in tears as, slowly the ducks who survived the early onslaught, fly lower and lower, as they get tired, and are popped off as they head back towards the water. At that moment I am ashamed that a fellow human being could do that. We can hear the men laughing in the distance and Ron is heading in their direction. "Leave it Ron," I plead. "It's the way of the country," I offer in

The long silent lane

Just left to rot

someway of an explanation for the slaughter of these birds. But Ron is on a mission. I hope and pray that the men do not appear around the next bend as we now head up a long lane. My prayers are answered until, suddenly, through a gap in the hedge, Ron sees seven or eight armed and laughing men heading towards us. Ron stands firm, hands on hips and calls them all the names under the sun. Everyone of those names cannot be put into print but let me assure you that Ron was very angry. I manage to drag him away, reminding him that his blood pressure must stay low or he may miss out on his operation. He calms down, slowly, still muttering under his breath as we head up Ivyhouse Lane. For some time now it goes very quiet. Neither of us speaks. We just head along the lane in silence, with our own thoughts of the last few minutes, because that's how long it took to kill those birds.

We pass Old Coghurst Farm and head towards a crossroads. At the farm we found

The climb through the wood

the usual rusty machinery just left to rot by a barn. This time it looked like a combine harvester just left to rust away. And they say that they are poor hard up farmers? Once at the crossroads we turn left and, after about a mile, we pass Coghurst Hall Holiday Park and find a stile, on our left, and head out across a field, passing to the left of a clump of trees surrounding a pit. Our next stile is very difficult to find, but we are warned that this would be the case in our instructions. It is exactly as it is described '....broken and overgrown and hidden by scrub'. I didn't find it but Ron did.

We now cross two paddocks, scaling a post and rail fence to get to a new stile. We now head through trees and uphill with a fence on our right. And it is uphill. In fact it is very uphill as we climb towards a concrete garage and yet another stile. We stop to get our breath. Passing the garage and to the right of a bungalow we join a road and turn left.

After 250 yards we find the public footpath sign on our left and enter a woodland path. After just a short distance we arrive at a T junction. We are told to turn left here and, after 30 yards turn right dropping down a long narrow path where encroaching

Looking back at the climb

brambles hinder our progress. I get more cuts on my legs as we hear someone calling. Apparently, surprise, surprise, we are on private property and we are asked to walk back, up the hill, so that we can take the correct path. It seems that I turned right too soon. At the bottom, in the valley, we re-cross the railway line, this time we go over it, we then climb through a wood until we reach a road. Here we go left for a few yards and then right, over a stile. From here it is all uphill as we find our way through gorse, more cuts to the legs, and scrubland. Before we reach the top I have to stop a couple of times for a rest Every now and again the path divides but our instructions tell us to keep bearing right until we eventually reach an estate road.

Again our map fails to give the name of the road, or the estate, but once we get to the road we turn right.

After just a few yards we find the steps, between house number 16 and number 14, which we need to climb before reaching another road. We cross this road and, yes you've guessed, we reach another set of steps with a path leading us up towards North Seat. From here you get a good view over Hastings, on a clear day. Unfortunately today wasn't that clear and the hedges are very overgrown so we can't describe the view. But what I can tell you is that the walk is not for the disabled or anyone who struggles with hills. It is 6¼ miles of hard work. Very pleasant in places, granted, but hard none the less.

Ron is still muttering about the duck shoot and I was disappointed that we did not visit a church but we completed the walk in just over three hours, which was the time recommended by the writer, Ben Perkins. This was not one of my favourite walks and I believe it could show in the writing. It was a boring walk and I apologies for not making it more interesting. The scenery, as always, was worth stopping a while, but it was also a difficult walk in places, very hilly and the scrubland was vicious on some of the paths. The area where the car is parked is ideal if you ever want to bring children out for a picnic in the summer. Lots of seating and clean toilets are available. And it is all free.

Just one other thing before we head home. Both Ron and I have noticed what appears to be a habit of the people living in the eastern side of the County. We haven't noticed it in any other areas on our walks in Sussex. We first mentioned it in one of our walks around Rye, the habit of dogs fouling the path, it being picked up and put into plastic bags but then, not taken home, but hung out on a fence. We saw it again today. Why do people do that?

Why not take it home?

Chapter 10 - High Hurstwood

This walk is a favourite of Alan's (from Billingshurst chapter) and we have been invited to accompany him on the walk that he describes as a 'walk, with scenery'. This will make a pleasant change for both Ron and me. I will not have the worry of finding a route and following the map. I will also be able to concentrate more on the photographs that will make up the next few pages so that with my words and my pictures, hopefully, it will be of interest to you, the reader. I'm not exactly sure how it will be a pleasant change for Ron, but he insists that it will, somehow (?)

I always try to find out something about the places that we walk around with the assistance of my reasonable library of books on Sussex and the Internet along with a number of books detailing walks. But even with the help of my library, as it is, I can find absolutely nothing of the slightest interest about High Hurstwood. Is this an omen? In desperation I tried the Internet. I found a number of websites. They advertise the schools, the pubs (now Ron's interested) and I have found that the church was registered for worship in 1872 but the person completing the website about Holy Trinity Church, complete with some fantastic photographs[49], was a bit disappointed that the church was locked on the day of their visit. I also found that if you wish to hire the village hall, for a wedding reception, the charge for non-residents[50] is £350. I also found a website[51] which gave me 24 pages of properties for sale in High Hurstwood. Each of these pages displayed ten properties. But when I looked at their locations only one property was actually in High Hurstwood, and it was for sale for £1¾million. The one site that looked really promising and I thought would be of assistance was www.highhurstwood.com/gallery.html. This site advises that you are 'Welcome to the High Hurstwood photo gallery, please browse the thumbnails and click on the thumbnail for the larger image. ...' Unfortunately the site

Holy Trinity Church

didn't actually work so I was unable to browse the thumbnails or get any information at all. I don't think High Hurstwood wants us to visit, but on a pleasant Saturday morning in November we defy all the negatives about the place and with Alan, straight out of the barbers, and sat in the back of the car, we head towards the village.

I'm not exactly sure how or why the topic of conversation got onto the subject of the Atom Bomb but, apparently, the man who actually dropped this marvellous human invention of total destruction, onto Hiroshima, has died at the age of 92. We also discussed Alan's father who was one of the first Europeans to release some of the Jews, who somehow managed to survive the awful holocaust, from the German Camps and we all noted that whatever it was that our fathers did during World War 2 they very rarely spoke, openly, about it.

---

[49] http://www.roughwood.net/ChurchAlbum/EastSussex/Buxted/HighHurstwoodHolyTrinity2004.htm visited 29/10/07

[50] http://www.buxtedvillage.org.uk/high_husrtwood.htm visited 29/10/07

[51] http://www.nestoria.co.uk/high-hurstwood/property/buy/start-230 visited 29/10/07

Also on the way Alan started to speak quite excitedly about Buxted. Now why this should be I have no idea but I started to wonder if he thought we were heading for Buxted Park and not High Hurstwood. It wasn't until we were approaching Buxted Park entrance that Alan told me to turn right and pass the school before coming to Holy Trinity Church, High Hurstwood, which is found up a dead end lane on the right.

I have to be very careful how I describe the next few minutes. But I feel I must share these precious moments with you all. I will apologise now if you are offended with the language, but without the actual words, it wouldn't sound the same. Only Alan has a little bladder problem. It could come to us all, as we get older, but poor Alan seems to require a toilet stop at regular intervals. Today was no exception. As we pulled up outside the church Alan says, "I'll just nip over the 'edge, 'cause I'm bustin' for a pee." And he disappears behind the hedge. "Cor, blimey," Ron and I hear him say, "there's only some sheep in this field and they've got a ram fer company. Yer don't want ter take yer eyes off a ram if 'es in a field with sheep, can be right buggers, they can." Ron and I continue getting our sticks out of the boot of the car when we hear "Oooh, yer b$&tard," from over

Electric fence

the hedge. "Are you alright, Alan?" I ask. "I've been 'it in me b%$$%cks!" he yells. And as I run round the fence I find him doubled over, clutching between his legs, with both hands. "How the hell did you let a ram get that close ter kick yer?" asks Ron, trying not to laugh out loud. "T'wasn't the ram," chokes Alan, "I was keepin' an eye

Fern clearing

on the dammed ram and didn't see the electric fence. Must 'ave pee'd on the wire, an' it zapped me. Bloody 'ell it's painful." And that's it for me. I am wetting myself with laughter. I'm sure that a short, sharp, jolt of electricity to that very tender part of Alan's anatomy must have been very painful but it takes both Ron and me a few minutes to calm down enough to make sure that Alan is ok and that we will be starting the walk. He assures us that he'll be alright and, still chuckling, we head across the field towards a kissing gate.

We pass through the gate and Alan produces a compass. "We're heading west," says Alan. I am comforted to know this fact, but if Alan is familiar with the walk, why does he need a compass? I don't ask. We follow the path, under the holly trees. "Not many berries on the 'olly," comments Ron. "Isn't that supposed to mean that the winter's going to be bad or is it the summer that's not going to be hot?" I ask but, for some reason, neither answers me. As we continue we pass some stables, seen through some of the largest oak trees I've seen. We go through another gate and follow the path through a fern covered clearing.

One of the things that I'm hoping to see and capture on this walk is the colours of autumn. I think that this is the most colourful time of year. Most of the leaves are turning to autumn gold yet some leaves still seem to be hanging on and remain defiantly green. Hopefully this will be captured for you all to see. Just as we get to the other side of the clearing Alan needs another comfort break. You can all imagine the banter between Alan and us as he stands up against another hedge. At the end of this path is another gate. This leads us onto Royal Oak Lane where we turn left and pass a house called Hadham House. "Bet yer 'e isn't a bin man fer council," comments Ron as we pass the gate entry system warning us of closed circuit TV cameras.

As we stroll uphill we ignore the lane to our right. One thing that I like and admire about Alan is his knowledge of all things country. It isn't long before he is showing me a plant called Wood Sage, "you can eat it," he says, "it tastes a little bitter, but it's not bad. Used ter be used as a mouth wash" It tastes vile! Trust me. I trusted Alan and popped in a lot and had to spit it out when he wasn't looking. A little further up the lane, "This is used by the French when they cook," continues Alan holding up yet another green hedgerow delight. "It's called Sorrel and has a vinegary taste to it. Try some." He hands me some leaves and it tastes nothing like vinegar to me. It was slightly tastier than the Wood Sage but it ended up in the same place. A little further up the lane we spot some Gorse bushes in bloom, "Is that early or a late bloom?" asks Ron. "Must be

It turns blue inside?

early," answers Alan as he surveys the bush with his critical eye. We head further up the lane, passing 'Cobbetts and 'Orchard Cottage'. "Better check the compass," says Alan. "It looks as if we're heading North East," he says. I'm still confused over the need for a compass but don't express my feelings in case there is some obvious reason for having it and I don't want to seem stupid. Alan is obviously pleased with the direction we're heading as he pockets the compass and says "we're heading in the right direction." We pass other, very grand properties. 'Holly Mount' is on our left, 'Russett', also on the left, made Ron comment about apples. A driveway on our right took you down to houses called 'Pickreed' and 'Penrhyn' or was Penrhyn the Welsh name for Pickreed? We head downhill towards 'Brackenwood' with 'Cherrywood' on the right. All names, that gives a picture, to our surroundings. We turn a bend and now head uphill, past 'The Fir Grove' on our right, 'Picture Tree' and 'Hillymead' on our left. I'm not exactly sure what Alan said as he pointed to a fungus growing on the side of the road but it sounded like "that's Balleteus Ed," or something like that. "Looks like a currant bun, it does." But unfortunately I really can't remember if he said you could eat it but, apparently, it turns a bluish colour inside. If you do see one I suggest you steer clear, just in case it is poisonous.

Alan inspects the 'early' gorse

As we walk down this lane there is the constant sound of barking dogs. Every house seems to have its own version of a guard dog. Some look ferocious and I wouldn't trust them as far as I could see them, while others just seem to like the sound of their own bark.

View across the countryside

But we turn left now and follow the drive, with a public footpath sign, to 'Grovehurst' and 'Grovehurst Farm'. The views along this drive are some of what I've been hoping for. As we pass 'Grovehurst', with yet another barking dog, we come to a view across the countryside with all the vivid colours of an approaching autumn. We walk for about half a mile just admiring the scenery before we pass a house called 'The Weald' and arrive at the entrance to 'Grovehurst Farm'. We now enter the farmyard and bear left, following the public footpath sign, leaving the farmhouse on our right. Two horse riders greet us as we head up the path which has turned into a well-kept bridleway. As we head up the

bridleway Alan produces, yet again, his compass. "We're still 'eading in the right direction," he say's as he studies the little needle. "We're now eading north ter north-east." I'm so pleased. But still not sure why we need a compass if we know where we're going. Perhaps someone can explain it to me later? We now arrive at a metal gate and the signs direct us left, continuing along the bridleway. When we reach the gate Alan notices that it isn't shut properly, "must 'ave been the 'orse riders," he says, "and they blame town people fer leavin' the gates open."

We follow the bridleway signs into a field. We need to keep the hedgerow on our right as we now follow a track down to an area that Alan knows as 'Singing Streams'. "There are little streams all down in this area," he explains, "on a quiet day all

Singing Stream(?)

you can hear is running water. It's a really peaceful place." Before entering 'Singing Stream' we need to pass through a gate in the far corner, at the bottom of the slope. Unfortunately the water level was alarmingly low through the small, narrow streams so we weren't able to experience the sounds of running water but it must be a very peaceful area. On our right is a gate, wide open, with 'Private Property' signs attached. A pheasant runs in front of us and for some reason this pheasant reminds Ron of an incident involving a member of our Royal family who has been 'interviewed' by the police over the shooting of protected birds on the Sandringham Estate. Two rare hen harriers, described by the Royal Society for the Protection of Birds, as the most persecuted birds in Britain, were killed on the estate last week. If the person is found guilty he could receive a fine of £5,000, or six months in prison. "Put 'im in prison," offers Ron, "A five thousand pound fine is peanuts to a Prince," he continues, "serve the bugger right, supposed ter be educated and does things like that. Make 'im do a year in prison" Ron has him tried, convicted and banished to the Tower before his feet can touch the ground.

We continue along the bridleway, passing streams as we head uphill. "I think this path will take us up to a road," says Alan. Now why should Alan say 'I think', surely he knows where he's going. "I'll just check me compass, again." I'm still confused about this compass thing. "Yes, we're still on the right track," he says. We must be on the right track, I think, because it's the only track. "We're now heading north." So that's really good, isn't it?

But first we arrive at a fork in the track. A footpath leads to our right and the bridleway goes to our left. We follow the bridleway to the left and soon arrive on

Uphill towards the road

Sweethaws Road. We again turn left. We have now turned left twice. Before we turned left, twice, we were heading north, according to Alan's compass. So explain to me this. Whilst walking up Sweethaws Road, which is steep, straight and uphill, Alan stopped, looked at his compass and tells us that we are heading north. How the hell can that be?

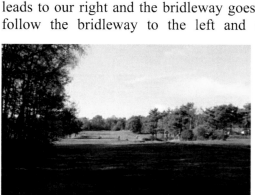

Crowborough Golf Course

Alan points out another plant. "That's Hairy Wound Wurt, that is. Used in the old days ter mend broken bones. Crush it up and mix it with egg white and put it on the broken limb. When it dries it goes solid and acts like plaster o' paris." He bends down again and snatches at the verge, "This is 'Bishops Bonnet'," he continues, "try it. It tastes of celery," he offers me a clump and the taste of Wood Sage slaps my memory, "no thanks Alan, I can't stand the taste of celery," I offer as an explanation. Ron also declined his offer, explaining that as the stuff was growing low, on a grass verge, anything could have been 'on it'.

The last direction sign

We continue along this road, passing some fantasticlly beautiful properties until we reach a driveway, on our right, leading to 'Ghyll Farm'. The public footpath we take leads us off to the left and is clearly signposted. "I think this path should lead us onto Crowborough Golf Course," says Alan. There he goes again. He thinks, but surely he should know? I look at Ron hoping that I will receive some comfort from my doubts, but all Ron says, with that beaming grin is, "You alright there, then, Graham?" Thankfully it isn't long before little flags and long grass fairways come into view.

The golf course looks beautiful and reminds me of many pleasant days playing the game. Some believe that the game of golf is 'a good walk spoilt' but I must say that I

A wonder of nature

found the game very addictive. You can play 17 holes very badly but on the 18th hole everything goes really well, and you're hooked. You've got to go round again. Unfortunately, for us, the signs around this course, for us walkers, are not very clear. We wandered around, trying to keep out of the way of flying golf balls, as we found one sign and looked out for the next. We eventually arrived at the 11th tee to find that the sign leading us out of the course had been broken and simply laid down, out of view. I'm sure that, at sometime, the users of the course have sworn at walkers for passing over their fairways when all that we are doing is looking for clear signs. You'd also think that with the fees paid by the members and non-members they could afford to ensure that signs, keeping walkers away from their precious fairways and greens, would be kept in a reasonable condition.

We find the pathway leading us away from the

Coloured dye

golf course and make our way along a narrow fenced path, heading towards Chillies Lane and the A26, main Tunbridge Wells road. It's along this damp, narrow path that I see one of those wonders of nature, fungi growing, in abundance, on the bark of a tree trunk. How or why it should grow on this particular tree and none of the others along this path I have no idea. But we all stopped to admire and appreciate its beauty.

Shortly after the fungi we arrive at the very busy A26 at the junction of Chillies Lane, which was, incidentally, the lane with the house for sale for 1¾ million pound. We walk along this road and past The Crow and Gate Inn, much to Ron's annoyance. Opposite the Inn is a telephone kiosk (vandalised) and behind the kiosk is a small green and a stile leading into a field. "We'll stop shortly fer a bite ter eat," says Alan, who has been carrying a 'Friends' bag over his shoulder since the start of the walk.

Trying to get to the chocolate

We follow the clear signs along the path, crossing the field keeping the hedge close to our left-hand side until we reach another stile. We now pass through a gap in the hedge. To the right of this gap is a metal gate. A large house is to the left of us as we pass through the gate and head towards yet another stile. Just on our right is a small field with a few sheep. "Looks like the red bugger's been lucky again," says Ron. Most of the sheep in the field have been covered by the ram with the red paint on his belly but he had missed a couple. They had blue dye on their backs. I have covered the reasons for these markings elsewhere so will not explain further.

At the end of the fenced path

Just past the sheep, at the next stile, Alan can't wait any longer for his bite to eat and opens his bag to produce a little lunch box. Inside, Alan's wife had supplied him with bacon sandwiches, miniature pork pies and a chocolate bar. "My wife can certainly make a nice bacon sandwich," comments Alan, "she ain't afraid ter put bacon in it, best streaky 'tis this, can't beat it." The three horses in the next field have obviously caught the scent of Alan's dinner and come over to see if there is going to be any left-over's. "Did you know," says Alan, "that if you give a 'orse stale bread it gives it wind, yer know." He really is a hive of information, but he manages to fight off the horses before opening his flask for a cup of tea.

You all know my fear of animals. In the next field are three horses and we have to get past them. Ron's words of 'don't run, they won't 'urt yer' fill my ears yet they don't, as always, seem to give me any comfort as I climb over the stile into the same field. The horses have decided to stand still, on the path; just inside the field, there is no way round them, so we've got to get them to move. And I surprise myself. I am reminded of words of encouragement from Teresa, when we rode Beaver in one of our exploits[52] as I lent against the neck of the big white horse and told it to move. To my amazement the horse moved out of the way so that we could pass by. The feeling I got from just that was brilliant, yet neither Alan nor Ron made any comment. But I was really pleased with my bravery.

We now walk across the top of the field, keeping the hedge on our right. I keep looking behind us to make sure the horses aren't following us. At the next metal gate we turn, immediately left and walk along a fenced path, downhill towards a stile. Again our direction marker is clear and we now follow the path through a wood. On our left is fencing, described to me some time ago as 'dear' fencing when it was meant to be <u>deer</u> fencing, to keep deer enclosed in woodland. "We 'aven't seen any deer fer ages, on our walks," says Ron. On previous walks we have been really luck and been able to witness the magnificent sight of deer, running wild, yet since the start of this book we haven't seen any. Just as the words leave Ron, on our left, we see two young deer, scamper away into the wood. I try to get a photograph but they're gone in seconds. But at least we had seen them. We follow the fence, along the path for over a

Harts Tongue Fern

[52] 'Left or Right Ron?' by this author and published by LR Publishing - Page 235

mile, crossing stiles and passing through gates. Conversation is about the beauty of the British Woodland and how seasons come and go. Alan points out where a badger has been furrowing in the undergrowth. "Do you know how I know that's a badger?" he asks. We both say no, "It's because a badger always digs a little 'ole and does 'is business in the 'ole before 'e rummages for food." I never knew that, did you?

Suddenly the deer fencing goes off to our left but we continue straight on towards a large white house. Just before the house a sign tells us to turn right. We head down

Cattle, just waiting to attack (?)

the slope towards a drive. In front of us is a large pond, complete with rowing boat. "'Ow about 'avin' that big 'un in yer back garden?" says Ron as we climb down a few steps and turn left, along the drive and head towards a gate and a public footpath sign. Once through the gate we head along a clear path passing a very beautiful tree. Alan stops and explains that the tree is an inhabitant of China and has been brought over to this country. It apparently is deciduous (?) and has a Latin name with about 500 letters in it. I will apologies for not taking down the name but it was much too long and Alan said it so fast I didn't catch exactly what he said. "Why do you know all these Latin names?" I ask, "'ad too," he explains, "I worked for the Forestry for over 20 years and yer need ter know all the names. Trained at Plumpton College I did." With that he stops and says "Look, that's Harts Tongue Fern, also known as *asplanium scolopendrium* (he spelt it for me) used 'fer burns. The leaves are full o'water. You can see the seeds on the back of the leaf." He turns the leaf over and small, long brown seeds are attached. He is amazing, just like a walking encyclopaedia. At the end of the walk, when I was dropping him off, he asked me if I minded him telling me so many things, "Don't want you to think I'm big 'eaded," he says. How can I, or anyone for that matter, think that of Alan? I have learned so much from him and Ron over the past few months. Things that you take for granted. Things that you may not realise the importance of have been explained and shown to me. I can't thank them enough.

Views across High Hurstwood

We continue along this path past more some Jacob sheep until we arrive at some gates leading us out onto a road. Here we turn left and after just a few yards we turn left again, passing through a kissing gate and head slowly downhill, for once, until we eventually reach yet another kissing gate in the far left corner of the field. Now I am really worried. In the next field are a herd of cattle. Recently, in our local press there has been a report of a 50 year old man, walking his dog, being attacked by cows. He sustained broken ribs, a punctured lung; he lost a lot of blood and needed to be airlifted, by helicopter, to hospital. Don't ever tell me again that 'they won't 'urt yer', because they can, they will and they do! This poor man is proof of it.

Standing right opposite the kissing gate we have to walk through is one of the meanest of the herd. He's big, he's black and he's staring at me as I approach the gate. "Don't show 'em yer scared," says Ron. But I am. I get through the gate as the big black one lowers his head and stamps his foot. Why am I being forced to go through first? The cow backs off as I get into the field. Its mates all look at me. They say animals can smell fear. Smell it, I was practically standing in it. Ron and Alan follow me and then they both walk past me and the cattle, ignoring them and me. To my relief the animals don't move as I race down the slope of the field heading for the next gate. Ron's immortal words are ring in my ears, "Don't run!" he shouts. But I'm off like a greyhound. I'm halfway down the slope and turn to see that the animals are still at the top of the slope, minding their own business. And it's now that Alan shouts to me "yer got ter stop an' admire the view from 'ere. It's a wonderful picture." And it was. This is exactly what I was hoping for. Full of greens and oranges and it stretched for miles.

The path continued for a few more yards, over a wooden bridge until we came to a gate which leads us out onto the road towards the church, where we started, over 4½ hours ago.

Alan has consulted his compass on more occasions than necessary and for what reason I am still not clear. The walk is nearly 8½ miles in length and crosses some of the most beautiful scenery and landscapes we have seen. The colours, although not clearly represented by the photographs are glorious in their richness and, although long in miles I will have to admit to the walk being exhilarating. But it is not for the faint-hearted. The hills are a bit steep and the animals could cause you some concern unless, like us, they don't worry you (?)

Unfortunately the church was locked so we cannot comment on its interior. I'm also a little surprised that High Hurstwood has only one church, and it's Catholic. Perhaps the church in Buxted Park is used by the non-catholic? There do not appear to be any shops to walk around in High Hurstwood and for all the time we were here we have seen just four people. So, perhaps that is why the countryside around High Hurstwood is so spectacular. There's no-one there to spoil it?

We will now have a short break from walking and writing. We have discovered that Ron is to have his long awaited operation, to repair his hernia, on the 4th December and he will need to convalesce for a few weeks. "I'll be back walkin' 'fore Christmas," he insists. "I been told ter walk after the op. It'll do me good." "Yes Ron, but lets get you over the operation and see how you feel then. From what I've heard, it can be pretty painful."

A beautiful stroll around High Hurstwood
Had a laugh just like we should
Alan taught us a lesson that made good sense
Never have a pee against an electric fence
Aresee©

Chapter 11 - Icklesham

Ron has had his operation. Thankfully, all went well and they had the technology to rebuild him. He has a scar. It is a smallish scar which is held together with stitches that will dissolve. "Got ter drink plenty ov fluid an' keep active," says Ron as he walks around the bar clutching his pint of Harvey's. "I think the hospital meant exercise, Ron," I offer, "like walking a couple of miles a day, outside, not around the bar at the local." "There's plenty o'time fer that when we start our walks again. In the mean time I'll concentrate on drinkin' plenty o'fluids first an' then work up ter the exercise."

Ron can't wait until we can go for one of our walks and has been pestering me since he came out of hospital. I am concerned that he will do some long-term damage but we have waited over two weeks and I have found a walk around Icklesham[53] which should not be too taxing. It's a 3¾ miles circular walk starting from, and finishing at, the Queens Head, Parsonage Lane and is described as 'a gentle undulating walk along field paths and tracks'. The fact that we start and finish at a pub appeals to Ron. "Exercise and fluid," says Ron, "just what the doctor ordered."

When I first told Ron that the walk is around Icklesham he said, "I played football there, against Icklesham Casuals. Scored a 'at trick, I did, and nearly got booked in the same match." "What do you mean, nearly?" I ask. "Tackled one o'the defenders, I did," Ron explains, "referee blew 'is whistle an' came runnin' over towards me with 'is book in 'is 'and. 'You were a bit late number 9' 'e says. 'I got 'ere as fast as I could,' says I an' the ref couldn't book me fer laughin'. Lucky 'e saw the funny side I suppose." It doesn't matter where we go; Ron always has a story to tell.

My very favourite website is back.[54] I view this site every time I find a walk to unearth snippets of information about the village we are about to visit. For some reason the site has been unavailable to me. But, thankfully, the site is working again. When I click onto Icklesham I find very little information. And what I do find is confusing. The details found on Icklesham tell me that the very first record of the

The Beatles - Ringo, John, Paul & George

village was in the year 772 when a land charter was signed by Offa, the King of Mercia. The village was then known as 'Icoleshamme' and dominated the River Brede. It was, undoubtedly, a prime target to the Normans in 1066, when they landed. The details on the website then tell me that in 1282 the King's treasurer was asked to visit Old Winchelsea to investigate the danger to the town from the sea. The report was to abandon the town and create a new town on the heights of Petit Ihamme, nowadays known as Icklesham[55]. I thought that when Old Winchelsea was lost to the sea, in the late 1280's, during the reign of Henry III, the new town created there was called Winchelsea. So, which is correct? I'm not sure, perhaps someone can enlighten me.

---

[53] Pocket Pub Walks – Walk 15 - downloaded from www.countrysidebooks.co.uk – fee paid
[54] www.villagenet.co.uk
[55] www.villagenet.co.uk/rotherlevels/villages/icklesham.php visited 10/12/2007

I'm also not sure if our walk will be anywhere near Hogs Hill but I am told that an old smock windmill, originally built in Pett but moved to Icklesham around 1791 been lovingly restored, and is currently used, as a recording studio, by Sir Paul McCartney (Younger readers may not be aware that Paul, along with John Lennon, was one of the founder members of the pop group, The Beatles, back in the 1960's).

The church at Icklesham is Norman and overlooks the Brede valley. An entry in the churchwardens' accounts is of fifteen shillings (a large amount of money in those days?) given to the ringers for "Rejoycing when ye rebels was beat," and is dated 26th April 1746.[56] This must surely be for the victory at the Battle of Culloden which took place on the 16th April 1746.

This isn't The Queens Head Inn?

Also recorded is the will of Joan Toyke, who lived at Icklesham, and part of that will reads; "ii busshells of malte be equivally devyded betwixt John Tokye and John Garlye so that they twoo buy me a fyrking of bere at the day of my buryall'.

But all that aside, our walk should start at the car park of the Queens Head. This building dates back to 1632 although it was first established as an ale house in 1831. The walk itself is part of the 1066 Country Walk, a long-distance route linking the town of Rye and Pevensey Castle. But our walk is Walk 15 from a book titled Pocket Pub Walks[57]. Our instructions advise us that the return part of the route is '…along less-well-used paths which require some care with navigation as it is largely unsigned.' I have warned the wife - if we're not back by the time it gets dark she is to notify the authorities.

So, on a very cold December afternoon, I pick up Ron from the Kings Head. I am still a little concerned that he'll be ok but, as he points out, the walk is described as '…A gentle undulating walk

But this is The Queens Head Inn!

along field paths and tracks.' "What can possibly go wrong?" he asks, "Be a piece o'cake this will. So don't you worry? I'll be fine." We make our way along the coast, through Hastings, towards Icklesham. The journey takes about an hour with the usual hold-ups along this very busy coast road. Matters aren't helped by the amount of roadwork's being carried out that need traffic lights. We hit them all at red.

"We need to find Parsonage Lane," I tell Ron. "It should be by the recreation ground." We pass a pub called The Robin Hood, "I wonder why a pub, in the middle o'Sussex is called The Robin 'ood? P'rhaps it's 'cause the beers expensive," chuckles Ron as he answers his own question. "By the way," he continues, "we just passed the rec." A quick look in the rear mirror, and I see a white van trying to climb into the boot of my car. We had to drive further down the road before I could turn round and

---

[56] Sussex by S.P.B. Mais published by The Richard Press, 1950 - page 183
[57] Walk 15 Downloaded to a pdf file from www.countrysidebooks.co.uk – visited 22/11/07 - fee paid

head back towards the recreation ground car park. But once we found it, we were fine. Another check to make sure Ron will be ok and off we go.

Our instructions start with the words; 'From the pub, set out along Parsonage Lane, walking away from the A259...' We are at Parsonage Lane but there is no pub. We are on the A259, at the junction of Parsonage Lane and we still can't see a pub. There is a nice house, but no pub. We decide to walk up Parsonage Lane and after about 100 yards, in front of us, is The Queens Head Inn. "Not that often we get lost before we start," says Ron, "still, at least we'll know where it is on the way back!"

Parsonage Lane soon becomes a rough track and then turns into a hedged path. We need to locate a 1066 walk logo, painted red which will direct us to a stile on our right. The sign was easily found as we head towards a stile. Our next instruction tells us to drop downhill along a right field edge. "I don't like the sound o'that," say's Ron. " 'ow far is the drop?" he asks. "It can't be that bad," I answer, "the description was 'gently undulating'"

Direction sign

But it was that bad. In fact it was worse than that bad. From our position, just over the stile, it looked like the edge of a cliff. The grass was white with frost and the path just disappeared. "I think now might be a good time to say I've left my walking shoes at

View across the valley

Towards a gate, but not through it

home." I tell Ron. "Now that would be a really stupid thing to do," says Ron, "especially with all this frost on the ground. The thing is, I forgot to put mine on, as well," And here we are, in the middle of a frozen field with me wearing trainers and Ron wearing his Sunday best. "Just 'ave ter tread careful," he says as we head downhill towards a stile in the bottom corner. "There should be a sign somewhere along this path pointing us in the right direction," I advise Ron, as we both slide down towards some trees and bushes. "I think I found sign, but it ain't goin' ter be much 'elp." Chuckles Ron, as he points to the sign which has obviously been thrown into the bushes. "The book says that the last bit's difficult ter navigate. Let's be 'onest," laughs Ron, "the first bit ain't too clever." I'm beginning to have that horrible feeling that things aren't going to go to plan as we continue to slip and slide to the bottom of the hill and our next obstacle.

After crossing the stile the walk levels out as we follow the edge of a meandering field hedge on our left. The views across the valley of the River Brede are exceptional. At least they would be if it wasn't for the mist. I did take a number of photographs, hoping that you could see how beautiful the area is but I don't think the pictures do the scene justice.

Rickety footbridge and stile

We now cross another stile and cross two more fields, heading for Brook Farm. I keep asking Ron if he's ok as we are now heading uphill on a track. "There's a young lady, out walking her dog behind us," says Ron. "How do you know it's a young lady?" I ask. "Trust me," is the reply and within a few minutes a young lady strides up to us with her collie dog, "Good afternoon, me dear," says Ron with his normal Sussex charm. "Hello," says the lady, eyeing Ron with just a little hesitation. "Beautiful day fer a stroll," he continues. "It certainly is," she replies, as her stride quickens slightly. We speed up as well. The lady realises that she's stuck with us, unless she stops and lets us go on or she breaks out into a run. But she seems to accept the situation and is happy to chat. She tells us that she regularly walks along this route. She buys fresh eggs from a farm just up the lane. She has children. Her children like to go out walking. Her children do not get tired when they have been for a long walk in the countryside. No, they don't sit in front of a TV or play video games and yes the Sussex countryside is very beautiful although today it is very cold and icy in places, yes she will be careful where she treads.

When we eventually arrive at the place where she buys her eggs we bid her a fond

Ron emerges from the path

farewell and both practically collapse with exhaustion. "Christ Ron!" I gasp, "She can certainly stride it out, and I'm knackered." We slow down to a stroll. "She can certainly stride it out but what a lovely lady. At least she spoke to us. Not like some we've met."

We arrive at the road junction with the A259 again. Here we cross the main road and go over the stile opposite, heading across the field towards a gate. Our instructions are very clear. Don't go through the gate but pass to the right and continue beside the fence. It is here that the instructions are not so good. We are told that '...the path will curve to the right'; we follow the curve to the right'...after 30 yards, you turn left along a woodland path'; there is no woodland path, there is a railing fence in front of us and a wood, to our left, but no path. "Have you any ideas, Ron?" I ask. "Is this the last bit?" asks Ron. "We're over halfway so I suppose it could be the last bit, why?" I ask. "'Cause it'll be the bit that's difficult ter navigate. The bits with no signs ter tell us which way ter go so let's go back ter the path and follow it till the end and then work out what ter do next." A logical reasoning process, I think.

So back we go to the path and follow it through until we come to the driveway leading to a large house. Presumably the name of the house will be at the other end of the very long drive so I am not able to tell you what the house is called. But what I can say is that our instructions now tell us to walk ahead with a close-boarded fence on our left. And what is in front of us? You guessed it; a public footpath with a close-boarded fence on the left. Ron doesn't say anything. He just has that smug grin on his face.

We now descend, again to a footbridge and stile where we bear left and follow the edge of a young tree plantation. We pass through a gate in the field corner and continue along a narrow path between a fence and hedge out to a lane. Once onto the lane we turn left and then almost immediately right onto the driveway leading to

Scrag Oak Farm. Once into the farmyard we turn left passing the outbuildings and continue along the fields' edge. The farmer must have spent days here, ploughing. Everywhere you look is ploughed, for as far as the eye can see. Again I have tried to capture the moment but the camera doesn't do the scene justice. In the distance, just in front of the setting sun, and on the distant skyline is Pett Church spire. It is a magnificent view but the light is beginning to fail. We must get on. We still have to look around the church at Icklesham.

The entrance to Scrag Oak Farm

Again, another field corner and we head through a wide gap. There are two stiles on our right and our instructions are to go over the second stile and continue direction, dropping gently (?) down the hill. At the bottom of the hill we go through a gate and start climbing uphill skirting someone's garden on the right. Just then a large golden Labrador spots us and heads towards us, hackles up and teeth showing. I freeze. Even my sons Labradors don't do that when they see me. Closely following this golden monster is a Heinz variety, obviously bolstered by his mates' bravado. Just as quickly as they arrived so did the owner who called off the dogs who now, enthusiastically, started licking our hands. "Sorry about

that," says the owner, "we don't see that many people up here. They startled you as much as you startled them, I suspect." "The dogs are ok," says Ron as he makes a fuss of the Labrador, "but can you tell us if this is the right path to Knockbridge Farm?" "It certainly is," comes the reply. "But a tinsee word of warning. If the dogs are out in the farmyard they may try to come at you or chase you. If you pretend to pick something up from the ground they will, invariably, run orf. Just thought you ought to know." "Thanks fer the tip," says Ron, "we'll bear it in mind if we 'ave to," and we head for the

Ron, doing the natural thing!

gate. As we get to the gate Ron says, "sounds like 'e were born with some silver in is gob." "Let's hope we don't have to chase the little doggies' orf." I mimic. But He wasn't listening. Two collies come hurtling round the corner at us. As suggested I bent down to pick something up and the dogs both stopped. "Looks like it works," I whisper to Ron. "Don't you believe it," he whispers back, "they ain't runnin' orf. Try throwin' what you got in yer 'and." "I haven't got anything in my hand. I was only pretending." I can feel my legs shaking as the dogs slowly head in our direction. Slowly Ron bends down and picks something up from the ground. Both dogs stop. Ron pulls his arm back, as if to throw something, and both dogs hurtle away from us, and head for the buildings. "How did you do that?" I ask. "Tis easy," replies Ron, "ma'y pretendin' is obviously more superior to your pretendin' that's what made the little doggies run orf." I was impressed. "But now," Ron continues, "one must relieve oneself before one gets scared somethin' silly." With that he drops his stick and carrier bag and heads for the hedge.

Just left to fall and rot?

We eventually come to a road. Here we turn right and head towards a road junction where we turn left. After a few yards we turn right, again, this time along an access drive to a pair of garages. We go over the stile by the gate and head along the edge of an orchard. The strange thing about this orchard is that it looks as if none of the apples have been picked. The ground, all around the trees, is covered with fallen apples, yet every now and again, there is one tree that still bears fruit. Of course we didn't pick any of the fruit, that would be stealing, but the one that happened to fall into my hand tasted beautiful. Ron though some of the apples may have been Russets but the one I tasted was like a Cox. Even so, I wonder why so many apples were left to fall naturally to the ground and not harvested.

At the end of the orchard we turn left onto the road and pass a really nice converted twin Oast House called Manor Farm.

It is just past the Oast House that we bear left onto a grassy track which leads us to Icklesham Church. Unfortunately the church was locked so we were unable to see inside. It is a shame, in today's society, when a church, for its own protection, has to lock its doors for fear of vandalism or theft. It must be said that locking the church doors does seem to be in the minority. Most of the churches we have visited have, thankfully, been open to the public. Some have welcomed us with open arms and shown us around their magnificent buildings. Others keep a discreet distance. There is always something to see or find in a church and it was disappointing not to be able to see inside this one.

From the church it is just a short walk back to the car and on our way home. The light is getting worse but when I

The sun sets over Icklesham

turned round for a last glimpse of Icklesham I couldn't resist taking this photograph as the sun is setting.

The walk was very pleasant even if the instructions were a little 'orf. The hills were steeper than expected and some of the stiles and bridges needed a little tender loving care. As ever, the views were worth the visit and the people we met were approachable We did notice the habit of letting dogs foul the path and the owners putting it into plastic bags and hanging it from a fence but, as we've said before, it is a well-known habit in this part of Sussex.

Thankfully Ron was fine with the walk and has suffered no lasting problems. In fact he can't wait for our next one. As we walked back to the car he pointed out that even the council are now putting out signs to warn people of our presence.

Warning

Graham & Ron in the area

Icklesham was a walk with variety
We met people from a different society
The view when the sun set
Is one we will never forget?
Aresee©

Chapter 12 – Jevington

It is Christmas time and my daughter has decided to leave home. It is not a surprising decision; after all, Michelle is 33 years old. But it was the speed in which things happened that was alarming. One minute she was looking for a flat in Hailsham somewhere and the next she was moving in and we were helping with Chrissie decorations. But she is the last to fly the nest and I know that her mum will miss her, even though she only lives the other side of Hailsham, she phones everyday and is 'popping in' every other day to leave her washing. So we now have the Pollard residence to 'ourselves' for short periods, just me and the wife. I'm already starting to think of down-sizing. But, over the Christmas period, we had more visitors than we are used to, so perhaps we'll stay where we are? One thing that did result in Michelle's move was a clear out of things cluttering up the house, because I found a book that I hadn't seen for ages. If you are familiar with Hailsham you must remember Robertson's Toy Shop. Mr Robertson, the owner, once wrote a book titled 'Hailsham and its Environs'[58]. The book tells the story of the area from about the year 340 to 1982 and is a fascinating insight into how people used to live, work and play during these times. It is full of anecdotes and facts that are truly remarkable. How the author managed to research so much and put it into such a book is a credit to his dedication. If you don't have a copy of this wonderful book it is a must have buy for next Christmas (see footnote for details).

After much searching of my other books and journals for a walk beginning with the letter 'J' I have had to settle on Jevington. This wasn't my first choice. Ron managed to complete Icklesham without any problems but that walk was only 3¾ miles so distance wasn't a problem. There are a number of listed walks around Jevington but due to the location they are all hilly. Long, in distance, as well as hilly. But my very first choice for the walk beginning with the letter 'J' was a placed called Jolesfield but I couldn't find a walk near the place. For anyone not sure of the location

Doesn't look too steep?

of Jolesfield it is near West Grinstead and the burial place of one of my favourite Sussex men, Hillaire Belloc. There are, obviously, lots of walks in that area but not one touches the village of Jolesfield so; I'm sorry Ron, but Jevington it is. What I have tried to find is a walk that is not too long, but the one I settled on is still 7 miles. Unfortunately it will be hilly. I just hope Ron will be ok.

On December 22nd 1917, during World War I, tragedy struck Jevington, when an airship, based at the Royal Navy air station in Polegate, was returning to base after patrolling the English Channel during the night. Unfortunately, the night was foggy and the pilot mistook one of its sister ships for the lights of the radio tower where it was to land and actually came down on top of the ship. Two of the heroes of the night, air mechanic Harold Robinson and boy mechanic Eric Steer, ran to the

---

[58] Hailsham and its Environs by Charles A Robertson pub. by Phillimore 1982 ISBN 0 850 334 34 9

burning remains of the airship and managed to remove all of the bombs[59]. This saved the lives of the injured crewmen and both Robinson and Steer were awarded the Albert Medal[60].

James Lambert, the watercolour artist, was born in Jevington in 1725 and became the illustrator of the important Historic researches of Sir William Burrell. Many of James Lambert's drawings are now in the British Museum, one of which is a drawing of Hailsham Church completed in 1780[61].

In 1751 England fell in line with the rest of Europe over the New Style calendar. Until that time the New Year, in England, began on March 25th. The Roman Catholic countries on the continent had adjusted their calendars way back in 1582. Due to our lateness in converting the calendar the authorities decided that September 2nd 1752 should be followed by September 14th (a loss of eleven days) in order to iron out the accumulated errors of centuries. As you can imagine, this caused some confusion. But it is not as confusing as the date difference between us and our continental friends. A memorial in Jevington Church seems strangely undecided:

Near this place lyes ye
body of
NAT.COLLIER
M.A.
late Rector of this
CHURCH
who dyed Mar:ye first
169½

Collier, presumably, died on the first day of March 1691 according to the prevailing calendar, but over the water 1692 was already two months old. His plaque with its queer 91/92 alternatives seems to be having it both ways.[62] There are a number of other reasons why I wish to visit this church but I will have to curb my enthusiasm.

The instructions for today's walk are taken from The Argus[63]; a book used by us many times. The walk uses sections of the South Downs Way, the Jubilee Way and the Wealdway starting and finishing at Jevington and is described as a downland walk; which for those people not familiar with the jargon, means it will be bloody hilly.

We start from the public car park (free *and* long-term) and head back towards the village centre. The first turning on the right leads you to Jigg

Until you look back

Cottage. The cottage isn't named after a dance but after the Landlord of the local inn.

---

[59] People of Hidden Sussex by W Swinfen & D Arscott published by BBC Radio Sussex, 1985 Pge 92
[60] First introduced on 7th March 1866 and named after Queen Victoria's husband, Prince Albert – the medal has now been replaced by the George Cross.
[61] Hailsham and its Environs by Charles A Robertson - Page 110
[62] Dead & Buried in Sussex by David Arscott – Published by SB Publications 1997 - Pge 64
[63] The Argus East Sussex Walks by Ben Perkins – Published by Southern Publishing Co. - Page 58

His name was James Pettit (or Jevington Jig) and he was the ringleader of the gang of highwaymen, smugglers, horse-stealers and general lawbreakers who terrified the district in the 18th century until they were caught and hanged in 1796[64].

The next turning on the right is the one we require, Willingdon Lane which is a cul-de-sac. At the end of the lane is a gate, which we pass through, and are instructed to fork right from the main path and head for the top right corner of the field. Top is the right word for it. As I said from the start, I had my suspicions about this walk and after only 100 yards I'm looking for the oxygen cylinder. The strange thing is, it didn't look that steep, it felt it but didn't look it. That is until you turned round and you could see for miles.

Once at the top we have to climb a stile and join a track. And guess what, according to the instructions we are now on part of the South Downs Way which will take us '…steadily up on to the Downs.' The word 'steady' implies gradual. His words not mine. I check with Ron to make sure he is ok. He's got that silly grin of his. He's fine. I'm flagging. Little did I realise there was worse to come. A lot worse. At the top, we continue over a track. Just then I hear what sounds like horses hooves behind us. I turn and see four horses racing up the hill. Due to libel laws I will not disclose the trainer of these steeds. But Ron says, "Bloody useless they are, run like camels. Especially when I puts money on 'em. Most ov' 'em are named Simpson somethin'. Cost me a few bob them 'ave." Ron is not impressed as they

Old stone marker

flash past us, towards a gate and turn right, galloping along the field edge. "There should be an old stone marker here, somewhere," I tell Ron. Just as we find the marker the horses are back. "Are they runnin' soon?" asks Ron. We are informed that all the horses will be racing over the next week, either at Linfield, Brighton or Plumpton Racecourse. "'Ave ter keep me eye out in the paper," says Ron, "may be worth a little dabble." "But you just said they run like camels," I can't believe what I'm hearing but Ron continues with "yer wouldn't think so ter watch 'em on the gallops. They all looked pretty fast. I'll just 'ave a little flutter. You never knows."

It is only a few more yards to reach one of the highest points on the Downs. At last we have stopped going uphill and can see the views across Eastbourne are remarkable. The sun is out, it's getting warm and you can see for miles.

View from the top of the Downs

We continue along the ridge, marvelling at the views for about a mile. The fact that we are at the top makes you feel good. I'm pleased to have made it this high. This area is somewhat familiar to me. "Is there a dew pond around here?" I ask Ron. "What makes yer ask," says Ron. "It just looks familiar up here. My son used to walk his Labradors, Pip and Tess, up here and they always ended up in a dew pond. There was also a plaque up here in memory of a lost aeroplane crew. I remember seeing it the last time I was up here." I thought the plane

---

[64] Hidden Sussex by Swinfen & Arscott a BBC Radio Sussex publication - Page 84

was German but Ron seems to think it was American and it ploughed into the side of The Downs because the pilot didn't realise where he was?

We are about to make our first mistake. We are now approaching The Eastbourne Downs Golf Course. I've played here, many times, and I've always found it a difficult course to get round. Ron seemed fascinated with the play. "Can you see the size o' the 'ead on 'is stick?" ask Ron, "it looks like a soup ladle. Even I could 'it a little ball with that damned thing!" "It isn't as easy as it looks," I offer in way of explanation. "Not only have you got to hit it but it's also got to go in the right direction." The man stands at the tee as both Ron and I watch. He steadies himself and winds the club back and hits the ball, "Lovely strike," say the other players, "Bloody 'ell," says Ron, "where'd the bloody ball go?" "That's one of the reasons I gave the game up. Couldn't see where the ball was. Most of the time, it stayed at me feet. But every now and again you will hit a ball, just like that man did, and it makes you want to play again. It really is a strange game."

Dew pond used by Pip & Tess

The distinctive crown logo?

A little further along a fairway Ron watches as a man hits a wayward shot and the ball plugs into a bank, "look at that," Ron chuckles, "'e'll need a bucket an' spade ter dig that ball out. Damn silly game, if yer ask me." We have now missed our turning. We were so engrossed in watching the golf that we missed a turning, to the left, which would have taken us across the golf course and out at Eastbourne Youth Hostel. "Never mind," I say, "We'll continue along the edge of the course and then turn left at the Club House. The Youth Hostel is just down the road, on the left." So that is exactly what we do. At least we are going downhill.

We manage to find the Youth Hostel and the path we need to take. We are advised that the next 3½ miles of our route '…is marked by a distinctive crown logo but one or two of the signs are missing'. Lucky old us. Missing signs, where have we heard and seen that before? But we will soldier on. We go down some steps and turn left along a wide track that follows the edge of a housing estate. As we walk I wonder if the people living on the estates are aware that this path exists. Probably not, although we do meet a few people who give us a merry seasonal greeting as we pass.

Another helpful sign?

The instructions now become a bit of a puzzle. Things we should see we don't, stiles not mentioned in the instructions we climb over and paths veering to the left we turn right. All I am aware is that further along our walk we should come to another Golf Course, Willingdon, and I think I can see it in the far distance. So we head in that direction and don't worry about the instructions. After all, both Ron and I are now experts at finding our way around. Aren't we?

Our instructions are still telling us that the paths are well signposted but as you can see from the photo's this is far from the truth. We do manage to arrive at the golf course, which is just visible through the trees. "Is this the golf course that Arthur plays on?" asks Ron. "It certainly is," I reply. "Per'aps we might see 'im and shout 'ello.," says Ron. "I'm sure he'll appreciate that Ron. And if you wait until he gets onto the nice smooth bit with that funny flag on before you shout he will think it's a really nice thing to do. Especially if he is playing the game for money." I think Ron took me seriously because the next minute he's looking through the trees telling me that "'e ain't in sight!"

Ron, trying to find Arthur

Steady climb uphill

Again our instructions seem out. We should be crossing a sunken bridleway. "What the devil is a sunken bridleway?" I ask Ron. "'Tis a bridleway that floods," is Ron's reply. "Are you serious?" I ask. "'bout as serious as you were, with me callin' out 'ello ter Arthur, back at that there golf course."

I don't seem to be able to make sense of the instructions. We seem to be heading uphill all the time and our instructions tell us to go down. But there is no down. We haven't seen a sign for ages so I'm not sure now if we're even heading in the right direction. Eventually we find what Ron decided was a sunken bridleway which, literally, was a depression in the ground, running downhill to our right. "According to the book there should be a narrow path running parallel to the sunken track," I tell Ron, but all we could find was a wide track leading us slightly to the left. We take this track, but it can't be right. When we stop, I read the instructions further down the page and see that we should come to a panel fence. "I saw a fence down by the sunken bridleway," says Ron. So back we go. And there, through the trees and down a slope, is a panel fence. When we get to it there's a small sign, about a foot off the ground with a crown and a white arrow on it directing us along a path. "Would 'ave been 'elpful ter 'ave that sign a bit clearer," says Ron. But at least we were back on track. For now!

Then it all goes wrong again. The path climbs steeply. Very steeply. Someone has put steps in the ground to help us get up this hill. "It levels out at the top," says Ron but as I look at the next instructions I read '....go over a crossing path, fork left and after a fairly substantial climb...' and I'm not sure how to tell him. Again the instructions don't seem right. I don't know how or why we seem to go wrong but after this 'substantial climb' we should find a 'steady descent'. But all we found was a substantial climb. It was very hard work. The more I kept telling Ron that we should be going downhill the funnier Ron thought it was. After what seemed ages of slogging uphill, without going down, we eventually arrived on a road near the top of Butts Brow (one of the highest points on the South Downs). I think I know where we are and point this out to Ron by showing him the map. "What we have to do now, to get back on the right track, is walk down the road to the bottom of the hill and we should pick up the path on the left." So down we go. As we near the bottom of the hill we can see where we should have come out of the woods. But I still can't explain where we went wrong. "Be funny," giggles Ron, "if, when we gets back on the footpath, we 'ave ter go up ter

View as we reach the top

top o' Butts Brow." "I wouldn't find it funny at all." I tell Ron but would you believe it? As we climb the stile onto the footpath it is practically vertical. Thankfully some kind person has put a seat, in loving memory of Ray and Betty Castle, halfway up the hill. I just had to stop and rest a while. "Look at that," exclaims Ron, "you can see 'ailsham church from up 'ere." He points with his thumb-stick, but try as I might, I couldn't see it. "Plain as day, 'tis, you can't miss it," he continues. "I'm sorry Ron but I can't see it." But Ron kept on and on, so in the end I just said that I could see it just to keep him happy. Apparently it's on the horizon in the picture and is plain as day. But we need to get on and, looking up the hill towards the top of the downs, I'm not looking forward to the next few minutes.

"Startin' ter get cold," says Ron. The temperature does seem to have dropped. The sun is now covered by cloud and, in the distance what looks like mist is rolling in. The highest point on the Downs is a place called Combe Hill. If you stand at Combe Hill, facing towards Jevington and turn round 180° you will see that you are slightly higher than Butts Brow. Ron thinks it's hilarious.

Steep hills draw you to the edge

To all those people, if there are any, who have not visited the South Downs, you must climb to the top and see the view. There really is no other sight like it. But be warned. In places the paths run perilously close to a long drop. On more than one occasion there was a feeling of being drawn to the very edge. It is a strange feeling but it does exist. Ron believes that some people don't jump over Beachy Head, our famous suicide venue, but are drawn to the edge and, literally, fall. That could be a fact, so please be careful.

Our instructions now seem to be vague, again. We are told of paths that we can't see and we see stiles and gates that are not described. But Ron assures me that we are heading towards Jevington village. We walk through a flock of sheep that, thankfully, totally ignore us. "Fancy bein' a shepherd up 'ere," says Ron, "After walkin' all the way up 'ere you remember that you took the sheep down yesterday," he giggles.

We find the enclosed path and eventually come out opposite the Eight Bells pub. Here we turn left and pass The Hungry Monk restaurant, the home of bannoffi pie, and head towards the Church of St Andrew. A magnificent Saxon church which, due to neglect had to have a lot of renovation work carried out in the 1870s'. In one of our previous walks we found a Tapsell Gate. A strange gate, that opens from a central axis that was at Friston church, and we were told that there were very few of these gates that still existed. Well, we've found another one at Jevington. A marvellous invention, for a gate, that works really smoothly. Part of the

Tapsell Gate

restoration work in the 1870's involved taking soil away from around the base of the churches foundations to stop damp getting into the walls[65]. This is evident by the two levels of ground. The graveyard at the Tower end of the church is higher than the path. The church is unlocked so we have to enter and we are not disappointed. It is a wonderful place. It may be that it is the Christmas festive season that the church has an abundance of flower arrangements but they certainly added something to the feel and smell of the old church which is a credit to the people of Jevington. Whilst we are wandering around, the door opens, and a gentleman introduces himself to us. "Just had to follow you in," he says, "because I couldn't help noticing the smock." Ron explains the reason for the smock and that we are writing a book about our walks. The gentleman then tells us that he has written a number of walking books and that his name is Len Markham. I said "That name is familiar," and I realise that one of our future walk is taken from a book written by Len titled 'Kiddiwalks in East Sussex'[66]. While he and I discuss the pitfalls of publishing, a young lady pops her head into the church and greets Ron like a long lost friend. Apparently she is the sister-in-law of a brother married to a friend of mine who used to work at the same school as I and was given our book as a Christmas present. Both Ron and I were now being treated like local celebrities.

We manage to leave our new-found friends and take a stroll around the graveyard. "I expect ol' Climpson would be buried in this church. Played cricket against 'im loads o' times. A real canny player 'e was," reminisces Ron, but we couldn't find the grave. But we did find a grave of someone of significance. The grave of Sir Hartley William Shawcross GBE, PC, KC, born in 1902 and died at his home, in Cowbeech, in 2003, at the age of 101. Sir Shawcross was the lead British prosecutor at the infamous Nuremburg War Crimes Tribunal.

And basically that was the end of one of the hardest walks we have completed. It wasn't helped by poor instructions or the amount of vandalised signs. But we did complete it in the suggested time of 4 hours. Ron has remembered the name of the

---

[65] St Andrew's Church, Jevington – The Victorian Restoration 1872-1873 – booklet purchased at Church. Written and compiled by Rosalind Hodge
[66] Kiddiwalks in East Sussex by Len Markham published by Countryside Books

pretty lady in the church. Apparently she has two sisters who, according to Ron were, and still are, 'lov'ly ter look at. Fancied all three, I did.'

Before we leave Jevington I have to advise you of a first. I didn't mention it earlier in the chapter but whilst walking along the top of the Downs, by the dew pond, I managed to find a penny, lying on the ground, before Ron saw it! I'm sure that this will never happen again. After all, I normally can't see a church in the far distance but Ron has the eyes of a hawk.

Finally, as this is the festive season, both Ron and I would like to wish everyone a Happy Christmas and a prosperous and healthy New Year and we would also like to remember those no longer with us, with all our love and thanks. X

Jevington was a stiff uphill walk
Done on good old Sussex downland chalk
I'm still trying to work out how
He marched me up, three times, Butts Brow?
Aresee©

Chapter 13 – Muddles Green

The year 2008 is upon us. Where does the time go? It seems only yesterday that Ron and I started our walks. But it is now well over a year since we took those first steps around Arlington Reservoir. I have learnt so much over these past 18 months and, luckily for us, we have managed to cover a few miles of this beautiful county of Sussex and shared some of our stories with such a lot of people.

From the contents of these pages it must be obvious to everyone that both Ron and I get enormous pleasure from learning about things in Sussex. We also enjoy walking, that goes without saying. We do get things wrong. We do go in the wrong direction and on some occasions, get lost. Ron is known to get his words mixed up. There is an old Sussex saying which you can sometimes associate with both Ron and I in times of torment: 'Arse-upards and arse-ackards'[67]. We both admit to getting it wrong, but at the end of the day that's what makes us human. At least we are not afraid to admit it. But it's not every time we walk that we get it wrong.

Christmas and the New Year are a bit of a blur. Apparently, the amber nectar worked exceedingly well over the Christmas and New Year festivities. Especially when I called into our local hostelry, The Kings Head, to wish, one and all, a Happy New Year. My good lady wife, Emelia, was my driver for the evening, so I was able to sample more of the nectar than usual. She, bless her, ensured that I got home safely. I know this because I woke up in my own bed the following morning. I can remember most of the evening but not the going home and getting into bed bit. I also can't remember arranging, with Lyn, a walk for today. She has changed her shift pattern so that she could come with us, she has advised all her friends that she will be out today, walking with Ron and me. And I had forgotten all about it. Until Lyn phoned to wish me and my wife, a Happy New Year, and to find out where we were walking this week. But I came clean. I admitted the errors in my ways and promised not to touch a drop again. Well, not until next time. But, what I did do was to hastily find a walk that, I hope, will serve the purpose, and is aptly called *M*uddles Green.

It is a short walk, only 2 miles[68]. As I have to work in the morning it can be comfortably carried out in the afternoon before it gets dark. There is a pub, but I will abstain, after all a promise is a promise, and the walk is graded as 2 which means it is easy going, walking on the level. That'll make a change from some of our previous walks. Ron doesn't seem to have suffered any ill effects from our hilly walks so I'm sure that he will be only too pleased for an easier time. Then, perhaps, he will stop ribbing me about how many times we headed up and down Butts Brow on our *J*evington walk.

From my book 'Sussex Place Names'[69] the name *M*uddles Green is derived from the property of a Tudor landowner, Nicholas Moodell of Waldron and is recorded in 1547. I have also found that a certain Mark Anthony Lower was born in *M*uddles Green on 14th July 1813. He died in London in 1876 after a life devoted to collecting source material for, and of, Sussex. He was a pioneer member of the Sussex Archaeological Society and has written several books on all aspects of Sussex[70]. And I'm sorry, but until now I had never heard of him. I have checked the internet for his

---

[67] 'Sussex As She Wus Spoke' by Tony Wales – SB Publications – 2001 – Page 8
[68] Route 43 – East Sussex County Council Leaflet obtained from www.eastsussex.gov.uk
[69] Sussex Place Names by Judith Glover – Page 154
[70] 'People of Hidden Sussex' by Swinfen & Arscott – Page 105

books and for one in good condition you can expect to pay, well in excess of £200 for a copy of 'The Worthies of Sussex' or £800 for a copy of 'A Survey of the Coast of Sussex' both written by Mark Anthony Lower. I won't tell you how much his book on Queen Elizabeth I is selling for, but if you have access to the internet go to www.abebooks.co.uk and sit down when you search for his books. Perhaps I should put my prices up?

But it is a cold and wet Monday afternoon that finds the three of us heading for Chiddingly Village, which is where we start today's walk. When I left home it had just started to rain. All the way to Chiddingly it rained. It rained hard. It rained very hard. But, as always, the instant we got out of the car the rain stopped. "Told yer it was a clearin' up shower," says Ron with that smug look on his face.

As I said earlier, we do get lost. Today we got confused at the start but things worked out ok. During our first

Chiddingly Church

walks, some 18 months ago, I thought that our instructions were old, so when we were told that a post was here or a stile was there and we couldn't find it then, perhaps, since the route was written, some things can change. But today's instructions were straight off the internet. The ink was still wet when we arrived at Chiddingly. We followed the instructions and walked past what used to be the village stores, still showing the original windows but now a private residence. The next instruction was to turn right opposite the Eight Bells ("We're actually passing a pub that's open," whispers Lyn, "and Ron hasn't said anything.") and head up the road for 260 yards to

Left or Right hand stile

the junction with Honeywick Lane. But there is no junction with Honeywick Lane. The only lane we found was Parsonage Lane which leads to Honeywick Lane. Now, do we turn right up Parsonage Lane, until we get to Honeywick Lane or, as our instructions say, do we turn left onto the footpath that I've found, opposite the junction? Now can you understand the problems we have? "I'll look at the map supplied with the walk," I tell Lyn and Ron. "According to the map we turn left opposite the junction and walk along a path besides Chiddingly Place." "But the building along this path ain't Chiddingly Place," points out Ron, "'tis Place Farm." So now, not only are the instructions wrong but the map isn't good either. We decide to follow the footpath alongside of Place Farm and hope that at the end of the path will be the stile needed to continue. Luck was with us, well perhaps luck had nothing to do with it, because we managed to find the stile in the bottom corner of the field. "'Tis one o'them posh stiles," says Ron, "got 'andle on both sides so's them left 'anded or right 'anded people can gets over." I'd never noticed it before but with a taller piece of wood, either side of the stile it certainly made it easier to get over.

Sunken sign

We follow the route into the next field where we find another 'posh' stile. The next field is narrow and an area has been fenced off by the farmer with a portable electric fence. "Shame Alan ain't 'ere," says Ron, "'e could 'ave told us if it were live or not." Because of the heavy rain the ground is a bit boggy and as we follow the path we start to slip and slide. Keeping the hedge to our right we head towards another stile leading us into a small section of woodland. From here we continue until we reach a junction with a signpost. "I'm only wearing walking boots," says Lyn as we look at the signpost under water, "I'll need wellies to get over to the other path." But we manage to find a hole in the fence so we can get through without resorting to water wings.

The path now leads us up a slight hill, "there was no mention of hills," says Lyn. "This ain't no 'ill," says Ron, "yer need ter go up Butts Brow three bloody times ter know what an 'ill is," says Ron chuckling. He just can't leave it alone. He has to have a dig every now and again, but I'll get my own back someday. "The instructions say that it is generally level," I tell Lyn, "look, we've just started to go downhill now." The path levels off and starts to head downhill towards an opening in the hedge which now leads us to a path.

Never far from view

The path leads us, eventually, to the road at Muddles Green. But all along this path fallen leaves have lined the ground and, although slippery, it looks like an autumn blanket. I read somewhere that a place was so peaceful you could touch it. That is how this pathway felt. Not a sound could be heard, no birds, no traffic noise just peacefulness. Also, all along this walk there aren't many places where the church at Chiddingly disappears and as you walk along this pathway, between the trees and bushes the church spire can be seen.

I have also read that the village of Chiddingly is said to resemble Rome, due to the seven hills of the parish. Stone Hill, Gun Hill, Thunders Hill, Burgh Hill, Holmes Hill, Scrapers Hill and Pick Hill. The church spire is one of only three stone built spires

Pose for the camera

in the county and its 130 feet is visible from all parts of the parish.

At the end of the path we arrive at the road at Muddles Green. For those not aware, there is very little at Muddles Green. In fact, apart from the school, with it's large sign for 1906 prominently displayed on the apex of the building, and a few houses, "bet there ain't many who vote labour round 'ere," says Ron, Muddles Green is nothing exceptional. "Isn't this walk number 13 in the alphabet?" asks Lyn, "that it t'is," replies Ron. "In that case," says Lyn, "we need a photograph. Stand by that post and I'll take it." With that, Ron and I are both up against a signpost, as Lyn takes a snap. Ron doesn't look very impressed, and haven't I put some weight back on?

We turn right and walk along the road looking for a junction leading to Scrapers Hill. "There's that word again," says Lyn, "I don't do hills." "You ain't seen a 'ill till you've been up Butts..." starts Ron, "Shut it Ron, or I'll have to publish some pictures of you dressed as a lady of pleasure," I have had to resort to threats now to keep him quiet. "Yer wouldn't do that, would yer?" he pleads. "Trust me Ron," is all I say. But it works.

We walk past the school and come to a Commemorative Garden on our left. "Bet it looks pretty, when it's got something growing in it," I

Commemorative Garden

comment. But perhaps this time of year is not the best time to look at gardens. "Is this where we turn left?" ask Lyn. "'Fraid not, this isn't the junction with Scrapers Hill," I reply, "we have to go further along the road and Scraper Hill is on the left. I wasn't being clever I'd sneaked a look at the map when everyone else was looking at the garden.

It is only a short distance to the turning to Scrapers Hill and our instructions tell us to turn left and then turn left again onto a signposted footpath. I must admit that since the hiccough with the start of the walk the instructions, since then, have been spot on and we've managed to find all the signs without problems.

We now climb two stiles, close together, and need to look out for a footbridge. Again, due to the rain, which thankfully has not started again, the path is very slippery but we manage to find our way, along

Playing Pooh sticks

the path until we come to a stile on our left and a small wooden footbridge on our right. "Do we go right and over the footbridge?" asks Lyn "or do we go left and over the stile?" "According to the map, we continue ahead," I reply, "then why didn't the man who wrote the instructions, say that?" demands Lyn. All of a sudden I feel it's my fault, but the instructions do say '...reach a footbridge. After the bridge, follow the route ahead...' so we press on ahead and come to, would you believe, a footbridge. Now I don't know what it is with both Ron and Lyn when they get to a bridge with flowing water that makes them become children but they have to giggle and play Pooh

Reflections

sticks. With this bridge they were no different. I will admit that taking photographs of reflections in water is one of my favourites subjects and I managed to get a reasonable shot of Lyn and Ron leaning over the bridge trying to see whose stick emerges first.

Although the picture is a little 'strange' I do think that it captures the moment reasonably well. Don't you?

It isn't long before we reach the end of the path and emerge by the cricket field. "Have you played cricket here?" I ask Ron, knowing what the answer might be. "I certainly did," he replies, "scored 35 not out an' saved the match. Was playin' fer 'ailsham. There used ter be a tree in the outfield. If yer 'it the ball, an' it 'it the tree, yer couldn't be caught out. Same as if yer 'it the sight screen. Couldn't score a four 'cause the ball didn't cross the boundary." Now I am confused but we did notice the large trees which seemed pretty close to the pitch. Is it called a pitch?

The Jefferay Monument of 1612

From here it is just a small walk, through the graveyard, to the church. All I will say about this church is if you haven't seen inside then go and take a little look. It is an incredible place. It isn't, in my opinion, a sit down church those are few and far between, but it is certainly a place with an abundance of history. One of the most outstanding features of the church is The Jefferay Monument. And it is one of the most impressive and important pieces of monumental sculpture in Sussex, as there are only 2 known examples, in England of erect figures in monuments of this period. The other monument is in Spilsby in Lincolnshire. Sadly the monument has been disfigured and although the damage is attributed to the puritans of the 17th century there is no foundation in fact[71]. But please go and see for yourselves. It is a truly wonderful church.

I am not, normally, a religious person. But every now and again something somewhere will jog the memories of the past. Tomorrow would have been my sister's birthday. Unfortunately she is no longer with us and I purchased, at the church, a small card with a few words which hit home. I reproduce them for you:

Lord, help me to remember
that nothing is going to happen today
that You and I, together, can't handle.

Finally, I also purchased, again from the church a prayer that I have seen many times before in my travels and, sometime ago lost my original copy. The last few lines of the 17th century Nun's Prayer says:

Give me the ability to see good things in unexpected places,
And talents in unexpected people.
And give me, O Lord, the grace to tell them so.

Amen

---

[71] Chiddingly Church Guide – purchased at the Church - £1

Chapter 14 - Nuthurst

It had to happen sooner or later. I'd find a place to walk and then be unable to find anything about the place. **N**uthurst is that place. The walk should be pleasant enough, but the only thing I can glean from my many Sussex books about **N**uthurst is that lots of people pass through it, or round it, but not that many people want to stop in it. Within the village lie the remains of Sedgwick Castle, once the home of the Braose family,[72] and dates back to the 11th century. Of course Nuthurst has a Parish Church, dedicated to St Andrew. It also has a pub, The Black Horse. I went onto a website[73], to find out about **N**uthurst. At first the site looked interesting. It had bright colours and I have reproduced the opening instructions here:

> *Many of the things to do in Nuthurst, West Sussex are shown on the map below, including local attractions, land features and railway stations. Scroll down to find the map of Nuthurst, and continue down the page to find details of the attractions, landmarks and much more.*

All sounds very professional and promising, doesn't it? But it isn't until your on the site and start to '*...scroll down to find details of the attractions...*' that you find that there are, in fact, 73 (yes there are seventy three listed) '*...attractions, landmarks and much more'*. But not one of them is in **N**uthurst. Some are only a mile from the village, some are 18 miles away. But not one attraction is listed as being within the village.

In desperation to find something, anything, about **N**uthurst I resorted to some of my family history reference books. These have spellbinding titles, such as, 'West Sussex Land Tax 1785'[74], and 'Mid Sussex Poor Law Records 1601-1835'[75]. You can imagine that these are both gripping reads and unputdownable on a winter's evening with a pint of amber nectar in one hand, the book in the other and me sitting in front

The Dun Horse, Mannings Heath

of an open fire. But I did manage to find out that in 1801 the population of **N**uthurst was 456 living in 77 houses covering an area of 3,305 acres with land tax valued and collected totalling £184 4s 0d. All fascinating stuff you must agree. But what was surprising was that in the book 'Mid Sussex Poor Law Records 1601-1835 the village of **N**uthurst is mentioned on 31 different pages and most of these mentions are from people trying to settle into neighbouring villages after leaving **N**uthurst![76]

Our walk today is taken, again, from the

---

[72] 'Sussex' by SPB Mais – Richard Press – first printed in 1929 – page 204
[73] http://www.pagemost.com/Nuthurst-West-Sussex visited 16/01/08
[74] Various writers and available from Sussex Record Society, Lewes – ISBN 0854450491 price £25
[75] Various writers and available from Sussex Record Society, Lewes – ISBN 0854450505 price £25
[76] Poor Law records were kept to ensure that persons arriving at another village from their own could vouch for themselves as not being a burden on the parish that they wished to settle.

Argus[77]. We start in a village called Mannings Heath, walk towards and through **N**uthurst, past Monks Gate and back to Mannings Heath. A circuit of 5¾ miles of what is described as '…fields and woodland paths which may be muddy underfoot with few hills, all minor.' The weather this week has been horrendous. Flood warnings have been issued for large areas of Sussex and the wind has been gusting at over 70mph. Due to the rain and wind during Friday night I didn't sleep too well. But at 9 am the following Saturday morning I picked Ron up from outside The Kings Head and we both head for Mannings Heath.

The start of our walk

If you look on the Internet for Mannings Heath you will find lots of sites leading you to the golf course or the hotel. It looks as if all you will find at Mannings Heath is a golf course and a hotel. I did manage to find a couple of very desirable properties for sale with an asking price of over £490,000. Not a cheap place then. I believe Ron described Mannings Heath once as '…that posh even the 'orse shit don't smell.' I can't wait to see the place.

But wait I have to because things have changed. Let me explain by first asking a question. Why do people, who own horses, which are meant to be ridden, insist on putting that same horse into a horse box, which is so old that it is unable to travel at more than 30mph? It never happened years ago. If you wanted to get somewhere you'd saddle up the nag and head for the pub, but now things have changed. You put the horse into a box and then travel at 30mph or less, holding up streams of traffic behind you. Why the hell don't you ride the bloody thing to wherever you're going? We followed two horse boxes travelling at less than 30mph for over eight miles. Neither would pull over to let the

Muddy fenced path

stream of traffic pass. Not only is it frustrating but due to the frustration it then becomes dangerous because we eventually got past them by taking a chance.

I have now taken the wrong turning to Mannings Heath and find us heading towards Brighton. I find a road which will lead us towards Ansty, which will bring us back on course, and hope Ron didn't notice, eventually finding the correct route, over the A23 and onto Mannings Heath. We asked a postie for directions to The Dun Horse (strange name for a pub?) and parked, just up the road from the junction with the A281.

Our first instruction is to cross the road, opposite The Dun Horse. Be careful here, the road is remarkably busy and although the speed limit is 40mph the traffic seems to be going faster. But once over the road we easily find the woodland path we need to start our walk. After all the rain I have decided to wear wellington boots. Although not made for walking over 5 miles in, at least I'll keep my feet dry.

---

[77] http://www.theargus.co.uk/whatson/walks/westsussex/nuthursttomanningsheath/ visited 02/01/2008

We ignore a signed path to our right and proceed along a fenced path to the end. Here the path ends and we now head along the field edge towards the corner. Here we are to climb over a stile and turn right along a bridleway. Both Ron and I notice that both stiles, yes there are two stiles, not one as instructed, have a lot of wire criss-crossing the stile. "Look's like they don't want dogs ter be in the field," suggests Ron, yet someone has obviously pulled the wire to one side to let their dog through (?).

Wired up stile

We turn right and head along the bridleway. My decision to wear boots is already paying off. The bridleway is obviously very well used and is very muddy in places. Having the thumb-stick also helped in keeping our balance as we tried to avoid the really muddy parts. But it's not surprising that the conditions are so wet. I can't imagine guessing at how much rain has fallen over the past few days. The only thing certain is that during the summer we will still have a hosepipe ban in Sussex.

Ron's pet hate, rubbish

Our instructions tell us to continue along this bridleway for about half a mile, until we come to a pair of cottages. Both Ron and I chat away about things in general and it isn't long before we come across one of Ron's pet hates, Rubbish dumping or fly-tipping, it doesn't matter what you call it, Ron hates it. Should be shot at dawn; should be made ter clear it up; should be locked up; lowest form of life; could 'arm the animals are just some of the comments made, in the same breath, as we pass an area used to dump iron sheeting, bricks and coils of barbed wire.

Just as quickly as we arrive at 'the dump' we come to an avenue of trees with beauty that can't be described. With the wind blowing in the tree tops and the gentle sway of these tall pines, the peacefulness is stunning, yet eerie. So much so, that we both walk through this area without saying a word.

Tree lined path

We eventually arrive at the two cottages. Was it really half a mile? It seemed a lot less. How the description of cottages came to be we have no idea. The garage to one of these properties is the same size as my house. But cottages they are called. One, Finches Cottage, is a lot larger than the other, Bluegate Cottage. But they are both large. "Sod livin' all the way out 'ere," says Ron, "not a pub in sight fer miles. Lovely place ter be in summer but I can't see council comin' all the way up 'ere with a gritter in winter. Must 'ave ter 'ibernate, like a squirrel." It's true what he say's, the owners must have problems getting about if there is a lot of

The entrance to Sedgwick Park

Very muddy bridleway

More fly-tipping

Reflections

snow but as I explain to Ron, they probably own 4 x 4 cars so getting about may not be such a problem. "They must be well-off," continues Ron, "'cause they've got the lights on inside the 'ouse, and its middle o'day."

At the end of the bridleway we arrive at a drive and have to turn left. As we walk along this drive Sedgwick Park, with its mansion and ruined castle, are on our right. Our instructions tell us that the ruins of the castle cannot be seen from the paths we are taking which is a little bit of a disappointment to both of us. But, from a distance, the Manor House looked very impressive. "I wonder what the owner thinks of Gordon Brown," chuckles Ron, "bet 'e don't vote labour." We follow the path downhill until the drive bears left into another part of the Sedgwick estate. We continue straight on into a field and immediately turn left. In the distance we see two white horses being ridden by two young ladies. I can't see the riders as ladies but Ron insists, "trust me, them's girls," he says. "How can you be so sure, from this distance?" I ask. "'Cause they're wearin' pink an' purple," he replies. "And that means what, exactly?" I ask. "Take yer point," says Ron, "could be poofters. Let's 'ope we don't catch up with 'em." Because this bridleway is in constant use the mud is very deep in places. It becomes difficult to keep our footing as we slip and slide our way towards a farm track.

So far along this route the West Sussex Council have renewed or repaired all the signposts along each and every turn. As we've said before, whilst carrying out our walks, we have noticed that East Sussex signs are not as good as those in West Sussex. This walk was no different. If we did have one criticism of the walk it is the stiles. Not only are some of them in need of a little love and tender care some of them could also be a bit lower. Both Ron and I seemed to struggle over the stiles. Perhaps it was the mud on our boots and shoes that made getting our legs over the stiles difficult I'm not sure, but the stiles were becoming a problem for both of us.

I mentioned earlier about Ron's hatred of dumping rubbish in the countryside. Unfortunately we found some more. This time it was obvious that someone had installed a new bathroom and rather than take the rubble and old tiles to a dump decided to get rid of it in other ways. Ron is evil as he inspects the rubbish. I am unable to print the words that Ron used but I'm sure that those of you who know Ron will understand that he is a lover of the countryside and seeing this rubbish hurts him more than swear words can say.

But, on a brighter side. One of my personal favourite views, in the countryside, is water. Not just water but reflections. Although we have experienced a large amount of rainfall over the last few days, luckily for us the rain has held off, but it has made for some great reflections. With all the lying water along the edges of the paths it isn't long before I am clicking away with the camera capturing my favourite views. All along our route we haven't been far from water of some form, whether it is a stream, a pond or just a steady trickle down the side of a path. At least it draws Ron away from the fly-tipping and gives him something more pleasurable to think about. Little did I realise that worse was to come.

Nuthurst Church

Elizabethan 'dole cupboard'

But first we have to get to Nuthurst. We leave the bridleway and join a farm track. Here we turn left at a public footpath sign. We follow this route along the edge of several fields until it narrows to a path and enters woodland. Just inside the wood we fork right and come to a plank bridge. Ron stops, makes a wish and drops a coin into the water. He always does this whenever we cross water. "This walk's costin' me a fortune," he says as coins leave his hands yet again. We now climb to a gate and cross the middle of the next field. It always feels wrong walking across the middle of a field when we are always told to follow the 'Country Code' which tells us to walk around the outside. But it is clear, from the tracks, that the path does actually cross the middle of the field. Power lines are on our left as we walk towards the next gate and then veer slightly right across the next field. This gives us the first glimpse of The Church of St Andrew, Nuthurst. But before we get to the church we must climb a stile and continue up a path, squeezing between a garden on our right and the

13th Century Parish Chest

The Font

Looking towards the altar

church on our left.

It is now that we come up against one of my pet hates. Dog pooh. Collected in a plastic bag, which is all good and proper, but then left, usually on a fence for all to see. This time the person has excelled them selves and actually left the bag, tied up, in the middle of the path leading to the church! Right in the middle. I couldn't believe what I was seeing. All around us in the churchyard are snowdrops, daffodils and crocus bulbs, popping their heads above the ground. The churchyard has perfectly mown grass and well-kept graves yet in the middle of the path is this! Someone should be ashamed of themselves. Ron tried to pacify me by saying, "per'aps they're in the church an' are goin' ter pick it up on the way back." But the church was empty.

Pinus Pinea at £475

But what a church! Said to date from around 1130[78], in the reign of Henry I, it is a magnificent place. I had to sit down. It had that smell, that feeling that I only seem to get when I visit a certain kind of church. After visiting so many churches during the last year or so you'd think that I could recognise what makes me feel the way I do but I can't explain. I just feel odd. But I will just leave you with a few of the photographs and hope they will tell their own story.

We managed to drag ourselves away from the church and head towards The Black Horse. I could see that Ron was hoping for a little appetiser but we needed to press on. We turn right, just before the pub and head along a drive to Cook's Farm. On our left is a garden centre that specialises in exotic architectural plants. One that caught Ron's eye was

First broken sign

Pinus Pinea. I wasn't sure if it was the name that caught his attention or whether it was his horticultural abilities that were being honed to perfection before he started back to work. When I asked him why that particular plant caught his eye he replied, "did you see the b£$%dy price of that s&^%ing pot plant. It's only £475. Not surprisin' they've got so many left over, tryin' ter sell 'em at that price."

I drag him away and we follow the drive round to the left and where it divides we fork right passing to the left of a large storage barn. Just past here we fork left along a track which bears right. We then pass a shed and a metal storage container on our right. Are you as confused as we were? But, thankfully, all signs were in place apart from the very last one, which we found at the bottom of a hedge. The track we are now on leads us along a field edge and then into a wood.

Our instructions now advise us that care needs to be taken to ensure that the correct path is followed as many paths converge in the middle of the wood. Our instructions tell us to go straight ahead when we reach the converging paths, but as we are looking at the map to check our directions some of Ron's other pet hates are walking towards us. A Rambling Association. "Here's someone trying to follow a map," I hear one say. "Don't take any notice of that sign up ahead," says another, "been placed pointing in the wrong direction, so it has." "Is that right?" asks Ron,

---

[78] St Andrew's Church Nuthurst – A Guide and History – purchased at the church - £2

"And where are you lovely ladies 'eadin' on a fine day like today. Wouldn't be the church by any chance 'cause it is a lovely place." "We're heading for another lovely place," answers the lead lady walker, "we're heading for the pub." And with that they're gone as quick as they arrived. "Ladies after me own 'eart," says Ron, "only wish I was goin' with 'em." "Never mind Ron," I tell him, "when we get back I'll buy you a pint. But let's get back to the car first." And we head towards the converging paths. It was confusing because the sign, which was new, was pointing in one direction and our instructions told us to go in another. To add insult to injury, as we are trying to make sure that we would go the right way a land rover headed down towards us towing a trailer with dead pheasants hanging on a beam. Apart from duck shooting, another of Ron's real hates is pheasant shoots. I have to drag him behind a tree before he has too much to say to the occupants of the rover. The driver stops and I pray that Ron will not say anything. "Your heading in the right direction if you go up

Wild deer

the hill to the top and then down to the bridge," says the passenger. "That's very kind of you," I call back as I usher Ron up the slope. Again I can't print the words that Ron called these men as they drive off out of the woods. But trust me, Ron was not happy.

Once across the footbridge, more money and wishes from Ron, we arrive at a Y-junction and fork right. We cross a couple of fields in complete silence until we reach a lane where we turn right to reach a junction with the A281 at Monk's Gate. A little snippet of information gathered about Monk's Gate is that the hymn written by John Bunyan 'To be a Pilgrim' is set to the music from an old folk song which was called Valiant collected from Mrs Verrall from Monk's Gate.[79]

We now head along the road until we reach a 40mph sign and, again, risk life and limb to cross the road and head down a drive, turning right after a few yards and then through a gate at the end. It is now that I see, what I think to be the largest Rottweiler I've ever seen. Actually it is the bum end of a Rottweiler. It must have been big because its stub of a tail is higher than the next stile. It isn't until we get nearer the stile that I realise it was a wild deer. It obviously didn't realise we were near it because it didn't move; until I took the picture, and it was off like a flash. But it was a magnificent sight.

It isn't long now before we arrive at a riding stables and Ron, again, makes the comment about horse s*&t with no smell. We stand for a while admiring a very young lady jumping over some jumps and wondering why we can't do it. After all she made it look so simple.

From the stables we come out at Winterpit Lane, turn left and it is only a short walk back to the car. Wearing wellington boots was a good idea but my feet are really getting sore as I wait outside the village shop for Ron to buy a pie. He wouldn't listen to me when I said they would be expensive and not locally baked. He came out looking not too happy. I think the time it took to buy the pie because of slow service and the fact that it was pricey didn't help.

And here ends another walk which, for me, was very pleasant. For Ron I think it was a bit traumatic. With two pheasant murderers, two lots of fly-tippers as well as a

[79] http://en.wikipedia.org/wiki/Monk's_Gate visited 17/01/08

Rambling Association he'd had enough. But on the whole, considering the amount of rainfall over the last few days, we completed it in the dry. It could have been worse.

Nuthurst church was one you want to sit and ponder
Why people spoil our Countryside I often wonder
A beautiful walk, with wonderful scenery
A load of moron's spoilt the walk for me.
Aresee©

Chapter 15
Ouse (River) & Old Carriage Road

There can't be many hot-blooded males out there who don't recognise the name 'Charlie Dimmock'. She's the female with the large assets, and all that ginger hair. Used to work with a gardening chappie, who had a strange name Breastmarsh something or other. She did the water features in the gardens, you know who I mean? Since leaving that gardening programme she now has a TV slot doing 'River Walks'. I watched it the other evening, Thursday I think it was, and she 'walked' along part of The Thames. I have to admit I thought it was a bit on the boring side. Ok, she

managed to clear up some debris and put it in a bucket. She then spoke, very briefly, to some volunteers who were clearing a path. She discussed topics such as Charles Dickens and Great Expectations with an 'expert'. She then hopped onto a barge which took her up The Thames to Tilbury Docks. And that was it. But she kept boring me with her reminder that it was a 5½ mile walk. But throughout the half-hour programme she only walked 100 yards!

Isfield Post Office at TQ449175

So I thought Ron and me would try something a little different for this walk. I had intended to visit **O**ffham or **O**vingdean, the only two places I could find beginning with the letter '**O**', but I thought that they were a bit obvious. So I thought about that TV programme and started searching elsewhere and came up with the River Ouse. I thought that there had to be a walk in Sussex

which would touch on, go over, or follow this river. And bingo. Not only a walk along the **O**use but we visit a place (?) called **O**ld Carriage Road. Two **O's** for the price of one! The website address[80] gives you everything you need to know about the River Ouse. And I don't intend to go over the whole issue about conservation but will just say that all the work is done by volunteers and should you wish to help out then visit the website for all the information. Why all the work should be done by volunteers, when we pay so much in rates, baffles me but that is another issue. When was the last time you saw the Water Authority dredging out river beds and ditches? Yet when we have a little bit of extra rain and large areas and properties get flooded they blame 'global warming', the insurance companies increase your house insurance premium and then the Water Authority bans you

W. G. Grace

from using the water by issuing a hosepipe ban. Am I alone in thinking this?

As I said our walk today is taken from The Ouse website. One or two things worry me as I read about the walk after printing it off the web site. First I notice that we need to walk in compass directions. You all know that neither Ron nor I carry such an instrument. So when we are told to head 'North North West across the field' we could

[80] http://www.sussex-ouse.org.uk/ visited 22/01/2008

have a problem. Secondly the instructions are printed with 'Waypoints'. There are 10 different 'Waypoints'. Not too difficult except each 'Waypoint' has a grid reference. I will give you an example. We start our 4½ mile walk from Isfield Post Office. This is at Waypoint TQ449175. A closer look at the instructions tells me that we should also take with us an 'Ordinance Survey Map – Explorer 122'. But it is ten minutes to nine on a Saturday morning and I am due to pick Ron up, outside The Kings Head, at nine. So we'll risk it without a compass or an Ordinance Survey map. A decision we would soon regret.

Ron looking over White Bridge

Our first problem was finding the Post Office. I expected a large, prominent building but it turned out to be part of the cricket pavilion and found at the end of a gravel drive. 'Played cricket 'ere," announces Ron, "Never called them Isfield Cricket Club," he continues, "but was known as WG Gracefully. Named after, the cricketer, William Gilbert Grace. Some ov' 'em even wore beards, just like the great man of cricket. They we're a good team too."

We start our walk by heading onto a bridleway and walking down towards the River Ouse. We pass a very nice farm building on our left and look out for a small bridge called White Bridge. There must be a reason for calling it White Bridge but I can't see it. Perhaps it was painted white at sometime, I don't know. We cross the bridge and turn right, walking on the river bank. We have just left Waypoint 1 and we are now heading towards Waypoint 2. This is where our instructions tell us to go North-North-West. "Any ideas?" I ask Ron. "'Tis simple," he answers. With his thumb-stick he points out a direction. "How do you know that that's North-North-West?" I ask. "There ain't any other path ter foller, so it must be North-North-West." And off he goes. Striding it out, along the river bank. I run to catch up.

Reflections

From previous pages you will all be aware of my love of reflections in water and my enjoyment taking photographs. I make no apologies for the photographs in this chapter. I just love the effects and took a lot more pictures than can be put into these pages. Perhaps that's another idea for a book. Just pictures without my ramblings, now there's a thought?

As we head to the next Waypoint I read from our instructions that we pass a large hole to the right of the path. This is a crater left by a German bomb during WWII. As we approach it I explain what it is to Ron. "Can you imagine it, Ron?" I ask. "He's got one bomb left and Adolph tells the pilot to aim true and hit the heart of the British. Then he drops the bloody thing in a

The church in the distance

field in the middle of nowhere." "Bet 'e got a medal fer the animals 'e killed. Must a done some damage to our war effort," he chuckles. I have to say that the crater isn't that big, it looks a bit like a dent in the ground and there's nothing to tell you that what we are looking at is, in fact, a crater. Perhaps we're in the wrong place?

We are now on the Sussex Ouse Valley Way and about to approach the confluence of the River Ouse with the River Uck at an area known as Bell Hole.

We need to turn left (?)

Luckily for us it is marked with a large oak tree on the far bank. If I remember correctly a confluence is where two streams or rivers meet. I can see that two rivers meet so why I am told to look out for a large oak tree? Perhaps they have heard of our direction finding and need to ensure we get to the correct place.

Guns have started to sound, pretty close to where we are standing, and beaters are on the other side of the river as we now approach a stile. Ron passes comment as a few pheasants pass over our heads and manage to stay away from the guns. As we walk towards the stile pellets actually fall from the sky and land near us. We follow the sign on the post and make our way towards open fields as quickly as we can. This was a mistake. As we walk along the field edge I notice that the river has disappeared. "Ron," I say, "we must have gone wrong. The river isn't in sight now and our instructions tell us to turn left, opposite the church. We'd better retrace our steps, back to the guns, and check which direction we should be heading." So back we go. Once back at the church view we check the instructions. They tell us that at the church site follow the path towards a wood, but there isn't a path leading in that direction. At a stile, we are now at a stile, turn left, but the marker sign indicates that we go straight ahead. Again we continue ahead but this is not right. Again the river disappears and we are in open countryside. We should be heading along **O**ld Carriage Road. Back we go, yet again.

We can only think that the sign on the post is wrong. Instead of going straight ahead, as the sign shows, we decide to turn left and hope that the lane we are now on is, in fact, **O**ld Carriage Road.

We are now at Waypoint 3 and heading, according to our instructions, South-South-West and heading towards Agmond's Wood, named after a Barcombe family from the 14th century. The wood is of the old variety that Ron loves. He reminisces about an old tree in a wood near his home which had love hearts cut into the bark by the Canadian soldiers billeted around Hailsham during the war. Unfortunately the tree was cut down and will never be seen, or read, again. The stillness and beauty of the wood can't be described. All along the path we can hear birds in full song, Ron picking out the song thrush, the robin and various others. We come to a pond in the middle of the wood and just had to stop and think awhile. Just past the pond and a little uphill we come to a concrete and metal bridge over the Longford Stream. Our instructions tell us that this stream is an important Sea Trout nursery stream on the River Ouse catchment. But it's filthy. "You can't tell me that trout come all the way up here into this?" I ask. "No," explains Ron, "they don't come all the way up 'ere from the Ouse. But this is the stream used to top up the Ouse an' the sea trout use it to spawn 'cos the water is nice an' still." "It's nice and bloody filthy, too," I say as I point towards some sludge lying on top of the water. "You'll see," says Ron, "when we gets to the place where this stream joins the Ouse, it'll be a lot clearer."

In memory

South Downs

We shouldn't be here

Sleeper Bridge

We are now on to Waypoint 4 at TQ438178 (?) and heading South-South-West through a wood. The size of the trees here has to be seen to be believed. These mature Scots Pine trees must be over 80 feet tall and line the path all the way along this wood. The last time we saw trees this big was the tall pines at West Hoathly but these look much bigger and looked as if they were standing guard along the path. A fantastic sight.

A little further along the path we come to an area that has only recently been planted with trees. A brick square, with brass plaque informs us that the area was planted in February 2007 in memory of Arthur and Alice Sclater '...*who owned and loved the woods on the Newick and Sutton Hall Estates.*' It is signed simply J.R.S. and is a lovely memorial to J.R.S's parents.

At Waypoint 5 we turn left, by a small pond, so small we nearly missed it, and follow the path along field boundaries. The fact that the word boundaries is plural doesn't mean anything because we didn't, in fact, follow the path around more than one field, because at the end of the field hedge we found ourselves at a water trough which, according to the instructions was Waypoint 6 and we now need to turn left, or West. At the end of this path, on a clear day, we should get a wonderful panorama of the South Downs. I must admit that the day wasn't that particularly clear but the view was still tremendous. You could see for miles.

It is now that both Ron and I realise that we are in East Sussex. The signs have all but disappeared. The instructions also leave a little bit to be desired. Ok, we've been following the Waypoints but have totally ignored the grid references and compass directions for obvious reasons. The people who write these walks must appreciate that not everyone has access to a compass or a map. Some people, like Ron and me, just want to go out for a walk. Take in the surroundings, the wildlife and discover new parts of our county. But to be able to do this we need two things. Accurate instructions and clear signposts. We both appreciate that some landmarks will change, with time, and that paths will be diverted but surely any changes should be well signed so that trespass is not possible and getting from one point to the next can be achieved. I will explain the reason for this current rant; at

Waypoint 7 we are instructed to turn right (one sign) by an old stile and follow the

path (no sign) South-South-West (?) to Gallops Farm. We need to stay on the right-hand side of the fence. Is that the right of the fence or do we keep the fence on our right? It's a 50/50 chance that we get it wrong. And we did. We are told that we are now on the course of the old Lewes to London Roman Road (no sign). We are told to continue along the footpath along the West (?) boundary of the wood and at the bottom corner cross over the ditch using the sleeper bridge. Without signs we managed to find the bridge. But then we are told to pass the ponds at Gallops Farm. What ponds? What Farm? We can't see any ponds. It is now obvious that the Ordinance Survey map suggested at the start of the walk is a **must have** part of equipment. Rather than suggest that a map should be taken it should be stressed that this walk is not achievable without the map because the instructions alone are useless. We both wander around this huge field. We find a pond on the left edge. But the next instruction is to locate the T junction of footpaths. We didn't locate

We should be here

The Anchor Inn

a T junction. We then went back to the sleeper bridge and followed the field edge in the other direction. Again we found one pond and a footpath sign, but no T junction. We have no idea where we are. "Like the old times," chuckles Ron, "'Aven't been lost like this fer ages," he continues. There's supposed to be a green gate in a field corner, but I can't see one. Looking at our instructions there should also be a lane called Blunt's Lane but, although we can hear traffic we can't see anything. We decide to follow the path we are on and this eventually brings us out onto a gravel driveway. To our left is a large gate but dogs don't seem that happy to see us. If this is Blunt's Lane (?) we need to turn right to reach Waypoint 8. So turn right is what we do and it isn't long before Ron says, "Looks a bit familiar, this does." Within 100 yards of his comment we are back at Waypoint 5. We should have come out a little way down the road from The Anchor, on the river but I couldn't believe how far out we were.

We should have come out here

Rather than continue to Waypoint 6 and 7 again we decide to follow the footpath signs from Waypoint 5 which should take us

out to a road and, eventually, to The Anchor. It wasn't until we hit the road and turned left that we found out exactly how far out we were. If I wasn't so knackered I'd be bloody angry. We were heading towards Barcombe. The road just before the

Barcombe village sign informed us that The Anchor was 1½ miles up Boast Lane. It was a long, very quiet walk towards The Anchor. "Bloke that wrote that walk could never 'ave walked it," says Ron "must 'ave sat in 'is warm office, with a map an' just plotted it out." "How would he have known about a green gate, in the field corner?" I ask. "We ain't found a gate yet, an' if it is green it could 'ave been a lucky guess," is his reply. But just a few yards away from The Anchor, and 1½ miles up Boast Lane we found a green gate. Both Ron and I just look at each other.

So we are now at Waypoint 9 and we can pick up our instructions, which is to cross the old railway line and pass the Anchor Inn, we then cross a concrete bridge. The old railway line was closed during Beecham's cutbacks but it wasn't Lord Beecham who closed it. The line now, totally disused at The Anchor is in use at Isfield and is called the Lavender Line manned by volunteers, keeping the steam tradition for visitors and school children alive.

The Anchor Inn doesn't look like your typical 'local' pub. Not the place for two muddy walkers to drop in for a pint although walkers are more than welcome. "Bet 'e does some trade in the summer," comments Ron as we turn left after the bridge and head, again, along the river bank of the Ouse, this time on the opposite bank. The Anchor must be a wonderful setting for a summer wedding. Set as it is on the river bank with its large marquee at the back of the Inn.

Pill box in the distance

Again, reflections on the water help to give the place that little something extra as I drag Ron away from the demon drink and head back towards Isfield.

All along the riverbank are WWII pill boxes used for lookout and machine gun posts. The river must have been wider in those days, than it was currently, because all of the pill boxes seem to be a long way away from the river. I can't see, in the current position, how anyone could see anything coming up or down the river.

Too small to be of use at Hailsham

Since we started this walk, some 4 hours ago, we haven't met anyone. Now, as we approach the end, we are being followed by a young man (?) who appears to be talking to himself. Perhaps he is talking into a tape recorder, we're not sure, but every now and again he points to something and then speaks. As we arrive back at The White Bridge he becomes very animated with arms swinging about. We head away from him as quickly as we can.

It is only a short walk back to the car but we take a small detour across the cricket pitch. Tucked away, in the field edge is a roller. For those familiar with rollers, Ron wondered if it could tell any stories like the really big roller that use to be on Hailsham Recreation ground. Apparently Ron can tell a few stories about it but has promised that everyone's secrets are safe with him. "Anyways," says Ron, "this roller ain't a patch on the one from 'ailsham!"

Chapter 16 – Piltdown

After last week's long walk beside, around and over the River Ouse I thought we should have a leisurely stroll and have come up with a short walk around Piltdown. This walk includes part of the River Ouse, although a little upstream from last week. We've actually started a walk from here before, in our previous book[81], but on that occasion we headed for the village of Fletching. This time it is purely around Piltdown. To be more specific we start at The Piltdown Man Inn and, would you believe, we finish at The Piltdown Man Inn. Coincidence or what?

Another reason for this particular walk was that on completion of the River Ouse walk, Chapter 15, we were asked if we saw the WWII pillboxes along the river. As you know we saw the boxes and I passed a comment about them being a fair way away from the river bank and couldn't understand why. Another question asked was why there had to be so many boxes along this particular river. To be honest neither Ron nor I had any idea. So we thought that it would need some further investigation.

WWII Pillbox

Firstly we must realise that there are four principal rivers in Sussex, the Arun, the Adur, the Cuckmere and the Ouse, all of which have found their way, through many, many years to the sea. In the early days these rivers were the obvious places for invaders; after all we are an island. So some form of protection had to be built. In these early days castles were built by the rivers. Arundel Castle is on the Arun, Bramber Castle was on the Adur. The Cuckmere, although unnavigable, had Pevensey Castle and the Ouse was protected by the castle at Lewes. In those early days the rivers were not named as they are now. The Arun was called the Tarrant, the Adur was the Sore; the Cuckmere was the Wandlemestrow and the Ouse used to be the Mid-Wynd.[82]

At the start of WWII the great fear for England was an invasion by Germany forces. After all, nothing had stopped the advance of the Germans so far, until they

The Piltdown Man

came up against the bit of water between us and France. But England had to prepare for the worst scenario. Pillboxes (named pill boxes because they resembled the shape of boxes containing pills (?)) were erected on all rivers and beaches in preparation for the invasion. Not only were they used for protection of invaders coming from the sea and up rivers, but they were also used to mount anti-aircraft guns, should the invasion come by air. Which ever-way Adolph decided to attack, we were prepared. Fortunately for us, the invasion didn't happen. We

---

[81] Left or Right Ron? Published by LR Publishing – Chapter 40 – Page 178
[82] 'Sussex' by Esther Meynell from The County Book Series - Published March 1947

can only assume that the large number of boxes along the Ouse is because the Ouse, meandering as it does, through the centre of Sussex (Mid-Wynd) was thought to be an important enough target to warrant extra protection. But the grim reminders of what could have been still remain in place to this day.

Playground for the children

Talking of things grim, in 1912 Mr Charles Dawson FSA 'discovered' what he said was a fossilised skull at Piltdown. The top of the skull was human but the lower jaw bone was that from an ape. It was thought that this was the connection between man and ape. Tests carried out on the remains in 1953, however, have proved it to be a fake and not, as first thought a skull from over 150 thousand years ago.

Our walk today is taken from the East Sussex County Council Walks[83] and is Route 20 of the series. Thankfully it is only a short 3 miles starting from The Piltdown Man Inn and takes us, in a circle past the site of the 1912 find at Barkham Manor, across the Ouse at Sharp's Bridge, into the village of Shortbridge and then back to the Inn. That is, providing we don't get lost! An old friend, Peter, is joining us today. Being Welsh he is still a bit hung over after the win, by Wales, against arch rivals England at Twickenham over the weekend. Apparently it's the first Welsh win over the English at Twickenham for 20 years and was something to celebrate (?) It will be interesting to see if he manages to get up to join us.

But, as suspected, Peter didn't make it. We've tried his house but he's not at home, so we head towards Piltdown without him. The day is cold with a bit of a frost but the sun is shining and the forecast is good so all should be ok. On the way to Piltdown we discuss friends we met, last night, at The Kings Head. At last, Lyn has got herself a job working with children, something that she has been working towards for some time but the opportunity never seemed to arrive. Now she is where she should be, in a school passing on some of her knowledge. Both Ron and I wish her well in her new venture.

Mind your head, Ron

Sadly only four teams have decided to continue with the shove a'penny league in the Hailsham area because of lack of interest. I can remember when there were thirteen pub teams in the league. Ron can go even further back "...when the game was so pop'lar they 'ad to 'ave two leagues." In future years the loss of the game in competition form is a shame because it is one of the few pub games, apart from darts of course, that could be enjoyed by some of us old 'uns. One of the team members from the Kings Head arrogantly announced that he wouldn't be playing anyway because '...the current team aren't good enough to win anything.' Who was it that

---

said that it wasn't the winning but the taking part which was important? If the truth was told a number of really good players wouldn't play 'aypennies at The Kings Head because of this one player's attitude. But it is a real shame to loose a tradition in this way.

We park in the car park of The Piltdown Man which is situated on the very busy

The gate for what?

A272. It may be possible to park opposite the pub, in a lay-by, but we decided the car would be safer in the very large car park to the side of the pub. Round the back of the pub is a menagerie of animals for the children to pet and feed as well as one of the best play areas I've seen for some considerable time. The first disappointment for Ron is that the pub doesn't open until 11am and it's now only 10. "We'll call in when we get back," I tell Ron. "Perhaps we could 'ave a bite ter eat, as well," suggests Ron. "Do a set meal fer nine ninety five. Might 'ave ter try some o'that." From here

our instructions tell us to walk along the nearside pavement until we reach a place called 'Stonelands' where we then turn left down a path. This should be about 150 yards from the pub. But we can't find 'Stonelands'. We walk past a house called 'Stonecroft'. We are now over 200 yards from the pub so decide to head back to 'Stonecroft'. "Don't reckon much ter the instructions if they can't get the name o'the

One of the many ponds

'ouse right," says Ron. But, at 'Stonecroft', there is a public footpath sign leading down the side of the property. So we walk along this path and hope that we come to a stile on our right and into a field. The path starts off quite wide with trees leaning at strange angles before it narrows and winds along the hedgerow until we do, actually, come to a stile on the right. At least we must be on the right path.

One thing that is very noticeable now is that, although we have only just left a very busy main road we cannot hear the sound of any traffic. But what can be heard

are the birds in full song. Ron stops me as he points out the song of the robin, the song thrush and the great tit. They are all in full voice and it sounds fantastic. Once over the stile we need to follow the right edge of the field. This field was once a vineyard and has tall shelter belts placed strategically along sections of the field, all in regimental lines. Once through the vineyard we come to and cross a small drive and arrive at one of those strange phenomena that can only be Sussex. It isn't the first time that Ron and I have seen this type of thing. On one of our previous walks I can remember finding a stile, in the middle of a field, and once we found a locked gate, complete with brand new padlock, that you could walk round because there wasn't a fence. The gate now in front of us, protecting the entrance to the house, must have cost 'a pretty penny'. So much so that the owner may not have been able to afford the fence to be attached to that gate, because, like our previous find, there isn't a fence, and it is obvious that vehicles are driven round the gate.

Path through centre of field

Very fast flowing

Squeeze stile

Once across the drive we go over the small footbridge and turn left keeping the tall trees, another shelter belt, on our left. We are now about to pass the ornamental gardens of Barkham Manor, the place where the bony remains of the 'prehistoric man' were discovered (?) in 1912. Whilst very little can be seen of the gardens it is obvious to both Ron and me that the owners probably don't vote labour in a general election. I have to be a little discrete when taking photographs around houses and people, for obvious reasons, so all I took were a couple of pictures of the ponds at the bottom of the garden. Ron pointed out a plastic heron standing on the waters edge, placed there to scare off other birds. But I suspect that Ron thought I would assume that it was a real heron, but he caught me like that once before and I wasn't going to fall for it again. We continue to follow the field edge until we come to a large gap in the hedge. We bear left, through the gap, and then follow a clear path through the middle of the next field looking out for a cottage in the distance. Once over the rise we could see the cottage and headed towards it. Again one of the things that will always amaze me is the definition of the word 'cottage'. I have always believed that a 'cottage' is a small house. Plain and simple, 'cottage' means small. The 'cottage' now in front of us is massive; it must have at least five bedrooms, a long sweeping gravel drive leads you to a double garage and security cameras are on every corner. I will admit that the name of this property didn't include the word 'cottage', after all how could it?

We are now on a roadway leading us towards Sharp's Bridge. Why the bridge is named this I have no idea. I have tried looking it up in books and on the internet but I am unable to give you any clue to the name. Perhaps someone can enlighten us? It is obvious, though, that the area is prone to flooding. As we walk towards the bridge there is a raised walkway beside the road along with a water depth indicator which would, in times of flood, indicate how deep the water was. I suppose you would need that information for your insurance claim? One thing I haven't mentioned is that the river that flows under Sharp's Bridge is the River Ouse, and standing on a distant bank, to our right is a WWII pill box. Which, in times of flood, would have been totally submerged? Perhaps that's the best time to invade England, after a heavy rainstorm and whole areas are under water;

head up the Ouse whilst everyone's out looking at depth indicators so they can fill out the insurance claims. But, seriously, when we crossed the bridge I was amazed at how

New wooden bridge

fast the river was flowing. "'Ave yer noticed," shouts Ron above the roar of the water, "that all the time we've walked along this river we ain't seen any o'them signs that tells us not ter dive in the water and there's danger from drownin'. Yet when we was on the marshes an' the water was only inches deep, council 'ad put barriers round the water an' put signs up sayin' no divin' and danger of drownin'. Yet look at this, bloody water's as deep as 'ell an' travellin' faster than I can run yet there ain't a sign in sight. Don't seem right, does it?" You can't argue with him because he's right. I managed to get under the fence and got very close to the fast flowing river without any problems. I'm not saying we should barricade all rivers and ponds, far from it, but I don't understand why so much money is spent on signage around little places on the marshes.

Mystery machinery?

After some time watching the water we head up the road towards 'Sharpsbridge Farm' and a stile, on the left, leading us into another field. I must say that since the first mistake with the house name our instructions and the walk signs have been fantastic, which is making this walk a real pleasure. As we walk along the left field edge we head towards a squeeze stile. Most stiles are the normal step up and over type, but squeeze stiles are more user friendly in that you don't have to climb them, but simply squeeze through the gap. Ok if you're an average size but not quite so nice if your, what Ron would call, 'a little meaty'. But once through the stile we again cross the River Ouse, this time by way of a wooden bridge. We

are only a little way down river from Sharp's Bridge with its fast flow yet here the water is practically still and calm. The difference is amazing.

Across the bridge Ron grabs my arm, "Listen," he says, "What for?" I ask, "Can yer 'ear it?" he asks, "Hear what," I whisper. "Tap, tap tappin'" he says, "'tis a woodpecker. Fancy 'avin' ter do that with yer 'ead on a Saturday mornin'" and in the distance could be heard the rat-a-tat tap of the woodpecker as he head buts an old tree. It was a wonderful sound.

We now find ourselves walking along the bank of a stream. I have no idea what stream, it's not on our map, but our instructions tell us to follow the stream. So we do. It wanders through a wood and at one point is very fast flowing as it drops, like a waterfall, to a lower level. Another little mystery we found was at the bottom of this mini-waterfall was what looked like a pipe with some sort of mechanism attached to one end. It looked like the mechanism may have had a wheel of some sort attached to it but why this should be there we have absolutely no idea. Perhaps, again, someone could let us know the answer.

A couple of fellow walkers now advise us that it gets a little muddy further along the path but they didn't tell us exactly how muddy. There were raised planks in some places which helped us to get along the path but in other places the mud came over the top of my boots. So be warned, if you decide to walk this route, wear wellingtons, because it gets really boggy.

The path along the stream brings us out at Shortbridge, just by the old mill. It's obvious they've had a problem with flooding because sandbags have been left on the road. As we come out, onto the road there is one of the wooden fingerposts which advise of distances to other villages. One of the regulars of the Kings Head told us that he used to live in this area when he was a lad and, if his father asked him to go somewhere he always had to walk and everywhere was nearly two miles away. Both Ron and I noticed the mileage on the sign and also that one of the arms had broken off. When we get back to Hailsham we must remember to inform Phil, who makes and repairs these Sussex signs that one of his pride and joys needs some TLC.

Broken sign

Once on the road we turn left and immediately left again, heading towards The Peacock Inn. The mention of a pub makes Ron's eyes light up. Again, I disappoint him by turning left, just before the pub, and heading along the public footpath towards a small stile on our left.

Once in the next field we head along the right hedge emerging out at Piltdown Golf Course. We avoid any flying balls along the eighth tee and walk up the road towards Piltdown Pond turning left and then left again so that we are back at the Piltdown Man.

Our intention was to just stop for a drink, Ron had Harvey's 'Kiss', apparently not as good as Harvey's Best but a 'damned good substitute'. The smell of cooking was too much for both of us so we settled down, by the open fire and ordered an all day breakfast. If you're in the area, give it a go. The Landlord made us feel very welcome, but then he would, he was a Hailsham man. One of his regulars popped in and whilst chatting about things in general he informed us that he made sausages just down the road. His company had made over 3,000 lb of sausages this week, all with natural ingredients. How many sausages is that? All in all, the pub was very welcoming and the food was fantastic and very hot. Just what the doctor ordered after what was a very enjoyable 3 miles.

Both Ron and I enjoyed this walk, although only 3 miles it was pleasant and the weather was very good to us. The path was a bit on the muddy side towards the end but what the hell, winter is just finishing and we

Ron's find !

have the spring and summer to look forward to. We enjoyed The Piltdown Man so much they're having a Valentines dinner on the 14th February, the menu looks inviting so I might book a table for me and the wife. How's that for a recommendation?

On the way back to the car, walking through the car park, Ron swooped down like a kite onto its prey. I thought he'd hurt himself or had collapsed, but no, as he picked himself up he said, "that's over a pound I've found today" He'd spotted 20 pence under a table. Things never change.

Chapter 17 – Quedley

I thought the letter '**Q**' was going to cause me a massive problem. At first I was scratching my head trying to think of where we could go. The **Q**uay at Sovereign Harbour seemed the most likely place I could think of. Then I suddenly saw my book, 'Sussex Place Names'[84] and a place called **Q**uedley leapt from the page. Ideal, I thought. All I had to do now was find out where it was and if it still existed. I also needed a walk that would take me to or through **Q**uedley. And I found one. I couldn't believe my luck. I hastily printed it from the Internet[85] and put it in a safe place. It was that safe I couldn't find it when I needed it. I hunted everywhere, but I couldn't find it. So I had to go back on the computer to try and find it again. If anyone out there has used a computer you will be aware that what you type in is what you get out. Unfortunately, when I was looking for this walk through my search engine I typed in Q-u-i-d-l-e-y. Not a single reference to a walk came back, obviously. I started to panic. We are going on the walk on Saturday, today is Thursday and I can't find the

Lots of woolly friends of Peter's

walk instructions. I went back to the computer and typed in the name again, wrongly. Same result. I couldn't understand what I was doing wrong. It wasn't until my wife asked what the problem was and said that surely the obvious thing to do was look in the book 'Sussex Place Names' again to check the name that I realised my mistake. And bingo, the intended walk is back on my screen, printed off and safely deposited, ready for Saturday.

One of the things that really pleased me about this walk is that part of it is around Bewl Water. If you haven't had a chance to visit this place yet I would encourage you to go. It is fantastic. I read somewhere that the reservoir holds over 31,000 million litres of water and is the largest stretch of open water in the south east of England. It is a haven to a wide variety of wildlife and is one of the prettiest places in Sussex. The one thing that I wasn't looking forward to was the distance of 7 miles. But our instructions tell me that this is only a grade 2 walk which means '…A generally easy walk with some gentle hills, a few stiles and some muddy paths.' We'll see.

One little surprise I had was when I went to collect Ron, Peter who should have joined us on our last walk, but didn't, is waiting with Ron at The Kings Head. For those unaware of Peter I will give a little explanation. He is Welsh, and speaks the language fluently. He loves rugby (the game) especially since last week (?) He has been with us before, in the middle of summer, when he wore long johns and thermal vests. Sweated buckets, he did, as we

The start of our walk

---

[84] 'Sussex Place Names' by Judith Glover, Published by Countryside Books, Page 176
[85] www.eastsussex.gov.uk visited 13/02/08

walked around Firle[86]. He would also prefer us not to mention Welshmen and sheep in the same sentence. He finds the topic a little offensive, bless him. Yet he always seems to make the connection between his fellow Welsh compatriots and the woolly animals before Ron and me utter a word. We will see how it goes.

It's Saturday morning and it is cold. I had to de-ice the car before we set off. But the sun is out and the forecast is good as we head up South Road towards Ticehurst and the start of our 7 mile stroll. Everyone must be aware of the arrival of Tesco Superstore into our little town of Hailsham. One of the results of this brilliant piece of planning is that a number of good shops in our town have decided that they can't compete and have closed down. But did you know that it is also on the cards that a drive-thru KFC (Kentucky Fried Chicken) and a branch of Lidl's or some other superstore is also being planned to hit the town soon. So can somebody explain to me why, with all the extra traffic these schemes will undoubtedly bring into the town, we now have to have 'traffic calming' measures in South Road. The traffic hasn't

Large open field of broad beans

increased yet and, because of the narrowing of the road and that stupid zebra crossing on the bend, (which isn't switched on so drivers don't know if they need to stop and pedestrians don't know if they should walk across) traffic practically comes to a standstill at peak times. One old lady hit one of the bollards in the traffic calming scheme, a few days after they were installed, because it was dark and she couldn't see them, and closed the road for three hours. Is it me or is this what they call progress?

Ticehurst can be found on the B2099 and is one of those quant old Sussex villages/towns that haven't been invaded by multi-stores or traffic calming measures. It does have a free car park with an interesting way of segregation. If you only wish to stay for less than two hours you

Ron's famous carrier

park in a bay with a number 2 painted on the ground. If you wish to stay for up to nine hours you must park in a bay with a number 9 painted on the ground. Now ain't that simple? "But what if yer want ter stay all night?" asks Ron. "You're not allowed to," says Peter, "it explains it all on the sign over there." "We got a 7 mile walk, Graham," says Ron, "best take up two o'them nine 'our bays just ter be on the safe side."

After parking the car Ron starts to put on his Sussex smock, over his coat. "You won't need that coat on, Ron," I tell him, "you'll bake alive." He, reluctantly, agrees removes his coat and puts his smock on. In the meantime, Peter has started to get all his photographic gear together and is starting to look like a film producer, peak cap, dark glasses and cameras hanging from his neck. "What's the idea with all the cameras?" I ask. "It's my brother's birthday, next month," he replies,

---

[86] 'Left or Right Ron?' Published by LR Publishers, Walk 7, Page 24

"I thought I'd send him the book and do a little film as well. Be a nice present, don't you think?" "Depends 'ow the film comes out," says Ron. "Don't pick up the swear words, does it? Could be a problem if it picks up the swear words." "I'll edit anything nasty out," assures Peter, "It'll be fine."

Our instructions tell us to walk up the High Street, towards Wadhurst, until we reach a narrow alleyway on the right, opposite a private drive leading to Old Hazelwood. We found the alleyway without problems and turn right. "You expect some little urchin ter come out and pick yer pocket." The path is very narrow and it isn't long before we're passing the sports ground and heading along the path towards a copse. "Played football out there," says Ron, "scored 'at trick." There isn't a village or town in Sussex where Ron hasn't played football, played cricket or mown the grass. He will always comment at some time during our walks.

Before we get to the copse the temperature drops suddenly. In fact it is freezing. "Bet me coats nice an' warm in the boot o'your car," complains Ron. "It'll be ok once we get started," I say, with more hope than it sounded. "Could catch bloody pneumonia out 'ere before long," he continues. The wind was bitter as we head along the edge of a very large, open field. "What do you think the farmers planted in this field?" I ask Ron, hoping to get his mind off the temperature. "Looks like broad beans," he says. "Must be plenty o'money to be 'ad in growin' runners. Bloody field's enormous." We enter the copse and continue for a few yards until a sign points us to the right. Peter has run in front of us so that he can take pictures of Ron and me heading towards him. Our next instruction tells us to follow the waymark signs to reach Tinkers Lane. Unfortunately we missed the waymark sign lying in the hedge and headed in the wrong direction. As we approached the next hedge it was obvious that we had made a mistake. I say we but both Ron and Peter are blaming me. "Make sure you get this on that film thingy," says Ron to Peter, "only been out 'ere fer 'alf an 'our an e's got it wrong. Bloody freezin' cold an were 'eadin' in the wrong direction already." Whatever I say right now will not please Ron, so I ignore him and head back

A very, very small slice of Bewl Water beauty

to the place where we now find the broken waymark and head towards the opening onto Tinkers Lane where we turn left.

Some may wonder what Ron carries in his Harvey's carrier bag. But I can now let you into a little secret. One of the things he carries in the bag is a hammer. "Why do you carry a hammer?" asks Peter with camera poised and at the ready. "Well," says Ron, "sometimes, when we've been out walkin' we see's a sign that needs a little bit o'repair. So's I got the 'ammer an' a few nails an' other bits in me carrier so's I can repair the sign, see." He holds up the carrier for Peter. "How often have you used it?" Peter asks. "I 'aven't yet," says Ron "but if I do need it, I'll be ready." Ron's logic, again, can't be faulted.

Health & Safety at the extreme

We continue along Tinkers Lane until we reach the junction with Huntley Mill Road. Here we turn right and head along the road for about 150 yards before turning left onto a signposted footpath, which turns into a concrete drive. We continue along the drive until we come to a cattle grid and a junction with a bridleway. This is a point of the 'Round Bewl Water Walk', and from here we walk along the edge of Bewl Reservoir, which has to be one of the most spectacular and beautiful places in Sussex.The reservoir was man-made between 1973 and 1975. When Ron and I were here last year there were serious problems with water shortages. The reservoir level was very low and hose pipe bans were in force. Places now covered with water we could walk across last year. Some alarmists had mentioned that water rationing was a possibility but this never materialised. But looking at the water now we are amazed at how different it looks now that the levels are up to relative normality. You may remember that in some of our walks, when we get anywhere near water, we look out for signs warning of danger, risk of drowning etc. In

Abandoned machine

our last walk along the very fast flowing River Ouse there was not one sign warning of the danger. But here, right next to, what has to be the biggest expanse of inland water I have seen, you've guessed it. There is a sign warning, not only the danger of drowning but also that the water is cold! I will not comment!

I have a large number of photographs of Bewl Water should anyone wish to see all of them. Unfortunately, or fortunately, there is not room in the book for them all but I am warming to the idea of a picture book of Sussex

A 'walk around' gate

places. Watch this space.

As we walk along the waters edge we notice a number of joggers. All pass us by with a cheery wave and a kind word. One, a young female, jogging along with her dog, had a strange T-shirt on. It wasn't until she'd gone past us twice, once in the opposite direction that I realised what was strange. The wording on the T-shirt was upside down. Now Ron has a very ingenious reason as to why the wording on the T-shirt is upside down. Unfortunately I am too much of a gentleman to disclose exactly what he said in print but both Peter and I were rolling about with laughter when he said it. Next time you see Ron, if you dare, ask him.

Every now and again we have to walk away from the water and stroll through

The going gets muddy

some woodland before returning back to water. It was on one of these occasions that I spotted one of my pet hates. Abandoned machinery. And, again, we found one of those gates with no fence attached. What is happening to our beautiful county when machines are left to rot and gates don't have to be opened?

We walk along and around Bewl Water for over an hour. We stop to admire. We stop to take pictures. Every angle that you look is a perfect picture. I'm going on a bit, but believe me when I say that this really is one of the most idyllic places I have seen. I love it to bits. But all things must come to an end as we reach Rosemary Lane.

We cross the lane and head along a wide grass footpath. We can just about see part of the reservoir through the hedge as we head towards Ketley Wood. The temperature, thankfully, has started to rise and I notice beads of sweat on Ron's brow. "Getting a little warm, are we?" I ask. "All right, smart arse," Ron says, "luckily fer you I ain't collapsed with 'ipothermia. But I'm beginnin' ter feel the 'eat." That may be the closest I get to being told I was right. But at least he's got a smile when he says it. Because of the rise in temperature the frost has started to thaw and the path is a bit

Sign leading to Quedley

on the muddy side as we climb through Ketley Wood. Our instructions tell us to ignore any deviation in the paths but to continue ahead, in a straight line until we reach the main road.

Once at the road we turn left and then immediately right to follow a signposted footpath along the drive to **Q**uedley. I have absolutely no idea what main road we are on but I am sure that if I'd have known I still wouldn't have seen the little stone sign for **Q**uedley. It was nestled, on the ground, broken, under a hedge.

In 1605 it was spelt Quodleigh which

makes those in the know think that it was a local meeting place where local squabbles and arguments could be sorted out.[87] So, what is there to see at **Q**uedley? To be honest, nothing. At the end of the drive a nice houses and a farm (?) and that's it. Once past the house we turn left, where we follow a path which leads us to Dale Hill Golf Course.

Abandoned tractor

Later in this book is a description of how Ron, as my caddy, and I got on in the Kings Head Open Golf Tournament. Ron and I have decided to enter this 'fun' event as a team. In fact we are the only team. Others who have decided to take up the challenge are representing themselves, some are taking it seriously. But as we were at a golf course I thought I'd try out Ron's caddy technique. To our left, some way away is a yellow flag attached to a pole. "What club would you suggest, Ron, to get the ball on the green?" I ask. Ron scratches his head and says, "Not a bad distance, I'd say approximately 167 yards, I would recommend a 6 iron, soft and to the left of the flag, thus avoiding the trap in front of the hole." They were his exact words. I was totally gobsmacked and very impressed. But we'll have to see how he copes under the stress and strain of competition.

We make our way across the course, obviously avoiding all the flying balls along fairways. Players, although very polite and courteous, obviously wanted to see the back of us so they let us pass with a cheery wave. I think it was a cheery wave but sometimes my eyes aren't so good.

From the course we head into some woodland before emerging, again, onto the golf course. Across one more fairway, and another wave (?) and we are now on an

Overgrown and left

enclosed footpath. At the end of this footpath we have to turn left when we reach a drive. But it is along this path that we find more machinery just left to rot. We are actually passing what looks as if it used to be a vineyard with an orchard. Signs tell us that the fruit has been sprayed so you are advised not to be tempted. But it looks as if, some years ago, production just stopped. The owners or workers just dropped everything and left. The tractor by the shed, the bottles lying on the ground, what looked like vats in the shed were just abandoned?

The vines are all overgrown, the fruit trees have brambles growing up them, and the place is a tip. "The only thing wrong with this tractor," says Ron as he climbs aboard, "is the brakes 'ave seized up. Give ol' Des[88] a couple of 'ours an' ea'll 'ave it goin' again."

---

[87] Sussex Place Names by Judith Glover, Countryside Books - Page 176
[88] Des Pelling, one of our old drinking friends from The Kings Head

At the end of the driveway is Pashley Road, the main road into Ticehurst. Our instructions are to turn right and walk along this road for 500 yards, looking for a stile on the right. This has to be one of the fastest roads in Sussex. Traffic hurtles up and down this road at a fair rate of knots. I'm not sorry to find the stile and get off the road. It was a very hairy 500 yards. From here we head across a couple of fields following clear signs until we, again, come across a small section of Dale Hill Golf Course. We cross the tee and head for a path which leads us back onto the junction of Pashley Road and the High Street in Ticehurst just a short distance from the car.

St Mary's Church, Ticehurst

Of course no walk is complete without a visit to the local church. It is thought that this area goes back to the times of King Cnut (1018) when he granted the then Archbishop of Canterbury some land in the area. The place was called Haeselersc. The name survives today as Hazelhurst Farm in Ticehurst parish. Yet it isn't until 1197 that the church at Ticehurst is confirmed as coming under the 'blanket' of Hastings Priory.

The church isn't, in my mind, a sit down church. It lacked something. It was possibly too grand, too big and not my idea of a little village church. Don't get me wrong, the place is steeped in history. It is and always will be a place to visit if you are in the area. It is clean, the churchyard is well-kept and the whole place is a credit to its churchgoers. An interesting aside is that on the wall of the entrance is a list of all parishioners who served in both wars. Those who, sadly, did not return are remembered inside the church. But I haven't seen a memorial for every serving member of the parish before. It was a nice touch.

On the way home we stopped at The Jack Cade Pub. Thankfully, our mood was a lot brighter than that of the landlord who seemed to have a problem with strangers being in his bar. It was nothing he said, in fact he never spoke to us but looks can say everything. We didn't stop long.

A very enjoyable 7 miles. If you fancy doing it, don't be shy. You could always ask me and Ron to accompany you. This is one of my favourites and I wouldn't hesitate to do it again.

Quedley was a place so obscure
A house, a farm and nothing more
A pleasant walk, just the same,
Pete enjoyed it, he's glad he came.
Aresee©

Chapter 18 – Knucker Hole

At last we have come to the letter **K**. A little out of sequence perhaps, but I did have my reasons. From the start of this book I thought that the letter **K** would be the

Arundel Castle - Knights & Dragons?

easiest letter to find somewhere interesting to walk around. **K**ingley Vale is the oldest and largest elm forest in Europe. And it's in Sussex. The reason for leaving it a little later in the year was so we could experience some of the spring flowers. But then it all changed. I found **K**nucker Hole with its fascinating piece of history. I had to go and see the place for myself and try to experience some of the fantasy of dragons and knights that is **K**nucker Hole.

The actual walk is taken from The Argus[89] and is called 'Crossbush Circular' written by Eddie Start. It covers 6¼ miles, is a circular route and includes two churches, one at Lyminster and one at Poling. It also, of course, includes **K**nucker Hole. Let me try to explain, firstly, what a **K**nucker Hole is. A website[90] I found tells us that **K**nucker Holes are:

"Springs which rise in the flat lands of the South Downs. They keep at one level, are often 20 feet or so across and are reputed to be bottomless. The water is cold in the summer but never freezes, in a frost it gives off a vapour, being warmer than the air. Knucker Holes are found at Lyminster, Lancing, Shoreham, and Worthing and in many other 'Flats'."

Nothing too inspiring there until you use a little imagination, a fantasy, a daring and a good story. The **K**nucker Hole at Lyminster has every one of these and I will relate the story whilst walking by the Hole.

Again the morning is very cold and icy. We really shouldn't expect anything else in February. Ron and I are to be joined by Alan this morning who has asked if he could spend a few hours in some new countryside. Alan used to live in Kent but has been converted by the beauty of Sussex. I hope that today we do not disappoint him.

The starting point of today's walk is a hamlet called Crossbush, which is just ¾ of a mile from Arundel, on the main A27. Parking the car isn't a problem as we are able to use the main road where there is ample parking space. In fact we parked very close to the Convent for Poor Clares. I have since found out that the Clare referred to was associated with St Francis of Assisi and all she wanted to do was give herself to Christ in life and in poverty. She died in 1253 and was made a saint in 1255. It was in 1212 that St Francis led Clare to begin the Order of the "Poor Ladies" in San Damiano where the order lived in poverty making and supplying goods to give to others, expecting nothing but gifts in return. Clare remained there for 42 years, loving Christ in poverty and following in his footsteps.[91] We walk past the entrance to the Convent and head downhill towards Arundel Town. There is a cold fog covering the high

---

[89] www.theargus.co.uk visited 18/02/2008

[90] http://www2.prestel.co.uk/aspen/sussex/dragon.html visited 18/02/2008

[91] http://www.poorclaresarundel.org/Pages/ClareStory.aspx visited 20/02/2008

ground as we cross the busy A27 just after the turning to Warningcamp and head for a public footpath, on the left, just before Priory Farm. We are warned that the steps down to a small field can be slippery in the damp air so we all proceed with caution.

Frisky bullocks

The Queen's swans

Over the stile we now enter a small paddock. Luckily the thaw hasn't started and the ground is solid. If it had it would have been very muddy here. Across the paddock, in the far corner, is our next stile which we climb over and then uphill over the next field. When we look back we can still see the magnificent Arundel Castle through the haze. Our instructions tell us to cross over more stiles and plank bridges heading towards and to the right of the buildings of Broomhurst Farm. Everyone should know of my fear of animals. Unfortunately Ron had two of us to put up with, because Alan isn't that keen either. He didn't say as much but when, in the field just before Broomhurst Farm, four of the ugliest white bullocks seemed to be taking an unhealthy interest in us, I noticed that Alan moved just that little bit quicker. "Don't run," advises Ron, "they won't 'urt yer." "He always says that," I whisper to Alan, "but it never seems to make you slow down, does it?" "Are we safe?" asks Alan, "Course we are," assures Ron, "just don't show 'em yer scared." "He always says that as well," I whisper, "but they do look a bit frisky and they are heading towards us." Alan's steps get a little quicker and longer. One of the bullocks gets really close to Ron and starts treading the ground. Ron stops and stares at the animal. It's just like a stand off. Who will give in first? Will the bullock charge and trample all to death or can Ron win the battle of wills? Obviously, Ron was triumphant but they are big animals and can be a little scary if you're not too keen. Considering Alan was a little bit worried he didn't get too far in front of us because in the next field there were more bullocks. So he waited for us to join him. "Just walk towards 'em," says Ron, "they'll move out yer way soon

Knucker Hole, through the fence

enough." I've noticed that Ron always says that when he's behind me but, as we walk towards these bullocks they did wander off in front of us without paying us much heed. Alan looked decidedly happier when we got to the next stile. "Cor, look," chuckles Ron, "only got some swans in this next field, now they can be really nasty. Especially if they got young with 'em." You could practically see the colour drain from Alan. "Don't worry, Alan," I assure him, "we'll give them a wide berth so that they don't bother us if we don't bother them." All the time we were walking past them they kept watching us to make sure we were ok.

We now cross a footbridge and continue along an enclosed path besides the ponds known as Knucker Hole. One of the stories associated with Knucker Hole is from a very old poem called 'Beowulf'[92] which tells the tale of a dragon, known as a Knucker, living in Knucker Hole who used to terrorise the area. He lived in Knucker Hole and used to eat humans, crops and all other things. The King decided that the dragon must be killed. But no-one came forward until he offered the hand in marriage of his daughter. Then a brave knight arrived, fought the dragon and killed him by cutting off his head. They all lived happily ever after until the dragon's mother heard what had happened and challenged the knight to a fight to the death. Of course the knight, although much older and weaker couldn't be seen to back down, so agreed to fight. After a vicious battle the knight was triumphant again but was mortally wounded and died, shortly after the battle because of his injuries. This is just one of the stories associated with Knucker Hole; I will tell you another later.

Unfortunately, probably due to Health and Safety reasons, you cannot get anywhere near Knucker Hole due to the high fence but I did manage to get the camera lens squeezed through a gap to get a couple of photo's. It is said that the people from the local church at Lyminster, just a few yards past Knucker Hole, tied the six bell ropes together and lowered them into Knucker Hole to find out how deep it was. The ropes didn't touch the bottom[93].

The long roof of Lyminster Church

At the end of the path we come to a flint wall that marks the boundary of the churchyard of St. Mary Magdalene Church at Lyminster. The first thing you notice about the church is the huge roof. The earliest mention of Lyminster is in the year 901 A.D., when Alfred the Great bequeathed it to his nephew, Osfred, under the name of Lullyngminster.[94] King Athelstan, who reigned as King of Wessex from 925 to 939 used to come to Lyminster with his council to deal with governmental problems in the area. It was this King that is said to have offered his daughter to the slayer of the dragon at Knucker Hole. The church is well-kept and the gentleman clearing the churchyard was working well as we passed him along the path, heading towards the lychgate and out onto the road.

Here we turn right and head towards Church Farm. The instructions are a little confusing here and it's obvious that buildings have been removed and new ones erected because the description on

Welcome to Littlehampton

[92] Old English epic poem believed to be dated 8th – 11th century - http://en.wikipedia.org/wiki/Beowulf
[93] http://www2.prestel.co.uk/aspen/sussex/dragon.html visited 18/02/2008
[94] The Parish Church of St Mary Magdalene Lyminster – A short guide - £1.50 purchased at church

the instructions don't match up with what we are looking at. But we do manage to find our way to a meadow where we bear right and head towards a flint wall. We pass through a squeeze gate (kissing gate to us) and find ourselves on a main road. The sign in front of us says 'Welcome to Littlehampton' which worried me a little because I didn't think we were in that area at all. We now cross the road and head for the public footpath in the picture, where we turn left and walk across an enclosed path. This path takes us past a couple of paddocks holding horses and in the distance is a young lady coaching a young horse on how to be led on the reign. Even from the distance we were at Ron has fallen in love again. "Look at the way she 'andles that animal," he's started to dream; "she could tie me up an' drag me round that paddock anytime she 'as a mind to." How he knows I have no idea but his next comment was, "got a lovely personality, a girl like that." How can he tell?

We manage to drag Ron away, as we now head towards Lyminster Road. Here, we are instructed to '…walk on the grass verge, passing Old Vicarage Cottage.' I'm not querying the 'grass verge' bit but I notice that the next instruction tells us to head along the bridleway. But the bridleway is before Old Vicarage Cottage, not past it. So, we shouldn't '…pass Old Vicarage Cottage'. But Ron insists we do as instructed, just in case there is another bridleway. So we walk along the verge for another hundred yards and all we manage to find, or at least all Ron managed to find was a 2 pence piece, in the gutter. "Was worth it," he says.

All gate, no fence

Back to the cottage we head along the bridleway and through one of those gates, again. You know the ones, all gate and no fence (?) They must serve a purpose. We are told, in the instructions that this bridleway is over a mile long. Ron starts to reminisce. "This bridleway reminds me o'the last train out of 'ailsham, it does." "Why would that be?" asks Alan. "Just looks like the cuckoo trail," says Ron, "'twas 1968, if I remember right, train was packed an' toilet rolls were 'angin' out the windows, was like a party it was." I can remember this story and how it ends. "You'd have thought that the words 'last train at Hailsham' would have given them a clue, Alan," I take up the story, "Silly sods didn't think too kindly of having to walk home." "Didn't give it a thought," continues Ron, "loads ov'us there was with no way o'getting' 'ome from Polegate. Even worse if, like me, you 'ad no money ter pay fer a taxi. It's a bloody long walk to 'ailsham from Polegate Station. Course the station ain't were it used ter be. Used ter be further up the road than it is now. But t'was a fair walk."

As we started to relate stories I thought it might be a good time to tell another story about Knucker Hole. This time it involves a young lad named Jim Puttock (sometimes the name Jim Pulk is used). In this story the reward was offered by the Mayor of Arundel and not the King. Jim came from a village called Wick and he visited the Mayor and told him his plan. The Mayor then tells everyone around that should Jim ask for anything they must give it freely and be thankful that Jim will get rid of the dragon. All the people helped Jim in what he needed to make a big pudding. The biggest pudding anyone had seen. Jim put the pudding onto a big cart and somebody had lent him a team of horses to drag the load to the Knucker Hole. At the Hole he meets the dragon. The story continues, as told by an old Sussex hedger

"How do man" says the dragon, - "How do, dragon," says Jim.
"What you got there?" says dragon .- "Pudden." says Jim.
"Pudden?" says Knucker. "What be that?" - "Just you try" says Jim.

And he didn't want no more telling – pudden, horses, cart, they was gone in a blink. Jimmy ud agone, too, only he hung on to one o' them trees that blew down last year

"T'weren't bad" says Knucker, licking his chops. - "Like another?" asks Jim,
"shudn't mind" says he, - "right," says Jim. "Bring ee one Sadernoon."

But he knew better'n that, surelye. Fore long they hears en rowling about, and roaring and bellering fit to bust hissel. And as he rowls, he chucks up gert clods, big as houses, and trees and stones and all manner, he did lash about with his tail.

But Jim, he weren't afeared. He goes off to have a look at en. When he sees en coming ole Knucker roars out:

"Don't you dare bring me no more o'that 'ere pudden, young marn!"
"Why?" says Jim. "What's matter?"
"Colly wobbles" says the Dragon. "Do set so heavy on me I can't stand un, nohows in de wurreld"
"Shudn't bolt it so" says Jim, "but never mind, I got a pill here, soon cure that"
"Where?" say Knucker.
"Here" says Jim.

And he ups with an axe he'd held behind his back and cuts off his head[95].

Training to fly

Perhaps not such a good story but it's the way he tells it. There are other stories that involve poisons and the like and the Internet is a mine of information if you have the opportunity and time to have a look.

But back to our walk. We are now approaching the village of Poling but before we get there we notice, in the distance, a mown patch of grass, a windsock and three men working out of the back of their vehicles. It is until we get closer that we discover that they are about to start flying radio controlled helicopters. A little chat with one of the flyers tells us that he is training one of the other men to hover a helicopter. But to ensure the safety of the helicopter the 'teacher' had to fit a false undercarriage so that if it did come down in a sudden rush there would be minimal damage.

We stayed and watched for some time but I found it all a little boring. Yes it was nice to watch but once in the air what else can a helicopter do but fly off, come back and land. Job done. The helicopter we were watching just missed out the flying off

---

[95] http://www2.prestel.co.uk/aspen/sussex/dragon.html visited 18/02/2008

and coming back bit. It took off, it hovered and then landed. Still, I'm sure the guy learnt a lot from his lesson. The teacher didn't stop talking to him all the time he was flying. But we have to get on so we left them to the helicopters.

Poling village is a quaint but barren place. Some of the houses are thatched which give it a jig-saw puzzle type of appeal but the church of St Nicholas is reason enough

to visit Poling. The first thing Ron noticed, as we walked up the path, through the graveyard, was the distinctive monument placed for one of his cricketing heroes, Colin Cowdrey, who died at his home on the 5th December 2000, four months after suffering a stroke at the age of 67. From the memorial stone you will see that his title was The Lord Cowdrey of Tonbridge. He was appointed to the House of Lords in 1997 and was only the second England captain to achieve this honour after the Rt Rev David Sheppard[96] Now I'm not superstitious but I have since found out that Lord Cowdrey's real name was **M**ichael **C**olin **C**owdrey even his initials were steeped in cricket?

A fitting memorial

But the church is a beauty. Full of character and historically fascinating, right down to the original poor box dated 1797, placed by the door. It is truly a sit down church of small proportions but with big feelings. I sat, and felt very humble. Propped up against the porch wall is a small memorial stone which is reproduced below. I am unsure of one word. It looks like 'fireets' but the stone is well-worn, after all, it is dated 1740 but I feel the wording is apt:

Man-made pond as we head towards the A27

Here
Lyeth ye Body
of Alice ye wife of Rob[t]
the 27th of May 1740
The World is a round thing
And full of crooked fireet's
Death is a market place
Where all Men meets

If Life was a thing
That money could buy
The Rich would Live
And the Poor would dye

Our instructions, from the church are, again, a little confusing. Either my right and left aren't quite the same or the whole thing is confusing with half lefts then half rights but we eventually find ourselves in the correct place with open meadows and a large pond in sight.

We pass the pond and head towards the next meadow. We are now instructed to walk across the next field but the farmer has recently ploughed so the public footpath no longer exists. We have to walk all round the field to get to the stile that takes us into Decoy Wood.

---

[96] http://news.bbc.co.uk/sport1/hi/cricket/1055384.stm visited 22/02/2008

We follow the path through Decoy Wood and cross a plank bridge to reach the busy A27. But it is here that we see the notice telling us that the footpath is temporarily closed for 21 days. "They can't do that, can they?" asks Alan. "If they think we're walking all the way back they got another think comin'" says Ron. Attached to the prohibited sign is a map showing where we are and the part of the

path that is 'prohibited'. "There isn't an alternative route on the map," I say as we all look at the piece of paper hanging from the tree. We decide to ignore the sign and continue along the path, up the steps and onto the busy A27. Where the path comes out they have closed the lay-by with cones so all we do is cross the road, carefully, and head for the other carriageway, where we can see a footpath sign.

Our next path is a mile in length and takes us through a few copses all with lovely names; Quakers Corner Copse, Priors-lease Copse and Sailors Copse all must be named for a reason. All the time we are walking along the wooded path there is the constant drone of traffic in the distance, but the scenery makes up for the noise.

Path closed sign

We come to the end of the copse and head across the clear meadow, towards a stile in the opposite fence. It is Alan who first notices the herd of Highland cattle sitting in the distance. "Shouldn't they put a sign up somewhere letting people walking through the field know that they're in here?" asks Alan as his pace visibly increases. We did find a sign telling us that a bull was in the field. It was on the stile we were about to climb over, but on the other side. For some reason, as we cross this field Alan insisted on telling us that if you get chased by an

Highland Cattle

alligator, or was it a crocodile, that you should run in a straight line, or was it a zig-zag, so that the alligator, or was it a crocodile, couldn't catch you (?) "We'll remember that," says Ron, "Just in case we sees one on our walks."

We come to a small road and continue in a straight line, passing through another two copses called The Isle and Poling Copse for what seems like ages but turns out to be only ¾ of a mile. On each side of us is nothing but woodland. At one point, looking to our right you couldn't see very far into the wood because of the amount of trees. All was dark within, which gave a slightly spooky feel.

Unfortunately, in places, large amounts of litter could be seen, just dumped. One was an abandoned car, probably used by joy-riders and

Forest deep.

just left to rust. It was disappointing to see but I suppose it is now the way of youngsters of today, but it does spoil a good walk.

The path gets increasingly muddy now as we head towards a driveway belonging to The Old Coach House and back onto the road that will take us, eventually, back to Crossbush and the car.

This was a good walk, everything was included, churches, dragons, castles, knights in shining armour and a very pleasant woodland walk. It did seem longer than the 6¼ miles but that may be due to stops on the way. The weather, again, was favourable which obviously helps.

After **K** we should start to get back on track, with the alphabet. We only have eight walks left but I'm still struggling with the letter **Z**. I just can't find anything in Sussex that starts with the last letter of our alphabet.

We three had a pleasant stroll
Didn't see Mother-in-Law in Knucker Hole
Walked through fields of bull and sheep
The look on Alan's face forever we will keep.
Aresee©

Chapter 19 – Robertsbridge

Some may be aware of my love for Hilaire Belloc. One of my prize possessions is a book written by the great man titled 'The Four Men'.[97] The book was originally published in 1911 but I have scoured my copy of the book and can't find a date of publication or a date of printing so I'm unaware if it is a 1st edition or not. It looks old and much thumbed but, like I said, I love it. I have looked on the Internet and it seems that all of this title, if old, does not have dates. But all the descriptions I have found describe my book to a tee. The reason I am going on about the book is simply that the first chapter starts with the words 'Nine years ago, as I was sitting in the "George" at Robertsbridge, drinking that port of theirs and staring at the fire, there arose in me a multitude of thoughts.....[98]' This passage is dated 29th October 1902. So, what better place to start a walk beginning with the letter **R,** than **R**obertsbridge.

I have also discovered that I've acquired two walks around **R**obertsbridge. Both are circular, one is a Ghost Walk[99] which is only three miles long and takes us along some country roads and lanes around **R**obertsbridge, into Salehurst and back to **R**obertsbridge and describes spooky goings on along route. Or there is also a five mile walk[100] around the town

The George Inn, Robertsbridge

of **R**obertsbridge and is described as '...a typical country walk with some hills, stiles and muddy paths...' I was thinking that we may combine the two, but on the day before our walk it didn't stop raining through the afternoon and through the night, the winds must have touched gale force because the tiles on the roof at home were chattering. After looking at both walks again I decided that it would be better if we went on the smaller walk because we would be able to visit the church at Salehurst. If we did the longer walk we wouldn't see the church and we would have to struggle across the open fields and through muddy paths.

Old timber building

You may remember that I drive a school minibus and a couple of the girls from my bus, Ellen and Halle, kindly gave me a book of walks[101] for my birthday. The walk we will complete today is Walk number 2 from that book, and is a circular 3 mile route from Robertsbridge into Salehurst and back to Robertsbridge. Details of the ghosts which can be experienced are given in the book and I will explain as we get to them.

The weather today is cold and blustery. But at least the sun has put in a bit of an appearance and it has stopped raining. Just to be on the safe side I've brought along

---

[97] 'The Four Men' by H. Belloc published by Thomas Nelson & Sons.
[98] Ibid page 3
[99] Ghost Hunter Walks in Sussex by Rupert Matthews, SB Publications, Walk 2 Page 13
[100] www.eastsussex.gov.uk Robertsbridge Walk, Route 33 site visited 23/02/2008
[101] 'Ghost Hunter Walks in Sussex' by Rupert Matthews, published by SB Publications

some wet weather clothing discretely strapped to my back and have not told Ron that I have it. We arrive at Robertsbridge in good time, even if we did go the long way round. Sorry Ron.

The first thing I noticed about Robertsbridge was the houses. Now I expected them to be old. After all, the area was around in the 12th century[102] but some of the houses are very old with a capital 'O'. Which makes for a very quaint, pretty village with bags of character. Even the National Westminster Bank is a wooden clad building and fits in very well with the surrounding buildings.

We park the car in the free car park in Station Road. Again we are instructed to

park in the bay marked with a 9 or, if we do not intend to stay too long, in a bay marked with a 2. "Best be safe," says Ron, "an' park in the nine bay. You never know. Might only be a 3 mile stroll but it could take us hours."

The first part of the walk takes us towards the High Street and the Seven Stars Inn. It is here, in the 1980's that the pub suffered from a violent outburst from a poltergeist. Not content with the more usual tricks, this spirit turned destructive.

Fair Lane, Robertsbridge

Sheets, shirts and tablecloths were torn to pieces and glasses were hurled off shelves and tables. Now it is peaceful here, allowing visitors to enjoy the meals and ales that the pub offers.

We turn left and almost immediately right along Fair Lane. It is slightly uphill, as can be seen from the picture, and it isn't long before we arrive at the footbridge which takes us over the very busy A21. At the far side of the bridge we are instructed to turn left then right. This should take us into a narrow lane that is a continuation of Fair Lane. "If this is supposed ter be a continuation o' Fair Lane," says Ron, "why does that sign say Redlands Lane?" Through the bushes we can clearly see a sign, pointing down the lane in the direction we are about to go that doesn't say Fair Lane, but Redlands Lane. "Perhaps they've renamed the lane since the book was written," I offer. "Or," says Ron, "we be lost before we 'ardly started, again!" "Trust me Ron, we're heading in the right direction." Ron mutters

The busy (?) A21

something that I didn't catch, but I'm sure it wasn't a compliment.

We continue along Fair/Redlands Lane until we reach a sharp right turn. Here we are told that a field in front of us has some 'tumbled stones and ruined walls.' which should be the remnants of the old Cistercian Abbey which dates from around 1098[103]. "Can't see nothin'," says Ron, "nor can't I," I reply and it didn't matter how hard we tried neither of us could see any ruins. "Trouble is," says Ron, "we might not even be in the right place, if we're supposed ter be walkin' up Fair Lane." "I appreciate what your saying, Ron, but if you look over to the left, that must be Salehurst church." In

[102] History of Robertsbridge: Salehurst Parish & Neighbourhood, By JJ Piper- Second Edition
[103] Ibid

the distance, through a vine field, could clearly be seen a church. "But what I don't understand is that our next instruction is to turn right and the church is on the left." Our instructions clearly say '...turn right where a signed path turns off down to the Rother.' When we get to the sign it is pointing either straight ahead, or left. Not right. "Let's turn left," says Ron, "it must be a mistake in the book 'cause we need ter get ter the church an' the church is on the left." So with Ron making the decision we head down a little muddy path, heading towards Salehurst church. Or, at least, that's where we hope we're heading. "We must be 'eading' the right way," says Ron, striding it out down the path, "there's a bridge 'ere over the Rother." The water was running really fast and the usual 'don't dive' and 'risk of drowning' signs were in evidence.

Salehurst Church on the LEFT

Broken seat

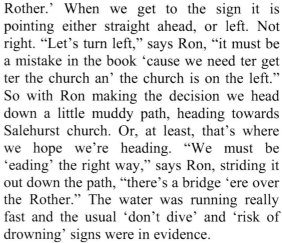

At the end of the path we bear slightly left and emerge at the church entrance. Now I have always been told not to take notice of the first impression. But I have to say; as we turned the path towards the church entrance I was not very impressed.

At the very front is a large tree with, what used to be a very pleasant place to sit. Now the seat is in a poor state of repair. The churchyard is no better. I have taken some photographs and will let them tell their own story.

Unkempt graveyard

Entering the West porch

The long nave

What I will say was that the church, inside is huge and not what you expect. To gain entry you must enter by the West porch. Once inside the porch you then pass through some glass doors into the Tower. Strangely, the font is here, and not inside the church nave or chancel. This font, known as the Salamander Font was, by tradition, presented to the church by King Richard I though no documentation exists today[104]. The font is believed to have been presented by the King as a thank-offering in gratitude to Abbot William, of the nearby Abbey, for his release from captivity in Bavaria.

It's a bit of a shame that he didn't supply the church with some dusters. The place really could do with some tender loving care. Not only was the outside a disappointment but the cobwebs inside looked as if they'd been in place for a few years as well.

The ghost in this area is that of a district nurse. She was killed at the corner of the church in 1930, on the road, when a car ran into her, throwing her from her bike and breaking her neck. She appears most often during the day, rarely being seen at night. She comes round the corner at speed, pedalling quickly, and then vanishes. "I wonder where she keeps 'er bike?" asks Ron with a chuckle.

As we stroll along Church Lane the sound of traffic is getting louder as we approach the busy A21 again. It is along this stretch of road that another ghostly cyclist is known to appear. This time it is the ghost of a young man who pedals along at dusk without lights on his bike. It was this habit which caused his death in the 1950's when he was run down by a lorry, the driver of which had not seen him. "That's made me mind up," says Ron, "there ain't no way that I'll be getting a bike. If it were dangerous in the 50's it'll be bloody suicidal now."

We cross the A21 and head along Northbridge Street, which was the original main road. It's only a short distance from here to the car and what ends a pleasant circular stroll. The scenery was good, the instructions a bit off but we made it back to the car. It was a shame about the church. All that history, but it needs looking after.

Hilaire Belloc 1870-1953

Robertsbridge from where Hilaire departed
Gave us inspiration to get started
To walk the Susses countryside
It's beautiful, the best we say with pride
Aresee©

---

[104] The Parish Church of St. Mary The Virgin, A short history and guide purchased at the church £1.50

Chapter 20 – Tillington

I know that after the letter **R** should be the letter **S**, but we did **S**altdean a lot earlier in the book so we have now jumped to the letter **T**. There are a few places that we could go to for this chapter but some we have already visited and some no longer exist, so I've tried to find a walk that is not too familiar with everyone. I was tempted by a place called **T**wo Mile Ash but I couldn't find a walk that included the place. **T**illington, is in West Sussex, and is in every walking book I own but this is the first time I've noticed it. So it only seems fair that we should visit the place. Historically the village is first mentioned in a charter dated AD 960 when the village was known as Tullingtun[105]. It is also mentioned in The Domesday Book. So it's old. It has a church with a rare shaped tower, in the shape of a coronet[106]. So it's unusual. A humble woodcutter from the area, John Sherwin, was appointed engraver to George III[107]. So it's famous with the Royals. All it needs now is for Ron and me to add it to our list of walks and the village of **T**illington will become popular. Who knows?

All Hallows Church, Tillington

Prior to making a decision I had a quick look on the Internet and found various walks in the area. One that appealed to me was 'A Parish Walk' found on the parish website[108] but it was only 1½ miles around the village which was a bit on the short side. But, as I said, a number of books have a walk around **T**illington but the one I have decided on comes from 'Village Walks in West Sussex' by Douglas Lasseter.[109] The circular walk covers 6¾ miles starting and returning to **T**illington via River and Upperton. Although it is a village walk it also includes some '…gorgeous rolling countryside.' Which probably means it's hilly.

But…… I have problems. Because of the distance we need to travel to get to **T**illington we must walk on a Saturday. So it's all arranged. But then I go down with double pneumonia. The wife said it was just a cold but, like all males, I was dying. So I had to put off the walk until the following weekend. Then my car played up. Nothing too serious, just the oil light came on, and stayed on. And before you all ask, yes I did have oil in the car. I daren't risk driving all the way to **T**illington and my mechanic couldn't see to the car until Monday. So I had to put off the walk again. Monday came and my mechanic said that he had replaced a part and that it would be ok. I arranged with Ron to head towards **T**illington the following Saturday, but guess what? The damned oil light came on again! And stayed on! Back to the garage I went. This time it was going to take over a week to repair and cost me over £600. It was time to get rid of the car. So I have traded in my beloved Daewoo

---

[105] Sussex Place Names by Judith Glover. Published by Countryside Books – Page 205

[106] Hidden Sussex by Swinfen & Arscott a BBC Radio Sussex Guide – Page 135

[107] People of Hidden Sussex by Swinfen & Arscott a BBC Radio Sussex Guide – Page 141

[108] http://www.tillington.net/parish_walk.htm visited 14/03/08

[109] Published by Countryside Books - Walk 5 – Page 24

and purchased a little Italian number. No, not a Ferrari, but a little Fiat. But guess what, I can't pick it up until Monday which means that the walk will have to be postponed, again. Then along comes Peter, our Welsh colleague, who very kindly offers to drive Ron and me to Tillington. So the walk is back on!!!!

I am very reliably informed that some of our readers actually go out and complete the same walk that Ron and I have done, fools that you are. If any one of you decides to have a go at this one – be warned. Read the instructions very, very carefully before you start. Do not think, like me, 'I've done walks before, I'll find my way around' because this has to be one of the most complicated walks we have had to try to follow. Not at the start, not at the end but right in the middle, when your miles from anywhere. It is also one of the loneliest walks we have completed. I confess to a little problem at the beginning. Let me explain.

Inside Tillington Church

The weather forecast for today is snow. It is the first week in April and the forecast is snow. How can that be? But today the sun is shining and the weather is warm and dry. It doesn't look like snow, but we are prepared for the cold. Peter is wearing a thermal vest. I have a large coat with attached hood and Ron has his Sussex smock. We all meet at The Kings Head, climb aboard Peter's people carrier and head towards Tillington which is on the A272 near Petworth. If I was driving I would have gone towards Haywards Heath, along the narrow A272, to Petworth. But Peter is a

chauffeur and says that it will be quicker to go along the A27 to Shoreham and turn right to get to Petworth. I'm just pleased to be going so I didn't argue.

Our journey takes just over the hour, so we arrive at 10 past 10. Peter is worried where to park his pride and joy and, after many um's and ar's decides to park by the village hall. From here our instructions are to walk back towards the village stores and onto the raised path leading to The Horse Guards. This was our first problem. From the outside it didn't look as if The Horse Guards was still a pub. Ron is gutted! Workmen

Windows of The Musician Angels

were all over the building, on scaffolding, repairing and painting the outside. We decided to head straight for the church and have a look round.

The outside is very impressive with its tower mounted by a Scots crown of flying arches. This is an unusual design for a Sussex church but, it is said, that the design for this tower was by the artist JWM Turner. But records show that Turner's first visit to the area wasn't until 1809 and the tower was constructed in 1807, however, some of Turners paintings of Petworth Park do show Tillington Church in the background. A painting of the church, dated 1834 by Constable is now held in the British Museum.

Unfortunately I am unable to find the origin of the name, All Hallows, dedicated to this church but what I can tell you is that it has to be one of the coldest churches we have ever been in. It is freezing and doesn't have that musty smell I have come to associate with a church. It is well-kept and is obvious, from the high sheen of the brasses, that it is well looked after and some pride is taken in its appearance only surpassed by the stain glass windows which are stunningly colourful. Just inside the door, on the left, hangs a beautiful plaque bearing the following prayer:

Thanks be to thee my Lord Jesus Christ,
For all the benefits which thou hast given me,
For all the pains and insults for which Thou hast bourne for me
O, most merciful Redeemer, Friend and Brother,
May I know thee more clearly, Love thee more dearly, and follow thee more nearly.

A very informative history of the church and its windows can be purchased separately,[110] by the door leading out of this beautiful church.

But, back outside we come up against problem number two. Where do we go from here? Our instructions do not tell us to go inside the church but to head for Cemetery Lane. We, obviously, didn't do that, so we have to go back outside the churchyard and to The Horse Guards before we can make a decision. "'ave yer seen that geezer watchin' us out 'is winder?" asks Ron. Peter had seen him but I hadn't until Ron pointed him out. "Been watchin' us fer ages 'e 'as," continues Ron. We walk past a turning, heading in what we think is the right direction but I don't understand the instructions because they tell us to find a lychgate. Surely a lychgate is attached to a churchyard. Yet the lychgate we are looking for has a coffin platform. But when we head back

Lychgate with coffin rest

towards the churchyard the gate there doesn't have a platform. "I'm confused," I admit, even looking at the map upside down doesn't give any clues. "Nosey parker's gone," Ron tells us, "No he hasn't," says Peter, "he's looking over his fence now." We walk on a little further towards The Horse Guards. "What are you looking for?"

nosey parker shouts. "We're looking for Cemetery Lane," shouts Peter. "You've just passed it," nosey shouts back. "Go back a little way and take the first turning on the right. That's Cemetery Lane." We all shout our thank you's and head back the way we came. I must say now that our instructions do not tell us to turn right into Cemetery Lane but that walking past the church '...takes you to Cemetery Lane'. With no sign to indicate that we were in Cemetery Lane this could have been anyone's mistake. Unfortunately it is not to be my last mistake of the day.

Large open field

We walk through the cemetery, which is nowhere near the church (?), and find numerous gravestones, all well-kept and maintained. Some just grab your attention, like the little boy aged 7 who died from an accident on 29th September, my birthday.

---

[110] 'A Guide to All Hallows Church' by Jeremy Godwin (revised 2006) and 'The Stained Glass Windows of All Hallows' text by George Warren, Photos by Keith Sandall - £1 each

A young flying officer who died in 1917 aged 24. A Major, from the Royal Medical Corp, with all those letters after her name. All make you feel so humble. We stay, wandering around the gravestones, for sometime before exiting at the far end, through another lychgate and onto a road.

Southdown sheep (?)

Our instructions are to cross the road and enter a large open field opposite the graveyard. No problem here except the field is no longer open but fenced off so there is only one direction we can travel in. To our right are a number of sheep. "They looks like Southdowns," offers Ron. "What's the difference to other sheep?" I ask. "These are stocky and short in the leg see," replies Ron. I will, again refrain from any connection with Peter, being Welsh, and the sheep except to say that it was about now that one of the sheep bleated, and Peter thought someone had called his name.

Also, Peter seems to be having a little problem with his equipment, photographic equipment that is. Some may remember the problems I had with a digital camera when Ron and I started our little escapades. Peter was now experiencing the same problem but with his digital movie camera. Due to writing laws I am unable to print exactly what he called this very expensive digital piece of science but every other word was a swear word and the more he swore the funnier me and Ron thought it was. But, due to this breakdown in digital equipment, this particular walk will not be available in the shops. Thank God, because it gets worse.

We are advised that at the fork in the path we should bear right. We didn't find a fork in the path. We found ourselves in a

View from the Vineyard

vineyard. Row, upon row of grape vines, as far as you could see to our right. But the views to our left were stunning.

Perhaps it was because the right fork couldn't be found that our next instructions didn't follow. All of a sudden we seemed to have gone to the next page and missed out the paragraph about hedges and stiles and pathways. We arrived at a sunken lane, with steps leading us down with another set of steps taking us back up into another field. But according to our instructions we shouldn't have reached there yet. It wasn't until I read further on that I found that we should cross the sunken lane and climb the steps opposite to enter another field.

We are now in another vineyard and can clearly see, at the other side of the field, the sign that we should be heading for. Except when we reach the sign our instructions tell us it is a three-way sign. The one in front of us is only two-way.

Entering Dene Dip Woods

Yet the road, and road junction, we should now be heading towards, is clearly at the other side of the gate.

We now cross the road and head towards the road junction. Here we turn left and now walk towards Dene Dip Woods. To our left are more of Peter's woolly friends and we manage to drag him away. The woods are getting ready to burst full of colour. Bluebells are growing either side of the path in abundance. "It'll be a real picture in just a few days," says Ron, "an' the smell will be wonderful." I have to admit that when we have completed walks in woods, where flowers grow, the scent they give off is so much nicer that home grown flowers. The stillness of the woods is eerie. Yet the sound of birds in song is such a joy to listen to. Ron tells us what song is from which bird and, as we walk along the path, everything in this world is just, I'm not sure exactly how I feel, but all is just fine, in a strange way.

As we exit the woods we arrive at an area known as Pitshill. As we head towards a gate in the distance, to our left is Pitshill House once the home of the Mitford family. Peter asked me who the Mitford family were and I had to confess that I had no idea. That was, until I got home, after the walk, and looked them up on the Internet. I am so glad that I didn't know then what I know now, because the Mitford family were somewhat controversial and can just hear what both Ron and Peter would have thought of the place had I been able to tell them the following account. The Mitford sisters, daughters to the 2nd Lord Redesdale, Nancy, Pamela, Jessica (Decca), Deborah (Debo), Diana and

Unity Mitford with Adolph Hitler

Unity once lived at Pitshill House which was the former property of Charles I and was given to Sir Thomas Herbert on the eve of the King's execution for high treason. I will include just some brief details of these sisters[111]:

Nancy b.1904 – d.1973 became a well-known and established novelist

Pamela b.1907 married Derek Jackson, founder of The News of The World newspaper in 1936.

Diana b.1910 and, in her youth, is said to have been a timeless beauty. She married Bryan Guinness, heir to the Guinness fortune. But in 1932 she met and fell in love with Oswald Mosely the founder of the British Union of Fascists. She left Bryan and became Oswald's mistress. She died in 2003

Unity b.1911. She became obsessed with Adolph Hitler, inviting him to the family home prior to World War II. It is rumoured that she and Adolph may have married. But on the day war was declared she tried to commit suicide by shooting herself. Her attempt failed. However her subsequent brain damage meant she had to be nursed, until her death in 1948.[112]

Jessica b.1917 – d.1996, also known as Decca, The Muckraker, was a known communist. She married Esmond Romilly, her 2nd cousin, in Spain, against everyone's wishes. She soon became a widow and decided to settle in America where she was arrested for being an enemy of the State because of her involvement with the communist party

---

[111] http://upbondageupyours.blogspot.com/2006/06/mitford-legacy.html visited 06/04/2008
[112] Picture obtained via Google search engine and www.thesun.co.uk visited 06/04/2008

Deborah b.1920, also known as Debo, is the Duchess of Devonshire. Her life differed greatly from her sisters. She was allowed to attend school prior to marrying Andrew the Marquess of Hartingdon in 1941.

The current owner of Pitshill House is the Honourable Charles Pearson. In 2006 it is recorded in The Independent newspaper[113] that Charles Pearson needed to redirect a public footpath away from the back door of his new home. Unfortunately this brought outcry from various Rambling Associations and the case has now gone to court. Mr Pearson is quoted in the newspaper as saying '...The issue is really

The current, deserted, Pitshill House

about public safety, not privacy.' Mr Pearson, who owns 53,000 acres of Aberdeenshire and Kincardinshire in the shape of the Dunecht estate and has an inherited fortune estimated at £70m, claims that his commitment to restore the property means that the footpath could be dangerous for pedestrians who are brought into contact with works traffic. Unable to carry out the work until the legal issues are settled, he has kept the property empty since he bought it. And that is how we find it today.

History lesson over. Back to the walk, which continues past Pitshill House and down a rhododendron-lined lane. It is somewhere here that things go really wrong. The instructions are very confusing. It tells us to look for a pathway; all we can find are bridleways. We are instructed to turn left at a three-way sign on our right or was

that a two-way sign on our left, that we have to turn right, or was it to the left. I am so confused. A slight slip on the wet path and my finger moves up to the top of the page and I now am hopelessly muddled. I have never seen so many footpath and bridleway signs leading off into so many different directions. But we keep walking. Now nothing makes sense. We should see a building in the valley to our right, but a farm building is on the left. And it's not in a valley. We should arrive at a three-way footpath sign, but the next sign is a two-way bridle path. But we keep walking. We eventually arrive at a four-way sign with a sign for Field Cottage. "It must be this way," insists Peter, starting to take control because, frankly, I was 'loosing it' and all the time Ron is giggling. It became more and more annoying the more Ron giggled, to a point where I was about to

A path to where?

give up and hand him the book and tell him to find our bloody way out. Of course we are now heading in the wrong direction. We should see a pond on our right. There is no pond. We should see a farm on our right. There is no farm and as we approach Field Cottage, the building is on our left. Ron is still giggling, I'm getting angrier. We

[113] http://www.independent.co.uk/news/uk/crime/mitford-home-to-make-legal-history-in-battle-with-ramblers-424117.html visited 06/04/2008

decide to go back to the last turning and head in another direction. We eventually come to a large building. "This is Rounadbouts Farm," says Ron, between giggles. "And how the hell do you know that?" I ask. "'Cause it says so on that, there wall," comes the reply. In large letters is the name of the farm proudly displayed on the wall in front of us? "This can't be right," I whine, "we shouldn't get to this farm until we've visited River. It should be on our right-hand side on the way back. We must have missed a left turn, miles back which would put us the other side of the farm building." I decide that the only thing we can do from here, looking at our map, is to complete this part of the walk in reverse. All we have to do is follow the map, backwards, and we should end up in the correct place. I could see that both Ron and Peter were not convinced. And they were right. Again it all went horribly wrong.

We emerge from the track at what I thought was Janes Lane. But I could be wrong. We walked along the road for sometime, ignoring all the signs for footpaths and bridleways. The houses were very pretty, some very large and pretty. Whatever possessed me to turn right at the end of this lane I have no idea. The map said turn right, but if you remember, we are doing this part of the walk in the opposite direction, so that meant we should have turned left. Doesn't it? So why in hell did we turn right? It is obvious that we are now walking away from the hamlet of River. So why did we keep walking? Both Peter and Ron have had enough. I can tell. Subtle hints, like they've stopped talking to me, and, when we get to a large gate and can see the hamlet of River in the far distance to our right, they don't wait

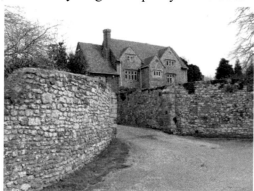

River House, Tillington

for me to advise them, and they just turn round and head back up the road. I am so confused now that I have absolutely no idea in which direction we should be heading until.......

Poser Ron at the pond

We pass a house called River House and straight away I know exactly where we are and in which direction we should go. Our instructions mention this house and it should be, and actually is, on our right-hand side. We must now be on course again, but both Ron and Peter still aren't convinced. Again ignoring footpath signs and Peter saying, "are you sure we don't go down this path or that path," we arrive at the entrance to Great Yew Cottage. "We turn right here," I tell them, "and then we come to a sign, after 400 yards, that will lead us into the woods." I'm really chuffed that we are back on track but Ron and Peter still aren't sure until we actually come to the sign and a path into the woodland.

I am worried about our next instruction, which I will now quote from the book, '…very shortly you will come to a rarity, a five-way sign. To ensure that you make no mistake have the waysign on your left-hand side, and walk ahead, into the right-hand track.' I'm sure you have guessed what happened. The waysign only had directions four-ways, not five and there were two paths, neither could be described as tracks, leading to the right and no prizes for guessing, we took the wrong one. But this time it was Peter who suggested the wrong right turn. That made my day. Not for the first time we turned back and found the correct path which lead us back to Roundabouts Farm. We, again, walked past the turning to Field Cottage and arrived at the pond on our right-hand side. I am now brimming with confidence. Nothing can stop me now.

As instructed we pass the entrance to Bucks Cottage and turn right onto Westland's Copse Lane before turning right again into Upperton Common. We are now on The Serpents Trail and heading uphill towards the hamlet of Upperton. And it really is uphill. Not too bad at the start but after about ¾ of a mile it gets really steep. So much so that I have to stop and take a breather. Ron and Peter must still be a bit upset about my earlier directions because they are up the hill long before me and have to wait at the top.

Once on the road at the top of this steep climb we now head downhill into the hamlet of Upperton. Again the houses here are stone built and the feeling of oldie worlde is remarkable. Unfortunately the scene is spoilt by the motor car, but none the less it was a picturesque place.

Just round the corner in the right-hand picture we come to Upperton cricket pitch and pavilion. "How many runs did you score here, then Ron?" I ask. "Never played 'ere," he says, "but, by God, 'tis a wonderful place ter 'ave a cricket pitch. Only one thing that is a disappointment, there ain't a pub in sight."

Downhill through Upperton

Would you believe it? After all the places we've been to, in Sussex, we have actually found a cricket pitch that Ron hasn't either mown the grass or played a game on. "But I'll tell yer one thing, that man on that there tractor, mowin' the grass, 'as the best job in the world."

After just a short walk down the hill we are soon back at the car. Peter, always ready to capture a moment on camera, heads towards some horses in a field. One horse in particular heads in his direction, putting his head over the gate for a quick rub. "There's a nice gee-gee," says Peter, "would you like me to take a picture of you?" he asks the very nice, very big, brown gee-gee. But, unfortunately, the nice big brown gee-gee tries to take a chunk out of Peter's nice jacket. Again I am unable to print what Peter now thought of the nice big gee-gee.

Mowing the crease

We thought about stopping at The Horse Guards before heading home but we still couldn't make up our minds if it was open or not so we all decided to head for another pub known by Peter, The White Hart at a place called Stopham with its beautiful bridge built in 1423 over the River Arun[114] Perhaps this could be the subject of another walk, who knows. But today, although frustrating at times, was, to quote Ron, "another bit o'Sussex we ain't seen before"

Finally, at the start of the chapter, I advised you that the forecast was snow. We were lucky during the walk and the weather stayed fine. But, the following day as I complete writing this chapter, it has just stopped snowing and we now have over 2 inches of the white stuff.

The Bridge over The Arun

Tillington, the walk with four 5-way posts
This is one walk we got lost the most
How we got back me and Pete will never know
"There, told you so," I can still hear him crow.
                                                    Aresee©

---

[114] http://en.wikipedia.org/wiki/Stopham visited 06/04/2008

Chapter 21- Upper Horsebridge

I am tempted to cheat with the letter <u>U</u>, but something tells me not to, because it wouldn't be right. I have struggled, over the past few days, to find somewhere to go in Sussex beginning with the letter <u>U</u>. From the books I have, I've looked at <u>U</u>pper Dicker and <u>U</u>pper Beeding but we have been to both places before and written about these walks. I have found, again, <u>U</u>pperton but we did that in our last walk with Tillington and the hamlet of River. There is, of course, <u>U</u>dimore and <u>U</u>pwaltham but I can't find a walk around either of these places. The one place I can find a walk around is <u>U</u>pper Bewbush but everything I can find on the Internet, and my supply of books, only gives me information on Bewbush and not <u>U</u>pper Bewbush so, as my wife, Emelia, says, 'technically, that's cheating'. Then my wife said, "What about <u>U</u>pper Horsebridge, after all, we only live round the corner." I knew there had to be a reason

for me marrying Emelia all those years ago. Of course it wasn't for her intellectual wit or her fantastic body, although that helped considerably, and for that matter, I didn't marry her for her business acumen. But it was her simple logic. She can see things so plainly. Why the hell didn't I think of <u>U</u>pper Horsebridge? It is so obvious and it is only just round the corner. But can I find a walk which will serve our purpose? A quick check on the Internet gives me a walk from <u>U</u>pper Horsebridge, along the Cuckoo Trail, out across the fields to Hellingly, back to <u>U</u>pper Horsebridge

Just one part of Horsebridge

and a well-earned pint at the 'other' King's Head. It couldn't be better. I can't wait to let Ron know and I think we might have some company on this walk.

Since starting our country walks, various friends have asked if they could join us as we find our way, or lose our way, around the Sussex countryside. Normally we have no hesitation in accommodating anyone who wishes to join us, but we now have only a few walks left, the weather is turning brighter, and lots of people have asked to join us. With only six walks left we may have to disappoint some of them. If we have let anyone down we apologise but we must end this book at the letter <u>Z</u>.

Like I say, today is to be a walk starting from, and finishing at, <u>U</u>pper Horsebridge. Horsebridge is a strange little hamlet. There is an <u>U</u>pper Horsebridge, a Lower Horsebridge and just plain ol' Horsebridge and they are all within a mile of each other. Being on one of the old 'London Royal Mail routes' the milestone marker, found

Old distance marker

in <u>U</u>pper Horsebridge, tells us that we are 54 miles from London. Did you know that there is a society which dedicates itself to the identification, record and research of these markers, known as 'The Milestone Society'[115] (?) unfortunately there doesn't seem to be anything on Milestones in Sussex on this particular website but, who

---

[115] http://www.milestone-society.co.uk/ visited 10/04/08

knows, someone, somewhere is bound to know something about these things and, hopefully, will be in touch. Anyway, back to our walk. Horsebridge is one of the few places we have found with two pubs, The King's Head and The White Hart, and no church. It's Ron's idea of heaven.

You wouldn't believe the difference in the weather. Only three days ago parts of Sussex were cut off due to heavy snowfalls, today it is sunny, bright and hardly a cloud in the sky, as I head towards our meeting point. I now have a new car, a lot smaller than my other car. Ron has suggested that I meet him and our companions for the walk, Pip, Helen and her dog 'Laika', at the car park at Horsebridge Recreation Ground. His reason for meeting me at the car park and not letting me pick him up as usual is, I believe, something to do with the size of my car and that he would rather be with Pip and Helen, two of his very favourite females. His excuse to me was that he was saving me money on petrol by not having me go backwards and forwards across Hailsham.

'Harvesters' by Jennifer Ulrich

The walk past the 'other' Kings Head to the part of the Cuckoo Trail that we need to reach takes us along the busy main road. Opposite the junction of London Road is what used to be, many years ago, a flour mill? I believe it was owned by MacDougall's at sometime but it has been derelict and a bit of an eyesore for many years now and has been vandalised over the years by some of our '…less edjercated morons…' to quote Ron. We also believe that some building plans have been sent to the local council which will mean that this area possibly as far as, and including, the now disused Hellingly Hospital grounds, is to be developed into low-cost housing, so the area we are now looking at will soon be full of houses. The one thing that worries me, personally, is that in heavy rain the area is liable to flood.

One of the tree 'carvings'

In our previous book we have walked along the Cuckoo Trail many times, but just for the next few hundred yards this part of the walk is new to us all, apart from Pip who uses the Trail to exercise her horse. But, and I know I am repeating myself when I say, if you have never walked along this Trail, get up, get out and give it a go. Even if you are wheelchair bound you can get along this Trail, it is better than good. This small section of the Cuckoo Trail, from London Road and past the old Hellingly Railway Station is typical of the other parts of the Trail that Ron and I have walked. The people are friendly and the paths are kept clean. Obviously we come up against some litter but it isn't 'in your face' or that unsightly that you feel you should complain to someone. I mentioned to a work colleague that we were walking along the Trail and he was surprised as he had heard that it was full of hooligans using

Ron with 'company'

motorbikes, scaring the locals and this is so far from the truth. All along our walk, past Hellingly Railway Station we met, and chatted to, a number of fellow walkers, some with dogs (one in particular who told us that the Harvesters carving, presented to the Harvest Forestry in 2002, is known as the 'piddle post' (?)) and cyclists both male and female, young and old. Not one hooligan did we see until, that is, we met Rodney, in his invalid buggy. No, but seriously, the Council have done a great job keeping the Trail open and clean. Even to the point of putting little signs up for younger children to read about foxes, mice, rabbits and badgers. Some enterprising person with a chainsaw, rather than leave tree stumps at the side of the path, has carved mushrooms and flowers in the remains. It all makes for a very pleasant and leisurely walk. I am just pleased with my surroundings and the stillness of everything. Although people are about you are on your own, it's difficult to explain but give it a try. I think you will enjoy it. Ron certainly did, although I'm not sure if it was the countryside or the fact that Pip and Helen were in our company.

Ron's only view of Pip

For those unaware, let me introduce our companions. Helen is the Landlady of our favourite Inn in Hailsham, The King's Head. Helen, and her husband, Darren, are thinking of changing the name of the pub. She did let slip what it might be but it's not up to me, in these pages, to disclose it, but I am in favour of the new name and it would, of course, not be confused with the 'other' 'King's Head' at Upper Horsebridge. Laika is owned by Darren and Helen and is named after the first dog to be sent into space. A complete explanation is given in 'Left or Right Ron'[116] so I will not go into the story again. Pip, according to Ron, is Piiiiiiiip. Just the mention of her name sends him into spasm. "If I were 20 years younger, an she played 'er cards right,

she could 'ave me" is just one of Ron's many dreams about Pip. But for now Ron is just happy to be walking behind Pip, occasionally tripping over his tongue, in true Ron fashion.

We pass under one of the old railway bridges, called Shawpits Bridge, and continue along the Cuckoo Trail for another 300 yards until we arrive at a point where a path crosses it. Here we turn left, climb the bank (sorry Helen) and enter a large field. Our instructions tell us to keep the hedge to our right as we cross the field. I have,

Laika, eating rabbit poo

throughout the walk, attempted to catch a photograph of Laika but it is uncanny that every time I point a camera at her she turns her back on me. Helen tells us that Laika has become a little deaf and the best way to catch her attention is to clap your hands.

---

[116]Left or Right Ron? Published by LR Publishers - Walk 46 – Page 203/4

This, Helen does, Laika takes no notice. She tries again, but no response, so we all have a go. Picture the scene, four people and a dog, in the middle of a field, the people are applauding something, and the dog's taking no notice. But I did, eventually, get my picture. Although Laika didn't stop to pose but carried on heading back and forth, looking down rabbit holes and, would you believe, eating rabbit poo (no, I didn't believe it either, until I actually saw her do it).

Two fields later and we have approached a wooden bridge, which I alone cross, opening both gates and ensuring that the gates are closed behind me in true 'country code' fashion. The others, including Laika, walked through the large open gate to the left of the bridge. The strange thing we found hanging on the gate was a sign, hand painted in white that read: 'PLEASE KEEP ALL DOGS ON A LEAD – SHEEP VERY HEAVEY WITH LAMB'. Can you spot the mistake? (I hope my proof-reader can!!)

We now approach some farm buildings. Why is it that if you see a building with a hole in the wall you have to go and poke your nose in to find out what's inside. That's exactly what Pip did only to be surprised by a young calf who was probably more scared than she was. We pass through a couple of gates and reach a covered walkway leading out onto Mill Lane, Hellingly. Here we turn right and walk along the road to Hellingly Parish Church. I have read, but am unable to find anything more, that a vicar of Hellingly, John Miller, was burnt at the stake in the year 1557. Whatever could a vicar do to warrant being burnt at the stake? Unless, of course, it was something to do with witchcraft? But, like I say, I can't find out any more.

Parents, protecting their young

The church is a beautiful structure, set on what once was a raised circle of land. I say once was because it has now, over the years, grown into a raised oval. It is, in fact, the only church in Sussex built on an undamaged ciric. A ciric is described, in our instructions, as '…a circular Celtic burial ground, raised to keep the dead dry…'. Also raised on the ciric are some wonderfully old houses which have to be seen to be believed. A photograph opportunity was to be had, with Ron dressed in his Sussex smock but when I'd turned round he had disappeared so the picture of the houses doesn't include Ron. The inside of the church was wonderful; it had the smell, the cold and the beauty. The only thing lacking was some information sheets letting us know about the place. But it was a pleasure to walk round and, at least, it was open.

Houses built on the ciric

From the other side of the church we head along the road towards the school. Hellingly School is one of the most popular schools in the Hailsham area and is a much sought after place for young children to attend. We turn left just after the school and head back towards **U**pper Horsebridge and the car, but before we get there we pass a cemetery. Now I have seen this cemetery many, many times before but never stopped to have a look. Ron, as we approach the cemetery, casually says, "me gran an' granddad are buried in there" and that simply means that we must stop and have a look round.

For me cemeteries are places of solitude and peace. I can wander around, at my own pace, and reflect on life and, to a certain extent, death. I marvel at some of the headstones. I read, and am touched by, some of the sentiments written about departed loved ones. I feel cheated if I find a grave with no stone or indication of who lies there. Ron tends to be a little different. He doesn't go out of his way to find people he once knew, or played cricket with, but he always, and I mean always, manages to recognise a name displayed on a stone. We have been to lots of cemeteries and the same thing happens... 'I never knew 'ee'd passed on..' or 'I used ter go ter school with im'... are all part of Ron's time in a cemetery. This one was no different. But what I also like to do is find the unusual headstone or a stone that tells a story. I have not written about our findings before but, from this cemetery, I feel the time is right to explain what I found.

I was surprised at how many young people are buried in the cemetery. Not children that died many years ago but of more recent times. The advances made with the materials now used for this type of remembrance will, hopefully, mean that the stones will be read for years to come, as opposed to the stones of the 17 and 18 hundreds whose resistance to weather is much less than desired. Within the cemetery is a black headstone for a young lad of 15 years of age, which has the most beautiful three verse poem on the reverse of the stone. When I first read it, I cried. There is another stone remembering a young man who played cricket. I also found the stone which remembered a mother and son who drowned on Christmas Eve 1963. They were aboard the liner Lakonia, which was owned by the Greek Line[117]. After sailing out of Southampton on a cruise, the liner caught fire. The ship was abandoned with the loss of 128 lives. She later capsized and sunk.

Ron remembered a story about a pilot who crashed and was killed in a field near the cemetery. We found the memorial to the flying officer from II (A.C.) Squadron, R.A.F. He crashed his Mustang AG611 on 11th November 1943. I have since found that the II (A.C.) Squadron of the Royal Air Force is the oldest fixed wing squadron in the world[118]. The squadron's basic role is to protect the Army and in 1943 the planes were used for reconnaissance work over France during the Second World War.

Seen on the walk back to the car, a Moorhen sitting on her nest

Unfortunately we were unable to find Ron's grandparents. Ron has an idea of the area that they are in but the grave is unmarked. He will ask for a marker to be placed so that we can come back and pay our respects.

In a way this was a sad end to a very nice walk. We will always enjoy the Cuckoo Trail as being open, pleasant, clean and friendly. Helen, with Laika, and Pip are always pleasant company so all in all we passed a comfortable, warm afternoon looking around a part of Sussex that, although very close to home, still held some surprises.

---

[117] www.simplonpc.co.uk/GreekLinePCs.html - visited 11/04/2008
[118] www.raf.mod.uk/structure/2squadron.cfm - visited 11/04/2008

Chapter 22 – Vines Cross

Never believe everything you read. How many times have you heard that saying? Yet I have done exactly that and then passed incorrect (?) information on to you in the last chapter, <u>U</u>pper Horsebridge. In that chapter I wrote about a vicar, from Hellingly, who was burnt at the stake. Whilst writing about him I was a little worried that I couldn't find anything else about the vicar, the Reverend John Miller.[119] Further checks were made since completing that walk and I have now discovered that his name may have been Thomas Mills.[120] No wonder I couldn't find anything, I was looking at the wrong name. Now that my interest was piqued I decided to look into the story of the Sussex Martyrs who were condemned for their religious beliefs. And, again, I have found conflicting information. I now have three names for the vicar at

The Brewers Arms

Hellingly; John Miller, Thomas Mills and John Mills[121]. I also have two dates for the burnings at Lewes, the 20th June 1557[122] and the 22nd June 1557[123]. Some sources say that a total of 36[124] people from Sussex suffered death by fire and another says that there were 33[125]. So take your choice, because I have no idea. All I can say, with some certainty is that a gentleman by the name of Richard Woodman, from Warbleton, accompanied John Miller or Thomas Mills or John Mills, to the stake on whatever day it was.

I am also reliably informed that <u>V</u>ines Cross, many years ago, were the Tug-o-War world champions. But do you think I can find anything about it? No. I can't find a year, a name, or a team sheet on the Internet. Is there a book out there, somewhere, that confirms this rumour? So, can we believe it? Is anything true? Am I really writing this or………….

Seriously one of the very few things that I have found out about <u>V</u>ines Cross is that it is a small village and, it is believed, is named after John Vyne, 'The Vintner' from Hellingly, who moved to the area in c1595.[126] The village once supported a school, bakers, and a village grocer but now has only a garage and a public house. There is a part-time Post Office which operates on Tuesdays and Thursdays from within Vines Cross Engineers.

Meet Oliver

[119] From 'Hidden Sussex', by W Swinfen and D Arscott a BBC Radio Sussex publication Page 76.
[120] From 'Hailsham and its Environs' by Charles Robertson, published by Phillimore- page 60/61
[121] www.villagenet.co.uk visited 14/04/2008
[122] From 'Hailsham and its Environs' by Charles Robertson, published by Phillimore- page 60/61
[123] www.orange-papers.tk.protmar.htm visited 14/04/2008
[124] Ibid
[125] From 'Hailsham and its Environs' by Charles Robertson, published by Phillimore- page 61
[126] www.horam.com/toedit/vinescross_edits.htm visited 19/04/2008

Our walk today is from The Argus and is written by Ben Perkins[127]. It is a circular stroll of 6 miles starting at the 'Brewers Arms' in <u>V</u>ines Cross, across fields and through woodland to Rushlake Green, and the 'Horse and Groom', continuing across some stunning open countryside to Warbleton and the 'Warbill-in-tun', and eventually back to <u>V</u>ines Cross. I say eventually because today we have a new walking partner, Sophie. I would describe Sophie as a very social drinker in as much that all the time you have a glass in your hand; Sophie will have a glass in hers. The fact that we have three pubs on this walk and I am going to encourage (?) them to pass a couple does worry me. Hence the start time of 9 a.m. I am hoping that the 'Brewers' and 'Horse and Groom' won't be open but the Warbill-in-tun will, and by the time we reach the Brewers again we will be too knackered for a drink and just want to get home. Well, that's my plan.

The walk is described by The Argus and Ben Perkins as '....A gently undulating walk along fields and woodland paths, mostly well signed...'[128] and we all know what that means don't we? Lots of hills, lots of mud and a good opportunity for us to get lost! But we will see.

The morning is cold, the forecast is rain but when I collect both Ron and Sophie from the car park by the King's Head the rain looks a few miles away. We have another walker with us today, Oliver, who belongs to Sophie. I am ashamed to say that I asked Sophie many times during our walk what breed of dog Oliver was. And I can only remember him being 3 parts Jack Russell. The other part sounded foreign. I'm sure Sophie will spell it out to me later. He is called Oliver because he can 'pick a pocket or two' especially if you leave your jacket or coat over a chair back in the King's Head.

Our drive to the starting point is reasonably short; <u>V</u>ines Cross is on the B2096 about a mile east of Heathfield so it only takes us a few minutes to get to Foords Lane and park the car. As I park the car Ron says "Cor, I'll be blowed, that's Basky Maskell." A man is in front of us doing a bit of weeding. Ron's out of the car in a

flash and heading in the man's direction. At first he looks terrified until he obviously recognises Ron and they greet each other like long lost brothers. While this is happening Sophie and I get changed into some sensible walking shoes. Actually I've gone a bit girlie and decided to wear wellies. Not just ordinary black wellies, these are green. (Sorry Ron) Once Basky(?) and Ron had said there farewells I asked Ron why he was called Basky. "No idea," says Ron, "they were all called Basky Maskell." "What do you mean 'all'?" I ask, "There were about five or six boys in the family an' a couple o'girls. But all

Sheep with lamb

the boys were called Basky. Never knew why, t'was just 'ow it was, t'is all." I didn't like to ask anything else. It sounded as if it was going to get complicated.

The first part of my plan worked a treat. As we walk along Nettlesworth Lane, in the Heathfield direction the 'Brewers Arms' isn't open so passing it wasn't a problem, although Ron kept looking back just to convince himself that the door was locked. Our instructions tell us to turn right at Boring House Farm and follow the concrete

[127] www.theargus.co.uk visited 04/04/2008
[128] Ibid

drive until it veers right. Here we need to bear right. Would you believe we got the first instruction wrong? We bore (?) right too soon, climbed a steep hill, and arrived at a stile, our instructions said we should pass a house, we saw no house, we should be at a gate and we were at a stile. Ron, not for the first time, can't believe it, "Fer Gods sake we ain't gone more'n a 'undred yards an' 'e's got us lost." It wasn't until we looked up and saw, in the distance a house with a gate on the right-hand side that I realised my mistake, so it was back to the drive and head towards the gate.

I'd noticed that all the sheep and lambs in the next field were numbered. Before I could ask Ron why he said "Must 'ave pretty clever rams in these parts," as we pass through the gate, into the field, "not only do they 'ave their wicked way with the sheep, they also keep tally by writin' the number on the ol' girls back!" What can you say?

Looking for wildlife in the bracken

Sophie lifts a leg

In our last chapter I spoke of Laika eating rabbit poo. When Oliver was eventually let off the lead he started running about doing the same thing, not with rabbits but with sheep poo. Are all dogs inclined to do this sort of thing? In a walk we completed with my son's Labradors I can't remember them doing it. Is it a fad that dogs are currently going through? Unfortunately it reminded Ron of a joke. "Two men lost in a desert. They're starvin' an' one ov'em says 'e'll go an' search fer some grub. When 'e comes back, two 'ours later, 'e says to 'is mate 'I got some good news an' some bad news.' An' 'is mate croaks 'give us the bad news first.' The other one says 'the bad news is I can only find one camel' an' 'is mate croaks 'what's the good news?', 'the good news is there's bucket loads ov it.'" We have to stop for a few minutes whilst Ron manages to calm down from his fit of the giggles.

One of the things that was stated earlier was that the walk was '...mostly well signed.'[129] We must say that although we haven't travelled too far we have noticed many signs, not just the usual public footpath signs but also signs placed, presumably, by the owner of the land. Credit must be given in the placing of the signs; they are clear, bright and easily seen. There really is no excuse to wander into private land. All the while we are walking Oliver is running about off the lead. But all the time he is loose we are constantly on the look out for fields with sheep or signs telling us to keep dogs on leads. Oliver is very good. He responds immediately to Sophie's requests to ''stay' when she needs to put on his lead. But even after this short walk his legs must be tired yet he doesn't stop.

We cross a stile and a footbridge and now follow the hedge for two more fields, passing under some electricity pylons. Our instructions now tell us to walk '...obliquely back under the power lines to find a stile beside a gate...'[130] Thankfully Sophie was better educated that both Ron and I, so we headed in the direction than

[129] Ibid
[130] Ibid

Sophie indicated and assumed we were walking 'obliquely'. We arrive at Furnace Lane and turn left.

After a short distance we turned right into a rough access drive which, just beyond a cottage, became a grass track. Whilst walking up the track towards the cottage we are passed by a Royal Mail vehicle, obviously out on delivery. For those of you who are not aware I used to be a Manager for Royal Mail. Since I left, about 4 years ago, I have, as I am sure most of you have, seen a steady decline in the presentation of the delivery staff employed by Royal Mail. Sometimes you would never know that the long haired hippie figure walking up your path, wearing jeans, tee-shirt and white trainers was, in fact, a postie. I must say that today my confidence has been restored. The lady delivering the mail to the cottage was not only very smartly dressed in full uniform, she locked the van when she went into the cottage to deliver the mail and she gave us a cheery greeting and wave as she very carefully manoeuvred her red van to ensure that we all, including Oliver, were clear of the van whilst she reversed and pulled away. I believe the van serial number was 257. If you are the lady post person reading this, thank you for restoring my faith.

Cascading water

We now walk, for some distance along paths taking us between Furnace Wood, on our left, and Wet Wood on our right before arriving at a path, turning sharp right, and heading for some bracken. Something catches Sophie's eye. Ron thought it might have been a vole, but by the time we got to the area where Sophie thought it was, it had, not surprisingly, gone.

Pheasant posing for the camera

Some will be aware of Ron's need to make a wish as he walks over bridges which span water. To-day he will part with a fair bit of cash and make a few wishes. As we leave the bracken and head down through a wood I can hear running water. It's not long before we come to the source of the sound, a beautiful area, with water cascading over stones. The water, as it flows under the bridge, looks a strange orange colour because of the iron that used to be mined in this area. But the whole scene is idyllic. Even Sophie and Oliver just stood on the bridge and took in the scene. If we see nothing else, throughout the walk, just to see this little stream would be enough for me. But we have to get on. We still haven't reached Rushlake Green and the 'Horse and Groom' yet. The pub must be open by now and I'll have to think of a way to steer both Ron and Sophie away so that we can have a drink at Warbleton.

We climb the small hill and come out at Furnace Lane again. Here we bear slightly left and then turn right and walk along the road until we reach a bridleway. Here we turn left and follow the clear path across the middle of a field and head towards a woodland which juts out towards us. It was along this field path that we came across a pheasant that appeared to be a bit cavalier. Normally you can't get too close to them before they give a cry and fly off but this one seemed to pose for the camera. That is, until Oliver spotted him and gave chase. Fortunately for the pheasant poor little Oliver's legs wouldn't go fast enough to catch the bird but as the pheasant took off Oliver jumped to catch it with Sophie shouting at him to 'leave'. But he had other ideas. He stood at the bottom of the tree looking at the resting bird until we caught him up.

We now drop downhill, keeping the woodland on our left. You way have realised that we have now completed a 'u' turn and, as we head to the bottom of the hill, we can all hear the sound of running water. Ron is already rummaging in his pockets to

try and find some copper to throw into the water, "I've only got silver," he says, "'as anyone got some change? This walk is takin' me beer money." But luckily the water we can hear is not crossed by a bridge so Ron puts his money back in his pocket. I have noticed that Oliver didn't appear bothered with anything on the walk that was bigger than him. Even dogs that sounded big, barking in the distance didn't seem to bother him. In fact nothing seemed to daunt him until we met water, then he wasn't so sure of himself. When Sophie threw a stick into the water and told Oliver to fetch he

Oliver, not so brave where water is involved

looked at her as if to say 'your 'avin a laugh' and froze on the spot. If he could feel the bottom of the water under his feet he was ok but no way was he getting in too deep.

From the pond we climb, gradually, until we reach a road. Opposite us, the path continues across three fields and this time we do cross a stream, where Ron makes his wish and deposits some cash. Across a stile we now appear to be in someone's back

garden but the signs clearly tell us that it is, in fact, a public footpath. At the end of the path we find ourselves opposite the large green which gives Rushlake Green its name.

Many years ago my grandparents lived at Rushlake Green. My earliest memory of them was when they lived at Pleydells Cottages. I believe it was number 3 but I could be wrong. Those were the days when the bucket used to be emptied daily from an outside toilet and candles were used. (Yes I can actually remember those days!!) I can also remember the bakers and the smell of

The Horse & Groom

fresh bread. Sometimes my mum used to give me some money and I was allowed to walk down to the shops and buy sweets at Daw's Stores, which is the only shop now in the village, all the others have long gone. My mum used to go to the only school in 'The Green'. I can recall the time when the old school was demolished and the block of flats were built in its place. Osbourne House, as the new flats were called, was the last home of my grandparents before they died.

Rushlake Green has a lot of fond memories for me. I met and 'got rid of' my first love in this village. I played in the local brass band and performed solo on the stage at the Dunn Village Hall during the Christmas Concerts. An inscription from 1763 was recently discovered on a pane of glass at Pleydells

Abraham Holman is my name,
and England is my nation
Rushlake was my Dwelling Place,
but not long Habitation[131]:

My first question, after reading this, was did they have glass in 1763 and would a humble villager be able to read and write? And I'm amazed to find out that glass was being used in years B.C... Although Abbot Benedict, in A.D.674, caused the windows of the monastery at Durham, to be glazed by foreign artists[132] it was many years before using glass for windows became common practice in Britain.

Rushlake Green today

Whilst I am disclosing all this important historical information to my fellow walkers we have managed to complete part two of my plan. Just a brief mention from Ron about how slow the service was at the Horse & Groom during our last visit to the village and we are past the place and now heading for the telephone kiosk, where we turn right and head along the public footpath.

We pass through a 'kissing gate' which has been dedicated to Ian Price who died close to the spot whilst repairing the power lines after the hurricane in October 1987. We now walk along the path for some time passing through a wood and, inevitably, more water. Ron performs his wishing act again and we then climb the hill to reach the lane opposite Kingsley Hill Farm. Here we turn right and, hopefully, fulfil part three of my plan, a short stop at the Warbill-in-tun. It was supposed to be a short stop but the warm greeting we received from everyone just made us stay a little longer than expected. Bryan, the landlord, vaguely remembered us from our last visit which was amazing in itself because it was nearly two years ago. Perhaps he was just being polite. Let's be honest, once you've

The very friendly Warbill-in-Tun

met Ron, most people don't forget him. Unfortunately, since our last visit, Bryan has lost his wife, Val, and there is a touching tribute to her in the bar area. All the staff, Vivienne the chef and Laura, Katharine and Lauren made us feel really welcome and all stopped what they were doing to have a chat with us. Bryan told us about the 'Lavender Lady', a friendly ghost who appears sometimes, but more often than not,

---

[131] People of Hidden Sussex by Swinfen & Arscott – A BBC Radio Sussex Guide – Page 124
[132] The New Gresham Encyclopedia (sic) Vol. V Fel-Gri – Page 348

just produces a fantastic smell of the flower. After hearing Ron's theory about 'it don't rain in Sussex on a Wednesday' Bryan immediately came back with, 'so it don't, but did you know that snow always arrives in Sussex on a Thursday?'

The Sussex Martyr Memorial

Whilst at Warbleton, I had to visit the church. Again, in my youth, I have been to this church many, many times. Both of my grandparents, from Rushlake Green, are buried in the churchyard, unfortunately the grave is unmarked, but I know where they are located. Also both of my children, Michelle and Anthony were christened at the church, one of the wishes of my grandfather Tom Churcher. Both Ron and Sophie were getting involved with liquid so I decided to leave them to it and wander over to the church. Ron insisted that Sophie should accompany me but Sophie thought I might like to be on my own. But once Ron has made his mind up nothing will change it so, bless her, Sophie came along with me but left me to enter the church on my own. Thank you Sophie. I'm sure, from my writings, you will understand that I am not particularly religious. But......... People react differently to the loss of a loved one. As you get older losing someone becomes a fact of life. I have lost both my sisters and both of my parents. Although I, obviously, feel grief I also feel great anger. Sophie has recently lost someone very, very close to her, her partner, Roy. As we walked back from the church I spoke to Sophie about her loss and, to my surprise, she also spoke of the angry feelings that she has experienced. Perhaps I'm not so 'strange' after all. So, again Sophie, thank you for our little chat.

On our return to the pub we managed, eventually, to drag Ron away from his liquid refreshment. It has now started to rain. Not heavy, but it was going to get us wet.

We walked back through the churchyard and manage to find, opposite the church tower and by the gap in the wall, the memorial to Richard Woodman,

Nature calls

mentioned at the start of the chapter which gave us the date of 22nd June 1557. From the card we were given at the Warbill-in-Tun there is a little piece written about Richard Woodman which could explain what he did that was so wrong, in 1557. It says;

RICHARD WOODMAN was a local ironmaster and church warden who was burned at the stake in Lewes on June 22nd 1557 having called his rector "Mr. Facing-Both-Ways" for being a Protestant under Henry the Eighth and a Catholic under Mary.

From this photograph, you will see the wall, and behind the wall is a large fir tree. Both of my grandparents are buried between the tree and the wall in an unmarked plot.

We continue through the gap in the wall and cross to the other corner, now heading down the centre of a field to reach a low bank. Here we turn left. It's amazing what a couple of drinks will do to people. As I was driving I consumed very little and,

Sophie, although a wine lover, didn't abstain but I'm sure she didn't drink that much. But Ron, I'm not so sure. Because, all of a sudden, Ron has become very verbal. All the way down the hill he doesn't stop talking. He even mentions a game of leapfrog and having problems leaping over the backs of females. Sophie tells him to behave. At the low bank we turn left and across the field is just a short walk back to the car. Of course nature has to take its course and, with liquid, what goes in, eventually has to find its way out. Rons liquid lunch was no different. But, even standing behind a tree, he didn't stop talking.

From this field we head back to the car. Oliver looks shattered and must be hoping for a nice hot bath and a long sleep of about two days. The rain is still falling and my instructions are now hardly readable. I hope I can make out my notes. I have scanned just a small part of my directions so that you are able to see the state they get into should you have rain. Thankfully we have been very lucky on our walks; most of the rain has been at the end. But can you imagine the fun we would have if we started our walk in the rain? We'd never find our way. I'm seriously considering a compass for the next walk. Just in case.

turn right. At a road junction bear left and at the next junction keep right, both roads signed to Warbleton Church. Walk up past the Warbill-in-Tun pub at Warbleton.

5. Just past the pub, turn left into Warbleton churchyard. The church stands high on a ridge, with views southwards to the South Downs and across the open spaces of Pevensey Bay to the sea.

t has a fine 14th Century tower and an even earlier nave and chancel.

The tower loft is reputed to have been used as a hiding place during the persecutions of Mary Tudor and, in the churchyard, is a memorial to Richard Woodman, a local iron-founder, who was one of the seventeen Protestant martyrs burnt in Lewes in 1557.

An iron-bound door of oak in the turret is said to have been made by Woodman.

Pass to the left of the church and, when opposite the church tower, turn left through a gap in a wall.

Cross a corner of the churchyard and through another gap in a hedge.

Drop down across a field where there should be a trodden path and then turn left along the foot of a low bank.

After about 250 yards, go right through a gap in the hedge and resume your previous

Soggy, rain soaked instructions

Chapter 23 – Washington

Some time ago I looked into my family history and discovered some things about my descendants. Nothing too outrageous but some little stories did emerge. The easy part was tracing my paternal side i.e. the Pollard line. The surname stays the same. I have researched back to the 1600's, and been able to verify back to 1837, with this line and still not left Sussex. But everyone's maternal line is a little different. Marriages take place and surnames change so that tracing the continuation back in time can take you in strange directions usually finishing at a brick wall. At times you are given information from other members of your family. For instance I was told that my Grandfather, Thomas Churcher, on my mothers' side, was born in Chailey, East Sussex in 1891. I have confirmed this with his birth certificate. The same supplier of that information told me that his father, George Churcher, was born in Steyning in October 1847 and that his wife, Mary (nee Jackson) was born in 1852 in **W**ashington. I was also told that they married in October 1873. But this is where something isn't all

The Frankland Arms, Washington

that it should be. I can't find a registration of marriage. But I have found the entry in the 1891 census[133] which shows the whole family residing in Ringmer and my grandfather is 3 months old. This document states that my grandfather, Thos. on the document, was born in Ringmer yet his birth certificate states that he was born in Chailey. So, which is correct? I am also unable to trace a registration of birth for either Mary Jackson or George Churcher. Civil registration started in 1837 so I should (?) be able to find them. But I can't! In fact I cannot find any registration documents for the whole family that make sense. And that is the sole reason for not looking too deeply at my maternal relations.

But with today's walk, around the village of Washington, I am hoping to find some names, perhaps in the churchyard, which could lead me in another direction in tracing this part of my family. But I shan't hold my breath.

The walk is taken from the book 'Pub Walks in West Sussex'[134]. Mike Power, the writer describes this 6¼ mile walk as '...*A ridge walk with beautiful views....*'[135] This, as we know by now, means it is going to be hilly. What we didn't know was how very hilly it was and how many miles off course we could get without really trying!

The start of the long climb

---

[133] PRO/National Archive Reference #RG12/796 Folio 39 Page 5
[134] Walk 36 – Page 84
[135] Ibid

The walk didn't start at all well. The drive to Washington, by Marian, was no problem. Today we are also accompanied by Alan and conversation, as it always is with Alan, is non-stop. But it was the instructions, and my 'map' reading that did us no favours at the start. Our instructions simply read *'Leave the pub and turn right....'* "But we ain't been in the pub yet," says Ron, 'so 'ow can we be leavin' it if we ain't been in it?" The instructions continue *'Almost opposite Stocks Mead there is a stile in the fence...'*. Needless to say we didn't find 'Stocks Mead' but we did find a stile opposite 'Franklands Mead'. "They must have changed the name," I offer. "Or there might be a 'Stocks Mead' further up the road," suggests Marian, who we all ignored and headed over the stile opposite 'Franklands Mead'. Our instructions tell us to walk diagonally across the field yet we were in an enclosed path. We should now head towards a wood, yet the only thing in front of us was a field of sheep. We decide to

turn right at this field, although our instructions didn't tell us to. We climbed another stile and we were in yet another enclosed path. After 30 minutes we were back were we started. Just up the road from The Frankland Arms. Luckily, a local lady is striding it out opposite us so I asked for directions. At first she told us that 'Stocks Mead' was at the other side of the pub but she then took us further up the road, passing two more stiles, passed the road leading to the Church of St. Mary's, until we reached a road called 'Stocks Mead'. So why didn't the instructions in the book say this? It could have saved a lot of time and a fair bit of bickering from my fellow walkers. All Marian kept saying was "I said to look further up the road, but would you listen?" We thank the lady and head up the hill towards the woods. And was it uphill? It was steeper than steep. It was practically vertical. It is now that I read the instruction that says we have to climb up the steep path. There was no mention of this at the start. We all had to stop after a hundred yards or so. Me, to get my breath, and Marian and Alan had to start stripping off some clothing. The weather, as expected today, was really glorious. Hardly a cloud in the sky and the sun was hot. Although very nice, it certainly didn't help us to climb this hill! I'd noticed that Ron hadn't attempted to wear his Sussex Smock.

The Quarry

As we approach, what we think is the top of the climb, we come to a quarry on our right. "Bet they didn't dig that bugger out with a shovel," giggles Ron. Although the quarry looked very big from where we were standing I don't think the picture does it justice. It must still be in use because we could see vehicles along one edge of the 'dig'.

It's still uphill

We pass the quarry and we are still heading uphill. Frequent stops are needed to take on water and deep breathing exercises. Marian keeps asking us about how long it will be before we get to Three Legged Cross. We keep telling her that we are going there on the next walk but she doesn't seem to take it in. "But aren't we going there today?" she keeps asking, "I thought we were heading for Three Legged Cross, that's what you told me." I started to think that it was the altitude we were at that made her the way she was but please, someone, explain it to her!! All the time we are walking uphill Alan hasn't stopped talking. He could talk for England. But the hill seems to go on forever. Looking at the instructions doesn't seem to give any idea as to when the path will level out, so we just keep climbing. My legs ache, the sun is beginning to burn and the slight breeze, as we climb higher, isn't helping the sunburn. We have been walking for over an hour and we haven't reached the top of the walk where we meet the South Downs Way. I'm shattered. Now Marian is worried because she hasn't brought any sun block and she is still asking about Three Legged Cross. If anyone reading this is under any misapprehension about this climb take a trip out to Washington and have a go. Both Ron and I had noticed a very large number of walkers and cyclists on this track but all were going in the opposite direction to us, downhill! "We should see a stile on our left soon. If we go over that stile we will come out at a dew-pond," I gasp as we set off again after yet another water stop. From our instructions I discover that this dew-pond was first constructed in 1870 and was the only source of water for the sheep. But we never did see the stile, or the dewpond. That is, not where I thought it was. My finger must have slipped on the map and I'd jumped a few hundred yards. So we were nowhere near where I thought we were.

Just one of the fantastic views

A distant sign?

But eventually, we did arrive at the top. And the view is extraordinary! I'm not sure how many miles you can see but it is certainly a long way. The fact that the day was so pleasant obviously helped but the view is stunning.

Just when you think it can't get any worse we have to start going uphill again. We are now up with the aircraft. There are planes up here doing acrobatic manoeuvres, Loops, rolls and tip stalls, all very fascinating and we stay here for some time just watching but more importantly having a long rest. We watch the hunting birds as they

Marian receives a text message

look for dinner but when we do get going again, things have started to seize up. Legs don't seem all that interested in moving in the direction you want them to and limbs are aching. I read further into the walk instructions and am pleased to discover that after a few hundred yards on the level we start to descend from the top of this huge 'mountain'. But our troubles have only just begun......

We are instructed to look out for a footpath sign which will be on our left. We should reach this sign after about a mile of level walking. We didn't see it. None of us saw it, I checked. So we kept walking, on and on we went until, in the distance, I could see a signpost. "This can't be right," I said to Ron, "We must have walked well over a mile before we found this sign." "Don't worry yer 'ead about it," he replies, "tis a sign an' it points left. Tis good enough." When we get to the sign nothing looks as the book describes. There should be a field, there's a wood, there should be a stream, there's a wood. "But nothing is as it should be," I advise the others. "I think this is the way to Three Legged Cross," says Marian, "so I'm heading in this direction." And down the slope into the wood she goes. Alan follows. But I'm not so sure. "This can't be right," I say to Ron, "nothing here looks like a field and the map doesn't show the path going in this direction." "It may not," agrees Ron, "but it is down'ill an we got ter go down'ill ter get back ter that nice pub, where we started from." And he's following Marian and Alan. I have no choice but to follow them down the hill. The instructions now don't mean a jot. We are way off course but we are getting off the mountain, I'm just worried where we will end up.

There now don't seem to be so many people going down the slope as there was going up. This may be because of how steep it was but every now and again an intrepid walker would be heading up the slope. I will say that the paths along here are used by lots of people and it didn't seem to matter if we met them going up or going down these steep slopes, all had a cheery greeting and a pleasant smile. But we were heading in the wrong direction. Marian's phone rings and she tells us it's a text message from our friend Lyn, who is sitting in the local bar at Hailsham and wants to know if Marian can join her. "Just text 'er back the word 'lost', she'll know what your doin'" chuckles Ron.

At the bottom of the hill we come across a young man and young lady playing on some makeshift rope swings. "'spect we spoilt 'is fun," whispers Ron, "didn't 'spect ter see us come round the corner like that, did 'e? Bet 'e thought 'e'd be ok fer some naughty." But let's be honest we were all young sometime, it just seems a bit longer ago to some of us. We quickly walked past the young couple and left them to it.

Eventually we arrived at a lane and everyone suggested that this was the lane we should have been on according to the instructions. Because there was a junction with three signs Marian insisted, not for the first time, that we had actually, arrived at Three Legged Cross. Nothing I seemed to say would discourage them as we slog on to God knows where. In the distance we see an elderly lady walking towards us with bags of shopping. In desperation, more than anything else I asked her if we could get to **W**ashington if we continued in this direction. She advised us that we needed to walk to the end of the road and turn left. But we'd missed the bus because she'd just got off it, because she had to get some shopping and she'd walked from the bus stop to here and she lived just up the road and wasn't it a lovely day for a stroll and have we walked far and why are you going to **W**ashington and it was only 2 miles. I think

Ron's money find

Alan has met his match. We managed to leave the lady, pass Chanctonbury Picnic Site and get to the road junction she described. From here we turned left and it must have been one of the longest 2 miles I've ever walked. At one point I was talking to the person behind me, who I thought was Ron, only to turn round and find I was on my own. Ron and the others had stopped to pick up some coins that Ron had found on the side of the road.

St. Mary's Church, Washington

We managed to find our way back to **W**ashington and The Frankland Arms. Our 6¼ miles has turned out to be nearly 11 miles, but who's counting? I think my tired legs will be complaining in the morning but before we head for the bar Ron and I decide to head for the church. Marian and Alan say that they will wait for us in the garden.

Unfortunately I didn't find any names that were familiar to me apart from one 'Jackson' who was mentioned on the war memorial, having lost his life in WW 1. This date would have been too late for my ancestors being in the area in the mid 1800's. Still it was worth a try. As we wandered inside the church it had a strange feeling that my great grandfather could have been married in this church all those years ago. But until I can find some written evidence it will still be speculation.

All of us can recommend the ale and food at The Frankland Arms. It was also nice, when I told them which of the pub walks we had tried to complete and that we had got hopelessly lost the young lady behind the bar said that we were not the only ones to get lost on that particular walk. Apparently she hears of walkers getting lost regularly. Which makes me feel just a little bit better.

Washington, was another walk that was rather hilly
Did we get lost? Don't be silly
Graham's instructions & Marian and Alan's talk
We just did a Washington – extended walk.
Aresee©

Chapter 24 – Three Leg Cross (X)

Not technically correct I know, but can anyone suggest a place, in Sussex, starting with the letter **X**? No, neither can we. I'm expecting even more trouble with the letter **Z** but that's still a couple of weeks away so I won't worry about that just yet. I have looked at various publications and maps hunting for somewhere, anywhere, that would fit the bill and start with the letter **X**. I found nothing, not even a place with a nickname that started with **X**. I then considered having the letter **X** at the end of the word but all I could come up with was Herstmonceau**x**. We have walked around Herstmonceau**x** a couple of times already so I then tinkered with the idea of a famous cross (**X**) roads but drew a blank. But, in the end, a decision had to be made. So we are going to veer off completely and do something very different.

If you remember, back at Chapter 12, Ron and I met a gentleman called Len Markham. Len has written a book titled, 'Kiddiwalks in East Sussex'[136] and one of the walks he suggests we have a go at is at Three Leg Cross. Now is that a coincidence, or what? Both Ron and I thought that as we tend to 'have a go' at the writers of these walks if they get it wrong, it would be rather nice to have the author with us when we do the walk. So Len, fool that he is, has agreed to come with us today. Just to make it even more of a challenge for Len we have invited a number of other people to complete the walk and, just for good measure, they are bringing their 'Kiddies'. So, not only will I give you Ron's thoughts but I will get some thoughts from the children and their parents on what they liked, or disliked, about our stroll.

But first I have a huge confession to make. I couldn't perform this walk with so many people and their children and suffer the indignities of getting lost, so to make sure that I had some idea of what to expect, I completed the walk, last week, with my daughter, Michelle. I'm sorry. But I had to make sure the walk was suitable for the age group we were hoping would join us. We also decided to make up a simple questionnaire, for the children, to answer questions on what they see. At one point of the walk it was muddy, but my daughter and I think that it should be ok but to quote Len's description of this walk *'...after rain it is not suitable for children under eight years of age.'*[137] This is a shame, because most of our children will be under eight. Let's hope it doesn't rain.

The Bull Inn, Three Leg Cross

Another thing that needed checking out by Michelle and I was how long the walk was going to be. Len had carefully planned a walk of 3½ miles but this could be shortened to 2¼ miles and it is the shorter walk that we will be completing. Not because it is easier, but because, when I attempted the longer walk with Michelle last week, the end was very muddy and uphill so Michelle and I tried to find another way back to the pub, and yes, we got lost!

I have tried to find out a little something about Three Leg Cross but without much success. I don't mean that in a nasty sense but there is very little to see there. The 1891 census[138] shows that there were just eleven properties in the village. The pub,

[136] From the Kiddiwalks Series – Published by Countryside Books in 2006 ISBN 1853069531
[137] Ibid - Page 49 - Walk 10 – Titled 'Three Leg Cross' - Backwaters
[138] 1891 census – British Data Archive - #RG12/778 pages 2 & 3

The Bull Inn, had not been converted to its current business at this time although the building itself is reputed to be one of the oldest in the country. Out of the eleven properties listed in the census a total of twenty-five children lived with their parents and all the male parents worked 'off the land'.

We all set off

The advanced party wait for stragglers

I must admit to feeling a little fragile on the morning of the walk. My brother-in-law, Andy and his fiancée Sarah got married the previous day and, although I did steer well clear of the amber nectar, the rich food was just too tempting. All week, prior to the walk had brought some heavy rain, until Thursday when everything started to look promising for the forthcoming wedding and the walk. But the forecast was rain on the Sunday. When I got up early Sunday morning and looked out of the window it didn't look too good. But as the day progressed, so the weather seemed to favour us and the well paid forecasters got it completely wrong, again!

The plan was to meet not just Ron at The Kings Head at 10 o'clock but everyone who was prepared to walk with us. So, in no particular order, we have; Sky, Megan, Abbie, Chloe and Kallum along with their respective parents and/or grandparents and friends. We will be meeting Len at The Bull Inn, as well as an Australian gentleman with his two sons, Henry and Ben. The total number on the walk would be twenty!

I believe it was Billy Connolly who once said, 'I love kids, but I couldn't eat a whole one'. And you have to say that kiddies of today want for very little. But have you noticed how some children are spoken to by their parents? I was walking through what's left of Hailsham since the new Tesco store was started, and I was amazed at how many times the 'f' word was used when talking to children. Not only was the word directed at youngsters but workmen, in the street, use the word as if its part of 'everyday speak'. I'm sure that none of the children on today's walk will be spoken to in this manner but I shudder to think what is to come of our future generations.

But I must explain about our walk. As Marian was the driver who knew a quick way to get to Three Leg Cross we decided that she should lead and we would all follow. As an ex-taxi driver Marian only knew one way to drive....fast. It appears that speed limits mean nothing to Marian. As I, Alan and my son Anthony, struggle to keep up and remain legal,

Lyn doing her own thing with Sky

Ben & Henry set off with dad and Ron

with young children on board, Marian is off like a rocket. But she couldn't lose us. My daughter and Ron are in the back of my car and Michelle tells us that she is treating this walk like one of her school trips. She has brought plasters, wet wipes, tissues and biscuits and Ron had the same idea and brought along a packet of jelly babies. So it seems that all eventualities are catered for. Or are they? We arrive at The Bull Inn, meet Len and his wife as well as David with Ben and Henry and prepare ourselves for a walk around Bewl Water.

Each child is issued with a little questionnaire and a pencil and off we go, turning left after The Bull and heading towards a farm track on our left. It is really strange that throughout the walk people have a different pace. Marian walks like she drives. My son, with his wife and daughters, all used to being in the countryside with the two Labradors do not walk, they stroll. Lyn, obviously not used to doing too much walking with a child in a buggy, had difficulty in deciding what speed she should go. Sometimes she would be on her own, far off in the distance and then, as if she realised she was on her own, would stop and wait for others to catch her up, only to speed off again. Len and his wife tried to stay close to Ron most of the time and I started to run backwards and forwards between all the groups until I decided that it was killing me and started to take it easy.

Heading down the enclosed path

The questions, set for the children, were meant to be answered as we went along. A picture was taken, the previous week, a question was set, and the children, once they had seen the picture and related it to what was in front of them, would then answer the question. Sounds good in theory and I had noticed that some were completing it as they should have done, with some help from mum and dad, but others had finished the questionnaire before we hit the first bend in the drive. I thought the whole thing was going to be a disaster. But as the walk continued, so everyone seemed to become

The beautiful blossom

more relaxed and laid back. Discussing everyday things with each other and just having a good time. The question set about who lived in the large hole on the side of the track was answered with various degrees of accuracy. Some, including Chloe thought it was a rabbit. Others thought it may be a badger. But little Megan decided that it was a wood lice, because she saw one, coming out of the hole. Michelle's idea, bless her, that it might be the home of a rhino was thought to be a bit over the top. I believe that it was about now that Sky decided to

Our first glimpse of Bewl Water

have a 'nappy moment' and needed a change of clothes. Unfortunately Sky was very shy and would only let her Nan get anywhere near her. As soon as a stranger approached her she opened her lungs and hollered!!

As we progressed down the track we did tend to split up but when we arrived at our first turning, just by the cattle grid, everyone was waiting for the last group to catch up.

Here we turned left and walked along the enclosed path towards Bewl Water. A wonderful smell from the blossom on the trees along this short path is breathtaking. This is a very popular walk and lots of people wished us a cheery 'good morning' as we walk along the path. At the gate we get our first glimpse of the expanse of water which is Bewl Water. This man-made 'lake' is outstanding, and as you may all know, one of my favourite places to walk. The freedom you feel is exhilarating. The openness, the wildlife and the smells all add to the enjoyment of this place. I love it!

Fisherman at Bewl Water

As we walk along the bank, fairly close to the waters edge, it did get pretty boggy and we had problems negotiating the mud and the stiles with the buggies. Here it is obvious that fishermen are doing what all fishermen do. Anthony, my son, decides it is time to put his two Labradors on a lead. When they see water they have to be in it. So, it's better to be safe than sorry. But as we walk on, a strange thing happens. I'm not really sure how to describe the next few minutes as they unfold in front of me but, like I said, we all walk at different paces so had started to spread out. Slowly, I noticed that the front few people had dropped back and, eventually, joined the larger, middle group. The group lagging behind had, mysteriously, also joined the middle group. Suddenly, without any warning two dogs, not on leads, ran round our group and attacked a dog owned by one of the fishermen. I do mean attack. The fisherman kicked out and struck one of the attacking dogs and promptly lay on his dog to protect it, sadly blood had been drawn but the dogs did, eventually, back off. But the strange thing was, as this was all going on, in the split second it happened I noticed that all the children in our group where now in the centre of a ring of protecting parents. Who were all screaming at the owner of the attacking dogs to get them off and put them on a lead. Did they all sense the possible danger to the youngsters? Is that what made them form a protective ring? I don't know but it all happened right in front of me.

Starting to feel tired

From this point we all seemed to keep together for a bit, talking about things in general. Henry started to get a little tired and wanted to be carried by his dad yet Megan, the youngest of the children, was still striding it out, holding anyone's hand that was prepared to let her. Nicole needed to know why a bus stop would be at Bewl Water, perhaps it was a River Boat stop is the only explanation she could offer and, of course, there was the inevitable disappearance into the bushes for natures call. But, I hasten to add that, for once, it wasn't Ron.

In some of the recent chapters I have mentioned the dogs walking with us and the habit of them doing things with rabbit pooh. We couldn't understand what Megan was saying as she pointed to the ground. She kept repeating the same word, over and over again and it sounded like 'turdy'. Her dad came to the rescue when he explained that Megan was pointing at sheep poo and saying 'dirty,' 'dirty'. It makes sense now.

Bus Stop?

The dogs have now escaped the lead and are enjoying the water as the pleasure boat 'Swallow' passes close to the bank. We all give the customary wave just so that the passengers

Pleasure Boat 'Swallow'

can wave back to us. This has got to be the life. Strolling along, not a care in the world, just watching other people enjoy the sunny day. We can't believe how lucky we've been with the weather. It's not too hot but we are probably starting to suntan because of the light breeze.

Just past this spot we bear right and head towards a stile and a gate. Once through the gate we head along an enclosed path until we come out, once again, at the cattle grid near the start of our walk, and here we turn left and head back up the long lane until we arrive at The Bull Inn.

All in all I believe that the walk was a great success. Part of it was difficult with buggies so I suggest that Len was right in recommending the walk for slightly older children. Having Len with us, obviously made getting lost impossible and his instructions, in the book are accurate. If I had one little itty bitty problem with the instructions it was how long the walk was. When I walked last weekend with Michelle it took us about 1½ hours. I believe, on average, I walk about 3m.p.h. As I had Michelle with me I probably walked a little slower but I still think, and so do the other walkers that the walk is longer than the 2¼ miles suggested by Len. When I asked Len how he measured the distance he told me that he used a pedometer, but if it was hilly, he might add a bit. So, not exactly accurate? But having said that, this was a beautiful walk, irrespective of the length. The water was beautiful, the bluebells smelt gorgeous, all the children were

Ben and Henry with certificates

fantastic, and although there were no prizes for getting the answers right on the questionnaire, well done Kallum and Abbie for getting them all right (Even if you did call the primroses daisies, and then corrected the answer)

My intention, at the end of the walk, was to stop at the Bull Inn for a meal. The building dates back to the 14th Century and is full of atmosphere. But last week I tried to book some places and was told that if the total number was going to be 20 then the chef would need to know if we wanted the snack menu, the carvery or the children's menu. We would also be asked to sit outside. I didn't think that was very good so I've invited everyone back to The King's Head in Hailsham where Helen and Darren were only too pleased to supply us with a buffet.

Unfortunately, Ben and Henry were not able to come back to Hailsham with their dad so Ron and I presented them with their certificates and everyone wished them a cheery goodbye.

All that remained for the rest of us was to head back to Hailsham, enjoy the hospitality at our local and award the remaining children with their own certificates – stating that they had walked with Ron and Graham, and didn't get lost.

Group photo at The King's Head

Three Leg Cross was a walk I couldn't wait
Bewl Water was picturesque, the kids were great,
Thank you Grans' and Granddads', mums and dad
For shear enjoyment and novelty, one of the best we had.
Aresee©

Chapter 25 – Yapton

I have one or two reasons for choosing the next location for the penultimate walk. One is that my wife's mum, Celia, spent some of her childhood in this area. She also met her husband, Sam at a pub called, would you believe, 'The Shoulder of Mutton and Cucumbers'. Honest, I couldn't make a name like that up! Sam and Celia married at The Church of St Mary the Virgin in **Y**apton. I can also remember my father-in-law talking of another pub called The Shakydoo (spelling?) in Ford, but that pub has long since been converted into an office block. My other reason for choosing **Y**apton is a story I read about 'The Shoulder of Mutton....' which involves a local rat catcher. Anyone who knows Ron will be aware that his father was the local rat catcher around Hailsham. I hasten to add that Ron's dad is not the 'catcher' in this story because this rat catcher's name was Seeby White. Another man who used to frequent 'The Shoulder of Mutton...' was the Thatcher, called Marley. The Rat Catcher took a fancy to the Thatcher's wife. So Marley and White struck a bargain at the bar. The Rat Catcher took Mrs Marley, the children and the furniture for 7s. 6d and a quart of beer. This is the last recorded incident of the old Sussex custom of wife-selling and is dated 1898.[139]

Yapton, as you may be aware is near Bognor. The Fire Brigade at Bognor were called to a fire at **Y**apton one night in the early 1900's. First the firemen had to be encouraged to leave the hostelries. They then harnessed the horses and drove, very quickly, to the fire. In fact they drove too quickly because, arriving at the fire, the old grey mare at the front had no sooner stopped when she collapsed and died. 'Well I'm danged,' said the fireman, 'I've never known her do that before!'[140]

The Church of St Mary the Virgin, Yapton

The walk I had chosen for today was an 8 mile circular, starting at Felpham, walking through Barnham and Yapton and back to Felpham. I was due to meet Ron at

Our starting point - The Shoulder....

9a.m. on Saturday. But at 8a.m. I had changed my mind. I really can't explain why but I just felt that an 8 mile circular, on a very hot Saturday, wasn't the thing to be doing. Also, although I had found the walk some weeks ago I had only just realised that we would not be visiting the church at **Y**apton nor did the walk include 'The Shoulder of Mutton and Cucumbers'. So I hastily turned to the computer to find me another walk.

My luck was in. I found a circular walk from **Y**apton, starting by 'The

---

[139] West Sussex Inns by Brigid Chapman published by Countryside Books ISBN 1 85306 023 2
[140] People of Hidden Sussex by Swinfen & Arscott – A BBC Radio Sussex Guide published 1985

Shoulder of Mutton…' called a 'Rife Walk'[141]. But, and there always has to be a 'but…' there are no directions supplied with the map. That will be ok, I thought, the map looked pretty accurate, and clear, we'll be fine (?) I quickly printed off two maps and headed towards Ron, who was waiting for me at you know where.

Ron knows we are heading into West Sussex. He is also aware that the walk is around **Y**apton but he thinks it will be by following instructions, as all the other walks have been. I'm not completely sure that I should tell him that we have no instructions and I decide to leave disclosing this until we get to **Y**apton. He's more than happy when I tell him that we will be starting and finishing at a pub. It'll be a nice surprise for him when we arrive.

The start of the walk

As I said, my mother and father-in-law were married at the church at **Y**apton so I decided that we would call in there before we started our walk. We turned into Church Road and St Mary's Church is about ½mile up the road, on the right. It is a very picturesque place. Typical of any village church. The grounds are well-kept and people are mowing the grass and tending to the graveyard as Ron and I walk along the path to the door. And my camera has decided not to work! Of all the times for this to happen. Is it an omen? I still haven't told Ron about my change of walk plans. "Per'aps it's the batteries," offers Ron as we wander round the inside of the church. "I put a new set in on Thursday; they shouldn't have run out already. I haven't used the camera since the last walk, apart from downloading pictures from Three Leg Cross." I realise I'm beginning to sound pathetic. But it's a long way from Hailsham to here and I didn't fancy having to come back just to take photographs. I try taking some pictures with my mobile phone but it's useless. As we leave the church I ask one of the people tending the graveyard if there is a shop that I could buy some new batteries.

He gives us directions to the local co-op and reluctantly, as we drive to the shop, I admit to Ron my change of plans. "That's ok," he says, "'tis a lovely day fer a walk." "But that's not all," I admit, "the walk I've chosen only has a map, we don't have any instructions." Now I've known Ron for sometime and the fact that he's gone quiet tells me he's not amused. Eventually he turns to me and says, "We can get bloody lost with instructions, we can be completely bloody lost without them!" "But the map is a good one," I plead. "It's got ter be better than bloody good. We could be out 'ere fer days." We pull up outside the shop and I leave Ron to simmer down as I purchase 4 new batteries. When I get back he seems pretty calm. The batteries bring the camera back to life and we set off.

Don't go down the steps

"Just in case," I whimper to Ron, "I've printed off another copy of the map so we could have one each." "Yer know what yer can do with that," he replies, "you ain't

---

[141] http://www.westsussex.gov.uk/leisureandtourism/prow/pdfs/The_Rife_Circular_Walk.pdf - visited 10/05/2008

blamin' me fer getting' us lost just by passin' me a map. Just like always," he continues, "you leads the way an' I'll foller yer."

We pass The Shoulder of Mutton…' and turn left up a signed public footpath. The map shows that we need to turn left so, nervously, I suggest that we take the next left. We climb down some steps and find ourselves in a street of very posh houses. I look at the map. Something's wrong. According to the map we should be walking along another footpath. As if Ron knows, he stops me and says, "We've gone wrong, already, aven't we?" What can I say? "It does look like it, Ron, yes." "I don't believe this," says Ron, "We've only been a 'undred bloody yards and we're lost already." I'm frantically trying to find a way out of this when Ron goes up to a gentleman and asks directions. It appears we turned left too soon. We are now in a street called 'The Pines' and need to make our way back up the street, up the steps and turn left along the path. Once we had done this we were, once again, back on track. I am desperate not to go wrong again and keep referring to points on the map as we head along each path. After each turn I show Ron where we are, what we are looking out for next and in which direction we should be heading. And it worked, for the remainder of the walk we didn't put a step wrong. Well, almost.

As I said this is a Rife Walk. The word 'Rife' is common to Sussex meaning 'a ditch on the moorland'[142] All along this walk there is a ditch close by. Some of the larger ditches are named and I will give the names as we cross them. Some are but small, insignificant waterways which were difficult to find. But some were magnificent, with moving water and wildlife to match. In fact, on reflection, on this

Overgrown stile

particular walk we actually saw everything. Fly-tipping aplenty, the most wonderful Sussex scenery, rusting farm machinery, birdlife in abundance as well as joggers, walkers, and dog strollers. We found some history but most importantly of all, we found our way back. And that may not be just because of my brilliant map reading but could also be for the fact that we are in West Sussex, and West Sussex paths are well signed. This walk was no different.

After our first error of turning into 'The Pines' we made our way towards the outskirts of a village called Bilsham. I can find nothing about this hamlet but it was an area where fly-tipping was pretty common. Any unwanted washing machines are dumped behind the trees. The signed path leads us past the hamlet and after a couple of left and right turns we head towards the outskirts of the next village, Flansham. It is here that the author Gerard Young used to live. He once described Flansham in his book 'Come into The Country' (1945);

'Like most villages, no one has ever heard of it and no one can ever find it. Even if I tell you the name of it, which is Flansham, it will convey nothing to you. It is a dead-end village; two lanes which lead to nowhere…'

Another claim to fame for the village was James Guthrie who ran The Pear Tree Press from 1907 to 1952 from his cottage in the village. During Festival of Britain year he wrote, designed and printed the book *From a Sussex Village*, in a limited

---

[142] 'A Dictionary of The Sussex Dialect' by Rev W.D. Parish first published in 1875 republished 2008

edition of 300 copies, selling it at 10/- (10 shillings – or 50p to you youngsters). The book is, obviously, about Flansham and its residents and is now a collector's item. James Guthrie died from a heart attack at the age of 78, while out walking. That's cheered Ron up!

Ryebank Rife

We now head towards our first Rife, Ryebank Rife. But just before we reach the Rife, on our left is what looks like an old church but it's been converted into a house. Although it has been made to look old it doesn't pull it off very well and seems odd. Past this church/house we turn left. When we reach the Rife I would normally be snapping away with the camera by now. After all it is water with its wonderful reflections, but I'm still not that sure that the camera is going to behave so I only risk a couple of shots. Also, if the map was anything to go by, I will have plenty of opportunity to take water pictures later on. So we press on. The sun is getting very warm now and I've noticed that Ron's skin has started to leak. Thankfully he has brought liquid refreshment. Luckily it is only water. Being out here, in this heat, with anything other than water would be plain idiotic. Ron reminds me that the two of us being out here without some instructions is pretty bloody stupid as well, but we keep walking.

Ron looks worried??

It is now that we need to turn right and head towards 'Hoe Farm'. Again the signposts are very good, although a couple of the stiles could do with some tender loving care, as we exit the footpaths and turn right along Hoe Lane. This Lane just seems to disappear at some point and we are now on an unmade gravel track. Please, God, let us be going in the right direction!

Another thing Ron and I have just noticed is the abundance of brand-new fences, gates and stiles. As we walk along Hoe Lane we bear right and pass through a very new kissing gate. The signpost tells us to walk across the next field, but Ron looks worried. Just before we passed through the kissing gate a sign, in bold red writing said, 'Beware Bull. For Safety please keep to path'. But there wasn't a path, and in the field were a number of cows. "Where's the bull?" I whisper to Ron. "Don't know," is the reply, "but don't run." We haven't got too far into the field when Ron prods me with his stick. I spun round so fast I nearly drilled myself into

Spot the bull

the ground. "'E's the big black bugger over there," Ron points with his stick. "Just the other side o'them cows, can you see 'im?" I'm not sure if it was fear that made me sweat or the prod of Ron's stick, but all of a sudden I can't see a thing as salty sweat drips into my eyes. The thing is I honestly believe that Ron was a little worried as well. He said not, when we got to the other side of the field but I'm sure I saw a flicker of dread as we entered the field of cattle. But once through the gate he became much more relaxed and, I noticed, not going on about the lack of instructions.

We continue along Hoe Lane, passing some really beautiful properties. Joggers seem to use this lane to go back and forth. One gentleman informed us that he was preparing for a race in what I thought he said was 'Orton' but I'm not sure exactly what he said. I should have asked him because a few minutes later he was heading back towards us.

We, eventually arrive at a bridge over Lidsey Rife, after passing, on our left, more fly-tipping. At least if Ron is having a go at the people leaving rubbish in the countryside he is not having a go at me.

Once over the bridge we turn sharp right and walk along the side of the 'Rife' for some time. We have heard the sounds of so many birds along this walk that I have lost count, and every time I pick up the camera to take a picture of this bird or that they just fly off. So I've decided that, when I get home I'll get pictures from the Internet and place them at the end of this chapter.

The wrong path

In the distance we can see the railway line as trains head from London down to the coast. A quick look at the map shows me that we should be heading towards and under this railway line. But we're not. We are actually walking parallel to the line. But we can't head towards it because the path we are on is enclosed, with barbed wire. So, I have a confession to make. In the distance, to our left, I can see a church. I hope that this church is St Mary's Church at Barnham. If we were to go under the railway line and turn right we should walk past this church. It looks as if the path we are now on, if we turn left, will take us to the same church. Looking at my map there

Ron admires the Roll of Honour

should be a turning to the left just ahead. And that is exactly what happened. We came out at Barnham Church and we can now resume our walk and Ron is none the wiser. Until, that is, he reads this!

Of course we have to go and have a look inside this magnificent building, which is recorded in the Domesday Book from the 11th century. Ron and I were particularly touched by the 'Roll of Honour' for the fallen during the Great War. With the names of the men it simply said 'Lived for England – for England we have died.' Both of us felt humbled by such a tribute.

Arundel and Portsmouth Canal

Back outside we headed back to join the walk on what once was the route for the former Arundel and Portsmouth Canal. Built between 1818 and 1823 it's life was short-lived.

By 1847 the Canal became unnavigable[143] through lack of use. Parts of the canal were sold off, parts had to be drained because salt water was polluting the wells but the canal was used, to some extent, for smuggling. The contraband was taken ashore at Climping, known to the locals as Yapton Beach. There is a tale that the vicar at Yapton gave a sermon on the evils of smuggling, without knowing that the contraband had been hidden beneath his feet in the pulpit.

We walk along the bank of the disused canal for about a mile, dodging sheep droppings, past the Barnham Mill, until we reach, once again, 'The Shoulder of Mutton and Cucumbers.' Inside the pub we are greeted by the landlord and staff and enjoy a cool refreshing pint. Patrick, one of the customers attempts to answer my many, many questions about Yapton and the stories spoken of by my in-laws. For that I thank him sincerely. Unfortunately we are told that this old establishment is due to be demolished and replaced by blocks of flats. So, this time next year, the pub which was in the Guinness Book of Records for having the longest pub name in England will be no more. Because of the history of the place we have decided to come back with my mother-in-law to have one last look at the place where she met her husband, all those years ago. .

| Chaffinch | Great Tit | Green Woodpecker | Kestrel |

| | Reed Bunting | Reed Warbler | Robin |

Linnet

Skylark   Swallow

Yapton was a walk that set the heart ringing
Beautiful countryside and so many birds singing
Barnham, with its lovely remembrance to its fallen
The welcome at 'The Shoulder of Mutton', back we will be calling
Aresee©

All images obtained from www.rspb.org.uk visited 25/05/2008

[143] http://en.wikipedia.org/wiki/Portsmouth_and_Arundel_Canal visited 14/05/2008

The Letter 'Z' & The Problems it Caused

Well it has finally arrived. The last letter of the alphabet. I still haven't come up with anywhere in Sussex that starts, finishes or has a '**Z**' in it that we could walk around. But below are just a few of the considerations:

Drusillas **Z**oo

Herstmonceaux – pronounced 'Herstmon**z**oo'

Somewhere with a '**Z**' bend?????

Zion chapel – resting place of the onion pie murderer.

Японеряан – translated from Russian – **Z**abloodeelsa – 'I'm lost'

(Thanks for that Stuart but we're not that desperate)

I've considered going to a restaurant beginning with '**Z**' and writing about the meal, but I can't find one.

We could go to a club beginning with '**Z**' but Ron and I aren't clubbers.

So, after much head scratching and many weeks of searching we have called a halt. There isn't anywhere. People have suggested that as Ron and I have now been walking for over two years and completed 78 walks covering over 465 miles we could do with a rest. Perhaps we should fill the last pages with '**Z**'s.zzzzzzzzzzz zzzzzzzzzzzzzzzzzzzzzzzzzzzzzzzzzzzzzzzzzzzzzzzzzzzzzzzzzzzzzzzzzzzzzzzzzzzzzzzzzz zzzzzzzzzzzzzzzzzzzzzzzzzzzzzzzzzzzz but that would be silly. Some have suggested leaving the last pages blank………………

PTO…..

.........but that isn't on either, is it?

So, what we have decided on is a Plan <u>Z</u>. The last resort. The final fling. The last piece of the jig-saw?

I've always fancied taking part in a Treasure Hunt. I mentioned this to Lyn and Marian a few weeks ago and they have devised a Hunt for me and Ron to carry out. We've all decided to call it

Chapter 26 - THE TREA<u>Z</u>URE 'UNT

Lyn and Marian have been working on the 'unt for some weeks now and both Ron and I were getting a little impatient. The book has to be finished, and time was running out. A date was arranged for the walk but unfortunately this had to be postponed. I assumed that we would carry out the walk the following weekend but again, the walk could not be carried out for some reason. Lyn apologised for the delay but had one or two problems. She was off work for a week and assured us that the trea<u>z</u>ure 'unt was completed, on paper, but one or two things needed checking. Another week passed by with no indication as to when Ron and I could complete the walk. Marian called into our local on the Friday so I asked her when the walk could be completed so that a final draft of the book could be made. Her reply was, "Can't you do the walk without me? I'm knackered and I'm on holiday soon so I won't be available for weekends anyway." Lyn has had her own, personal problems with finishing the walk so, bearing Marian's comment in mind I have made an executive decision. We won't be doing The Trea<u>z</u>ure 'unt.

All of the walks, carried out in this book, are with Ron. He has taught me a lot about Sussex and its countryside. The fact that we seem to get lost, more times than not, is probably down to my map reading and poor instructions, rather than Ron's misdirection. So, what I thought I would do is a walk on my own. Just to test my knowledge of what I have been taught and to see if I could actually find my way round a map and get back to the starting point within a reasonable time without Ron's advice and comments.

Winchelsea Railway Station

Another consideration, in this book, was to find places that were a little more obscure than the normal Sussex places. We found Quedley, Didling and Ebernoe, Knucker Hole and Tillington but the other places were a little better known. The problem was that I was restricted to letters of the alphabet. Now I do not have that restriction. This is my very own walk. I can look at a map and pick out names of a place without the worry of the starting letter. That is what I have done today and found a lovely (?) walk around *Cock Marling*[144]. I'm hoping that a number of readers have no idea

---

[144] www.eastsussexcc.gov.uk visited 31/05/08 – Route 4 – 'Cock Marling Walk'

where this place is. I've never seen it before and have never been to the little hamlet, just west of Winchelsea.

The walk is described as a *'typical country walk with some hills, stiles and muddy paths (depending on the weather)'* and is 4 miles in length, starting and finishing, hopefully for me, at Winchelsea Railway Station. How many of you have got on a train and headed for Winchelsea? I suspect that not too many could answer 'yes' to that question, me included. I've been to Winchelsea on a number of occasions and must admit that I didn't know it had a railway station. In fact the town doesn't. The station is ½ mile away, in the middle of nowhere. But after an hour's drive from Hailsham, through Hastings, Guestling and Icklesham I managed to find the station. Parking is free, another bonus, a change of shoes and a quick phone call to the wife to let her know I was starting on the walk (bless her, she worries about me) I head back towards the main road, this time, on foot.

The first signpost

Today's weather couldn't be better, sunshine but not too hot with a little breeze now and again, what could be nicer? Since I am now writing about the walk it is obvious that I completed it ok. So what I will be trying out is a description of what I saw, how I felt, what I discovered and what I found wrong with my instructions as I progress along the way.

The walk back to the main road was really nice. The road was rather narrow and it surprised me how many excursion coaches pass me. It is just over ½ mile until I reach the road where I turn right and then immediately right again. If my directions are right Winchelsea town is now on my left-hand side. I'm not sure if the first sign I reached was placed to confuse or whether the name Winchelsea was painted on because that is the Town I am in. But the arrow was pointing to the right? So is Winchelsea on my right? I'm missing Ron already! But my instructions are clear, turn right at the sign and walk past a Southern Water entrance. Easy, I don't need Ron. As I walk along the track a strange feeling comes over me. I can here a plane, overhead, and when I eventually trace the source of the noise it is an old biplane. Suddenly I've been sent back in time and the feeling is surreal, only to be woken by the sound of a Southern Water van tooting at me to get out of the way.

Footbridge

At the end of the track I manage to find the stile, closely followed by the wooden footbridge. After the bridge I turn left and follow the hedgerow on my left. My instructions tell me to ignore the first sign with a turning on the right but to make my way, uphill, to the next signpost and turning on the right. I must say that I couldn't understand why it had just done that, because when I reached the second signpost and looked back, I could see the first signpost and it looked as if both paths were heading in the same direction, towards a gate in the distance. I am now conscious of other people heading in my direction. Looking back I can see

At the second, higher, signpost

a couple heading up the hill. I decided to pretend that I was looking at a map and making a decision on which way to go. In fact I wasn't pretending. I didn't know which way to go and the map I was looking at wasn't helping me much. "Good afternoon," calls the lady. I look up and return the greeting. The man doesn't look well. He's puffing a lot and although the hill was reasonably steep I didn't think it was that bad. "We're out for a stroll," pants the man who then turns to his wife and says, "I've had enough love, can we stop?" The lady explains that her husband is recovering from an illness and finds it difficult to climb. I must admit that I thought what the hell are you doing right up here then but actually said, "it would be best if you rested for a while here and then took a slow stroll back down the hill." "Your right," says the lady, "that's what we'll do, eh love. Just sit here, till you get your breath back and then head back home." While they find a comfortable place to sit I bid them farewell and decide to head down the hill towards the gate in the distance.

Both paths lead to this gate?

When I reach the gate it is obvious that the first path would have brought me here. So why was it necessary to go to the second signpost climbing up that hill? Never mind, my next instructions tell me to head cross the field and head towards a gate in the opposite hedge. Once through this gate I then need to head '...*towards the south-west corner of the field.*' I can only assume that I now follow the directions on the fingerpost and hope that it is towards the south-west. Across one more stile and I am now heading towards a pumping station alongside of the River Brede. This River is said to be 3 miles in length[145] and covered in weed during the summer months. But looking at the stretch I'm walking alongside it looks pretty good. I will admit now that being on my own is a bit scary. It's not just that Ron's not here to talk to, but the sheep are looking at me

The River Brede with the Pumping Station in the distance

funny. All along the bank, past the pump house, are sheep. Big sheep, little sheep and middle size sheep. I'm sure they know I've got lamb for dinner tomorrow. I'm even started to talk to the woolly darlings. But I managed, eventually, to get through it without Ron. I don't remember too much about this segment of the walk but I was mighty relieved to see the railway line I needed to cross next, just in front of me.

Another strange feeling. Perhaps being on my own I start to imagine things. As I walk towards the railway line I can hear a train coming. Or can I? If Ron was here I'd ask him. But he isn't. So, once I've managed to wade through the thistles and stinging nettles and actually arrived at the

Very high, narrow footbridge

---

[145] http://www.ukriversguidebook.co.uk/brede.htm visited 31/05/2008

edge of the line do I head across to the other side or wait until after the trains gone? What train? I can't hear anything now except birds in song. Ron, during our walks, has explained to me the song that each bird makes. I can hear the birds but I have no idea what breed they are. It's all a mystery to me. Birds fly in front of me but I'm unable to tell you what they are. Of course there is no train and probably hasn't been one for ages although it looks as if the line is still used. I manage to get over it safely and head for the next 'obstacle', a footbridge. Not any footbridge but a narrow

The Plough

footbridge. Not only narrow but it seemed pretty high as well. I'm sure that the thought of sheep creeping up behind me actually got me over that bridge. I'm not sure why I was so worried. Was it the bridge, the sheep, the height or that I was on my own? I don't really know. But I admit that I had to stop for a rest, just the other side of this bridge. And I felt really stupid! Once rested, I head towards the road and turn left. Before I get to the road my instructions are a little off. The impression given by the instructions is that you arrive at the road. You don't. First you have to pass through a gate, enter another field full of yet more bloody sheep, cross the said field, pass through another gate and you then come out onto a road. Here I turn left and walk past a beautiful Oast House called Float Farm Oast.

Road Sign to village

My next path is on the right about 175 yards past the Oast House and is easily found. It's right at the top of the hill. Actually that's not true. Because, as I turn right onto the path, I see that this is uphill. This sunken path takes me further up than is healthy, again through sheep until I reach gate. Once through the gate I continue uphill, gasping for air, fending off attentions of yet more sheep until I reach a stile. Once over the stile I walk along the clear pathway leading to Udimore Road and Cock Marling. My instructions tell me to cross the road and follow the footpath signs, but I wanted to have a look at Cock Marling. Unfortunately it didn't take long. The pub, The Plough, although gives the impression of being a bit tatty outside, I am told the food and beer are excellent[146] so impressions are deceiving. I'm sure if Ron was with me we would have given it a try. At the other end of the village is a school for Nursery children and that's it. A few lovely properties in between and I have photographed the road sign just to prove the place exists.

I continue the walk by heading along a footpath leading to a place called Tuckaway. Just before the cottage I bear left and climb a stile into a field of yet more sheep. Where do they keep coming from? Here the signs and paths are a bit vague, but

---

[146] http://www.beerintheevening.com/pubs/s/14/14899/Plough/Cock_Marling%22target=_blank%22 visited 31/05/2008

I managed to find my way to the correct place without too much wandering about so the instructions can't be that bad. At the other side of the field of sheep I pass through a gate, cross the drive and immediately turn right along a bridleway, and back towards Udimore Road. Once at the end of the bridleway I turn left, cross the road and head for some cottages on my right. For some reason the instructions don't name the cottages but I can tell you that they are called Woodside Cottages and I need to turn right just past number one. One small word of warning; this part of Udimore Road has narrow verges running alongside of the road. I slipped a couple of times whilst trying to dodge traffic as it hurtles along this busy road, so if you are contemplating having a go with this walk take care here. Just past the cottage I turn right into Workhouse Wood. Why it's called this I have no idea. But it's spooky. Again I'm not sure why I'm so worried but I am. It's dark, it's damp, it's overgrown and it's slippery and it's muddy and I'm on my own. Anything could happen and I wouldn't be found for weeks. I have to tell myself not to be so stupid, but I can't help it. Luckily the wood isn't too long and I emerge, unscathed at the other side, with some relief.

Entrance to Workhouse Wood

My next instruction is to walk across the field, diagonally, to the next stile. Climb this stile and head towards the next, which is only a few yards away. I am now in a field of something, I have no idea what it is. It's tall, green and appears to have gone to seed. The path I need to follow isn't that clear and keeping upright is a bit of a problem. When I fell over for the fourth or fifth time I manage to grab hold of some of the foliage on my way down. I'll take it back to Ron, at The Kings Head and find out what it is. Eventually, at the end of this field and now downhill I come to another stile. Across this stile and into a little field of, yes, more sheep as I head towards yet another stile and the road.

My instructions tell me to cross the stile and head in the same direction as previous but what you have to do is turn left, walk for just a few yards and then turn right. This way it's just a simple walk across a field of wheat and your back at the Railway Station.

It's a nice walk. It's a bit hilly and is everything that the guide tells you. The scenery, as always, was stunning. I don't like animals so they were a bit worrying. However I managed to get round without being chased, bitten or butted so it can't be all bad. I will admit to missing Ron. It wasn't the same without him. I was seeing things that I didn't recognise and hearing things that I, possibly, imagined and let my imagination run riot. Now, as I'm hot and sweaty, at the car, a nice pint would go down well. Perhaps I should have stopped at The Plough. But then again, I'm sure a pint back in Hailsham will go down just as well.

After the completion of this walk it was with some hesitation that I accepted yet another challenge from the people who have given me so much, in producing these stories. Teresa, you may remember from Left or Right Ron[147], offered Ron and me a ride on Beaver. A friendly horse, from the stables where she works. The stables are in Potmans Lane. For the purpose of this story we will spell it as we pronounce it;

---

[147] Published by LR Publishing

Potman<u>z</u> Lane. (Please note the 'Z' because this is real desperation!) "You've got to progress from Beaver," explains Teresa, "and I've got just the horse for you. Her name is Baby and she's only 16½ hands tall." Now that sounded big to me but without even asking Ron if he would be ok with this ride, I accepted the invitation gladly. After all what could go wrong? But I had noticed the colour drain from Ron as soon as I mentioned 16½ hands. "Christ!" exclaims Ron, "that's a bloody big 'orse. What does Teresa think were gona' do with it?" he asks. "Just the usual," I reply, "but with extra's." "What the 'ell are the extra's?" asks Ron. "Nothing out of the ordinary," I explain, "just a little trot and, perhaps, a small jump." Hearing me say this brings

Teresa and Baby

home, exactly what I've let us in for. I didn't think. Ron isn't completely over his hernia operation and whilst apologising for accepting the riding lesson I would understand if Ron didn't want to do it. "I'll be there," insists Ron, "if only ter carry the equipment." "What equipment is that?" I ask. "Step ladder ter get on an' a bloody parachute ter get off," chuckles Ron.

Baby with Ron

A farrier at work

The day arrives. It's a nice sunny Saturday morning and Ron, me and Lyn set off for the final part of the book(?) We are greeted at the stables by Teresa, Lyn's daughter, who promptly introduces us to Baby. In the stable Baby looks surprisingly small(?) but once outside with a saddle on her back she looked her full 16½ hands.

Ron is first to try his hand at riding Baby. Lyn tells me that "Teresa will treat him gently; she's saving the trotting and the jumps for you." Baby is led around the paddock by Teresa at a nice sedate walk and Ron was fine with that. Before it came to my turn I had a chat with a farrier who was working at the stables. He tells me that there are more horses in England now than there was when horses were used on farms. Apparently everyone has a horse nowadays, for pleasure, but in the 'good ol' days' only the well-to-do and gentry could afford a horse.

But the inevitable happens. It's my turn to don the customary safety helmet and climb aboard Baby. As you know I have a couple of girls on my bus who own their own horses and I have been given a couple of tips. Relax, don't squeeze with your thighs unless you want the horse to go faster, sit up straight, are all tips to help me get past the sheer terror I now feel. But I have to say that Teresa (and Baby) treated me really gently. Yes I did manage a trot and no I didn't fall off. I'm sure Teresa steered Baby the way she wanted Baby to go and it wasn't my expertise that made Baby turn left or right. Yes I was glad it was all over. Thankfully I didn't humiliate myself and managed to dismount in true Western fashion.

Ron had brought carrots for baby (and Beaver) but the only way that we could give them to Baby was to break them in half and ask her for a kiss. Once she had raised her head and kissed us she was allowed to take the carrot.

It was heading back to the car that things didn't feel right. It must be a bout of indigestion, I thought. But it got worse. My neck and jaw started to ache terribly and the pain in my chest started to get really bad. We all got in the car and headed back to Hailsham. If I drive it'll take my mind off the pain, I thought. But it didn't. It got worse. I have to pull over. Pains were now in my left arm and I realised what was happening to me. I pulled onto someone's drive when Lyn asked, "Are you all right?" I had a heart attack 18 years ago so knew what I was experiencing. I have a GTN spray so used that as both Lyn and Ron start to get really worried. The GTN spray didn't work and I vaguely remember Lyn telling me that she had called an ambulance. I was then being man-handled out of the car by Lyn and laid on the driveway (?). I

I'm terrified!!

remember Ron sitting with me slapping me, telling me to talk to him. But after that I remember just bits.

The ambulance arrived quickly and two Paramedics kept asking me questions. I remember being put in the ambulance, being driven to hospital, Lyn phoning my wife. These are all vague memories. The pain in my chest was not vague. I can remember being given morphine and the pain started to ease as we arrived at The Conquest Hospital. I can't thank the Paramedics enough for their quick response in getting to me and for administering drugs so promptly. I have been told that time is muscle. Without the quick response of the Paramedics, one I believe is called Dave, I could have suffered a lot more damage.

Once at The Conquest I was under the watchful eye of Emma and her team (?) I was treated immediately and I'm sure this aided, again, in my recovery. They managed to subdue the pain considerably, before sending me on to the Coronary Care Unit. It was about now that my family arrived after going through hell not knowing how bad the attack was or how it would effect us all.

I stayed on the Unit over the weekend and was seen by Dr Dickenson on Monday. She advised me of the procedure that I would be going through, which involved having an angiogram. Should they find anything at all during this angiogram they would treat it on the spot. She also told me the worse scenario, open-heart surgery.

On Tuesday I was taken to theatre and whilst undergoing the angiogram Dr Dickenson found that an artery was blocked on the right side of my heart. It could not be opened with a balloon so a stent would have to be fitted. I will not go into how an angiogram is performed and a stent is fitted but I will say the procedure, carried out whilst you are fully awake, is not that pleasant and, for me, was extremely painful.

But, at the end of the day all is well. What is remarkable is that I had a heart attack on the Saturday, rushed to hospital, seen by a specialist on Monday, diagnosed and had the operation on Tuesday and released into the care of my loving family by Thursday? I now have to take it easy for a few weeks.

I have been back to the hospital to thank all who helped me through this: Maxine, for all the cups of coffee. Michael, the night staff nurse and Sally, the day staff nurse, Rachael, the Student Nurse to name just a few. Other nurses that came to my care are Mary, Sharon, Theresa, Sarah and Mai Lei. All angels in uniform. I thank you and my wife and family thank you.

I must give a very big thank to the couple where I abandoned my car. Jane and Tony came out, with others and assisted in directing traffic round me as I was laid on the edge of their driveway. Someone also drove my car back to Hailsham with Ron as a passenger because he was a little distraught. Of course I must also thank Lyn, who stayed with me in the ambulance, and then there is Ron himself who I owe so much to, even if he did slap me about a bit. Without them these words would not be in print. And without their quick response this outcome may not have been the same. Lastly there is Teresa. This 'event', after the ride on Baby, could have happened days before, or weeks after, my horse ride. You are not to blame, in any way for what happened on that day.

Trotting with FEAR!!!!

Chapter 27 - The Last Bit

Those that know of our exploits will be aware that, sometimes, I am blamed for some of the more outrageous things that we have done. From these pages you will be aware of my fear of animals, yet in our last book, and this, we went horse riding. I am not very good with heights. Again, in our last book, not only did we walk along the top of cliffs, but I also dressed as a fairy, complete with wings. Ice skating was another foolhardy pastime. All of these were blamed on me, after sampling some of the amber nectar at our local hostelry, The Kings Head. For this book I promised everyone that I would not open my mouth and land us in it.

Colin and Ron

So, I was somewhat surprised to find out that as part of the Remembrance Day celebrations for 2007 Ron had volunteered to dress up as a female for charity and work behind the bar at The Kings Head. "Did I volunteer us for this?" I whisper to Ron. "No," is the reply, "only volunteered meself an ol' Frenchie. You've no need ter worry." I breathed a sigh of relief. "How come you said you'd both do it?" I ask. "Don't rightly remember," he replies, "Frenchie an' me were speakin ter Pip an' the next minute it were all arranged. 'Ellen an' Darren agreed ter let us 'ave a go. An' Pip said she'd 'elp us out an' keep an eye on us. That's the bit I'm really lookin' forward to. Bein' close ter Pip be'ind the bar. She can teach me a thing or two. If only I were a few years younger she could lead me astray." He's now got those 'puppy dog eyes' as he dreams of things that will never be.

To celebrate the occasion I have produced a calendar with 12 different photographs which, during the year 2008, is hung behind the bar for all to see. But credit to them both, at the end of the day the till nearly balanced, the optics still dispensed liquor by the glass and all the punters were happy and the selected charity were a few bob better off. So everyone was a winner.

Our next 'silly' escapade was a game of golf. Not necessarily 'silly' but perhaps a little fool hardy. As you know I do like to play golf. I'm not that good but I'll have a go. On this occasion it was decided, after an evening of free flowing amber nectar that I would play in a new competition suggested by our Landlord and Landlady. This competition is now to be known as the Kings Head Open Golf Championship and will be played yearly. Not a bad thing, you might say, but for some reason, He above only knows why, I suggested that Ron

Golfers and trophies with their caddies

would be my caddie and that whatever club Ron told me to use, I would use without question. But some can take the game very seriously. Questions were asked about handicaps being fixed. But at the end of the day it is a game. I have been criticised on many occasions for not taking games seriously. But I firmly believe in the old saying that it's the taking part that matters. Even Mark Twain said that the game of golf was a good walk ruined. And he could be right. The organiser for this event was Alan (from Knucker Hole chapter). He did a great job. All was arranged and each player was handed a sheet with local rules and the lists of groups and the order of play. We were to play just 9 holes at Lottbridge Golf Club in Eastbourne. It would be under Stableford rules, whatever they are, and was open to any person frequenting the Kings Head. A total of thirteen people paid their dues and the game was arranged for Saturday 22nd March. The Saturday, before Easter Sunday.

In our group was Phil, who hadn't played for over ten years but had brought new equipment just for today, Peter our 'overseas' player, he's Welsh and hadn't hit a ball in anger for some time and John, who complained bitterly to anyone who would listen that when he rummaged in the shed for his clubs he found them to be brown with rust because of lack of use. Finally there was me and Ron. Now how could we take it seriously? Before we started Ron presented John with a small can of WD40 so that he could oil his clubs. What we were not prepared for was the weather.

For heavens sake it is supposed to be springtime. But from the start of the game it was so cold. Then the sun came out. Then it started to rain and got colder. Then the rain stopped and the sun came out. Then it started to get really cold and started to sleet. Then the sun came out again and the sleet stopped. Then it got really cold again. Then it started to snow. Then the snow stopped and the sun came out again. We had real problems seeing what we were doing and a couple of brilliant shots followed really bad shots which followed silly shots which followed even sillier mistakes, but with Ron's first class caddying we managed to get round. Once, on the eighth tee the sleet, hail, wind and snow was so bad we seriously thought about packing it in but, suddenly, the sun came out again. By now our group was soaked to the skin and freezing cold. But we only had one hole to complete. Hole nine. Ron suggested I use a 4 iron. It was only a par three and I overshot the green by yards and the ball went out of bounds. My next shot, with a 7 iron, landed on the green and I putted to score a 6. But I really didn't care. I just wanted to get in the warm, stripped off and under a shower. I couldn't feel parts of my body and the parts I could feel were soaking wet.

But, at the end of the day it was nice to be with so many friends. Ron was a great caddy, even if he did have a problem deciding what the difference was between an iron and a wood. After much deliberation and mathematical equations regarding handicaps and scores coupled with Ron's expertise we managed to get third place overall. Kevin, in one of the other groups became champion and also won 'nearest the hole' whilst Gary won the 'furthest drive' trophy. Good ol' Patrick came last and won a trophy that was the envy of us all. Some scores were settled and I do believe that some satisfaction was gained on a couple of occasions. But thanks must go to Alan, for his organisation, Darren and Helen, for the trophies, and Kevin, Bret, Arthur, Gary, Phil, Peter, John, Steve and Pat for taking part. A special thank you must go to Sue, who caddied for John. One very special lady. I must also mention the ***very*** attractive young lady who served coffee and breakfast in the club house before we started. She managed to warm us all up before we set out for the game. Ron was still falling over his tongue as we approached the first tee.............!

…..and finally

Some, who have read our previous book, 'Left or Right Ron?'[148] might have noticed one or two mysteries which we were unable to discover the facts, or origins, of. It may be a place or a 'thing' that we could not explain. One of the nice experiences of writing that book was the unexpected phone call, or a chance conversation from people who start talking with '…you don't know me, but I'm reading your book and I may be able to answer a problem you have...' or '…do you remember that bit in your book…' and that thoughtful person would then part with the information which explains our mystery.

The following are just some of the 'solved' mysteries and comments which have been passed on, by our readers:

Thank you to Mrs Powell who wrote to me after reading about Ron's father serving in the Royal Sussex Regiment. Her late husband served with Ron's dad during the war and was surprised to see Ron Senior's photograph in our pages.

Also we would like to thank Mr Bill Archer now residing in Wales, who wrote to me about being a mystery tour bus driver in the 1970's and calling into The Kings Head on a number of occasions with his passengers.

Nicky with her copy of Left or Right Ron?

We mentioned a very good friend to both Ron and me in 'Left or Right Ron?' Unfortunately John Delaney passed away shortly after the book was published. But both John and his wife loved the book so much that they brought a few copies. One was sent to their granddaughter in America who sent us this picture of herself reading her copy '…in a cabin in the mountains of Liverpool, Pennsylvania, USA' Overseas fame at last.

Walk 15 – Pluckley, Kent Page 62. A strange sensation when my mobile phone started to ring whilst I was standing in front of a very derelict and very old church at Little Chart. The church was built around 1250 from local sandstone but was now in complete ruins. I didn't know why or how a church should be in such a state. But a phone call from a reader solved the problem. Apparently, during World War II, the church at Little Chart took a direct hit from one of Adolf Hitler's Doodle Bugs.
Thank you, Mrs Bourne, for getting in touch and forwarding the information.

Walk 11 – Hellingly Page 42. This problem involved a picture taken along the walk and involves a rowing boat. The boat was in a field, obviously in need of some tender loving care but what I couldn't understand was why a boat, of this type and size, would be in a field and not on water. We have since discovered that the boat in the picture was, in fact, an old lifeboat which appears to have gone missing for some years (?). The members of the RNLI are pleased to have their boat back.
Thanks to you all for letting Ron and I know the full story.

---

[148] Left or Right Ron? Published by LR Publishers ISBN 978-0-9555919-0-7

Walk 29 – Rye Harbour Pages 127-131. Out of the 52 walks completed by Ron and me this was the one that really touched me. The circumstances which resulted in the complete loss of the crew from the Mary Stanford on the 15th November 1928 will always be remembered by us both. Not being able to enter the church because of locked doors, unfortunately, a sign of the times and an obvious disappointment. But I have since found out that services are only conducted on the 2nd and 4th Sundays and that the church is comparatively new, being built in 1849 with an extension completed in 1912. I still haven't had a chance or the time to get inside the church.

 Walk 33 – On page 147 we climb up Bo Peep Bostal and I wondered what a Bostal was. Since this walk I have manage to acquire a marvellous book written, originally, by The Rev W.D. Parish, vicar of Selmeston and first published in 1875. The title of the book is 'A Dictionary of the Sussex Dialect'[149] from which I quote the following:

Bostal or **Borstall**. *A pathway up a hill, generally a very steep one, and on the northern escarpment of the Downs; as the White Bostal near Alciston, the Ditchling Bostal etc.*

The explanation of the word Bostal goes on to say that it is a much disputed word and its origins are difficult to ascertain.

Walk 2 – As early as Page 8 we came up with a question. That question is still unanswered. Whilst walking along the bank of the River Cuckmere, heading back from the beach towards the Golden Galleon we spotted a new wooden post with the number '10' painted on the top. It was, as far as we could make out, the only post along this stretch of the river but we have no idea what it is meant to signify. Have you any ideas?

Walk 24 – This walk around Shipley was dedicated to our very good friend Sean Snee, who sadly and suddenly passed away before the completion of our book. It has been decided by one and all that an annual pool competition is to be held in his honour, at the Kings Head, and the proceeds from the competition is to be sent to his favourite charity. A lovely and fitting reminder to a very true friend. I was knocked out in the first round of this event in 2008 by my brother-in-law.

Walk 49 – Page 217 tells the story of me falling over and being awarded 10 points for artistic impression and 9.5 for difficulty. I really came a cropper. Luckily I managed to get the camera put back together and, at the time, it was only my pride and a cracked rib that hurt. Unfortunately I appear to have done more damage to myself than first thought. So, if you see me struggling to put my coat on, please lend a hand. I've damaged the muscles in my shoulder. No pain - no gain?

Walk 26 – This walk was about West Hoathly, where my family came from. Included in the chapter was a photograph of my grandparents, Beatrice and Stanley. Alan, who works behind the bar, at the Kings Head, brought a copy for his parents who lent it to their parents. It would appear that Beatrice was 'betrothed' to Alan's grandfather before Stanley, my grandfather. Unfortunately Alan's grandfather was blinded in the war and on his return to England was gutted to find out that Beatrice's parents would not allow the marriage.

Walk 52 – We visited Woods Corner for our last walk of the year. Unfortunately the pub at Woods Corner, The Swan Inn, didn't leave us with a very good impression. But we have been back since that walk and discovered that a new Landlord has made vast improvements to the pub and all is now much better.

---

[149] Published by Snake River Press ISBN 978-1-906022-15-0 Price £8.99

Walk 17 – On this walk we passed a very handsome and very old watermill. As usual I didn't take photographs because of intrusion problems etc. But whilst in hospital, recovering from my heart attack, the gentleman in the bed opposite turns out to be the owner of the old watermill. Small world, or what?

Walk 4 – I found a place for a friend to pick nettles to make twine and some sloe bushes so that she could brew her own sloe gin. I don't know how the twine finished up but if it was as strong as the gin you could tie anything up for ever.

And finally, really – from this book

Quedley – I mentioned that some of our postal delivery staff are not what they used to be but my faith was restored by the perfectly dressed post lady who delivered mail in the correct fashion whilst we walked around Quedley. Since completing the walk I have found out that the young lady's name is Jo. Thank you Jo, you're doing a great job.

High Hurstwood – For all those people who heard about poor Alan, who had a bit of a shock with the electric fence, he has asked me to let you all know that he is ok. His 'little' bit of pride (?) wasn't permanently damaged, although Ron and I have noticed that he now speaks with a slightly higher pitch to his voice.

Our Local has got Landlords new
There's a warm welcome awaiting you.
Pop in, and put them to the test
Whilst in, try a pint of Harvey's Best

I think you'll agree it has a unique flavour
Sip it slow, the taste you will saviour
There's darts, Toad-in-the-Hole, made of lead
Shove Halfpenny, where it's legal to have 'three-in- a-bed'

Sunday's the cunning have the table for card school
The brains of the pub do crosswords on a stool
There's 'Taff', 'Pip', 'Chris' and 'Helen'
I stand behind them – like a lemon

The word they are looking for I know and rub my hands in despair
If I give them the answer I'm sent to the naughty chair
I sit there looking alone and very sad
We have a new acquisition - a Helicopter Pad
The Landlord flies it around and around
But most of the time it's crashed on the ground
                                        Aresee©